700035363162

FREUDS'
WAR

For my husband Martin

'Dreams are often most profound when they seem the most crazy.'
Sigmund Freud

FREUDS'
WAR

HELEN FRY

First published 2009

The History Press
The Mill, Brimscombe Port
Stroud, Gloucestershire, GL5 2QG
www.thehistorypress.co.uk

British Library Cataloguing in Publication Data.
A catalogue record for this book is available from the British Library.

ISBN 978 0 7509 5112 8

Typesetting and origination by The History Press
Printed in Great Britain

Contents

Acknowledgements

My first thanks go to David Freud, Ida Fairbairn and Caroline Penney, the children of the late Anton Walter Freud. It is no exaggeration to say that this book could not have been written without them. Their immense support at every level, both practical and moral, has enabled me to complete this work. They have made available extensive family material and papers not yet in the public domain. That in itself was a huge privilege for me as a writer. My heartfelt thanks go to each of them for providing whatever help was necessary to complete the book, often responding immediately to requests for information, making the job of research and writing so much easier. They have also read and commented on drafts of each chapter.

The other person to whom I owe a huge debt of gratitude is Michael Molnar, Director of the Freud Museum, London. He has provided help with material from the Museum's archives and answered questions as they came his way. His extensive knowledge of the Freud family history and the available archives is invaluable for all researchers and authors like me. His constant support during the writing of this book is much appreciated. My thanks go also to Sophie Freud, Walter's sister in America, for help with memories of the period and to her publishers for enabling me to use extracts from her book, *Living in the Shadow of the Freud Family*. I would also like to pay special thanks to Erik Valentiner-Branth (a cousin of Walter's wife) and Olaf Krarup, both living in Denmark, for providing information on the family's involvement in the Danish resistance and the rescuing of Danish Jews during the Second World War.

To my friend and mentor Mary Curry, I owe an enormous debt of gratitude for her commitment and support of all my writings, this book being no exception. She has read and commented extensively on every draft of the chapters at every stage of writing and found research information which I would have missed. Her sharp mind and attention to detail ensures a high level of historical accuracy in this work. I would be lost without her friendship and humour. I am also indebted to Alexia Bradley whose practical help with typing has enabled me to complete this book on time.

A special mention and thanks must go to ninety-year-old Eric Sanders, one of Walter Freud's closest friends and comrades in SOE, for his extensive anecdotal stories about their time together in the British Special Forces. He has also provided material from his own secret wartime dairy and checked SOE material for me. His amazing sense of humour has made it such an enjoyable experience. He attributes any errors in the book to him! Eric has become a close, respected friend whose name has been added to my list of favourite veterans!

My thanks go to Professor Volker Welter of the Department of History of Art and Architecture at the University of California for help with material about Ernst Freud and his family. I am grateful to the staff and librarians at the Imperial War Museum, London for help with the Freud wartime papers deposited in their archives, also to Suzanne Bardgett for her encouragement and ideas. I would like to express my gratitude to Sonia Dell (daughter of the late Rudi Herz, an ex-Berliner in the British Forces), and veterans Willy Field and Harry Rossney for providing translations from German into English of a number of letters and documents from the Freud papers. This included Martin Freud's letters to his father Sigmund Freud during the First World War; letters from Martin Freud to his son Walter Freud during the 1930s and 1940s, and Walter's message from Zeltweg airfield to SOE HQ in Britain, a copy of which is in his personal Secret Service file. My thanks are also expressed to Ulla Harvey for translating from Danish into English the report on Nazi war criminal Gustav Jepsen. I would like to thank Eric Willis at Golders Green Crematorium for his help with information and for showing me the Freud memorial in the Ernest George Columbarium where the ashes of several members of the family are interred.

Acknowledgements

I am deeply indebted to Sophie Bradshaw, a truly remarkable and exceptional Commissioning Editor at The History Press. She makes all the work enjoyable, stress free and easy. Thanks for her patience and brilliantly clear mind to carry through all sorts of creative ideas. I would also like to mention my affection and thanks for others at The History Press, including CEO Tony Morris, Yvette Cowles, Peter Teale, Paul Savident, and Gary Chapman and his marketing team.

None of my books, including this one, could have been written without the huge network of support from my friends who always show an active interest in my projects. My grateful thanks go to my fiction writing partner James Hamilton for his practical support, loyal friendship and humour that spurs me on. I am also indebted to the following for their encouragement: my novelist friend Richard Bernstein, Daphne and Paul Ruhleman, Evelyn Friedlander, and Louisa Albani for her ideas and creative spark in our discussions together. Special thanks must go to my dear friend and fellow scholar Elkan Levy for his enthusiasm for all my writing projects.

Special thanks to my family: to my husband Martin who has supported me since the early days of my writing career. This book is dedicated to him. Thanks are due to our three boys Jonathan, David and Edward for their interest and help with computer technology at crucial points. My mother Sandra has been a tower of strength and practical help. Thanks to my son David for helping with the enormous task of the index.

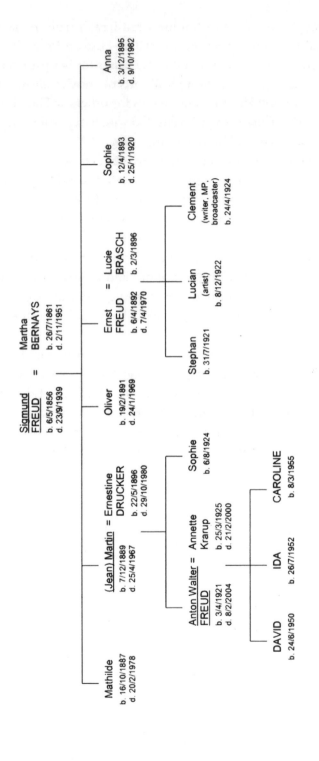

Sigmund
FREUD
b. 6/5/1856
d. 23/9/1939

=

Martha
BERNAYS
b. 26/7/1861
d. 2/11/1951

Mathilde
b. 16/10/1887
d. 20/2/1978

(Jean) Martin
b. 7/12/1889
d. 25/4/1967

=

Ernestine
DRUCKER
b. 22/5/1896
d. 29/10/1980

Oliver
b. 19/2/1891
d. 24/1/1969

Ernst
FREUD
b. 6/4/1892
d. 7/4/1970

=

Lucie
BRASCH
b. 2/3/1896

Sophie
b. 12/4/1893
d. 25/1/1920

Anna
b. 3/12/1895
d. 9/10/1982

Anton Walter
FREUD
b. 3/4/1921
d. 8/2/2004

=

Annette
Krarup
b. 25/3/1925
d. 21/2/2000

Sophie
b. 6/8/1924

Stephan
b. 31/7/1921

Lucian
(artist)
b. 8/12/1922

Clement
(writer, MP,
broadcaster)
b. 24/4/1924

DAVID
b. 24/6/1950

IDA
b. 26/7/1952

CAROLINE
b. 8/3/1955

Introduction

Freuds' War focuses primarily on the experiences of one line of the Freud family, that of Sigmund Freud's eldest son Martin and his son Walter Freud. In spite of this concentration, it overlaps at significant points with that of Sigmund Freud's life. Their personal perspectives on their father and grandfather are woven throughout the book. As their story unfolds, it soon becomes apparent that theirs is an extraordinary one. From the First World War to the Second, their lives are shaped by events which affect their future at every turn. Extensive information already published on the life of Sigmund Freud himself needs no re-stating nor will his theories of psychoanalysis be explored. Based on primary sources, *Freuds' War* uses interviews with Walter Freud's surviving son and two daughters. It makes use of family archives, papers and unpublished photographs in the family's private collection; unpublished material at the Freud Museum, London and Walter Freud's unpublished memoirs *Before the Anticlimax* are freely quoted. The Freud wartime papers and correspondence at the Imperial War Museum, and Sigmund Freud's diary annotated and published by Michael Molnar, Director of the Freud Museum, also provide insights. The book begins with Martin Freud's experiences of growing up in Vienna as Sigmund and Martha's eldest son, providing a window into life in one of the most prominent of Viennese households. The story then spans the turbulent years of the First World War in which three of Sigmund Freud's sons fought. They, like so many Austrians, were

fiercely patriotic and did not think twice about fighting for their country. Ironically less than twenty years later that would count for nothing
when the Nazis annexed their country. At the end of the First World
War, Martin was taken prisoner by the British and spent nine months in
a camp in Italy. His wartime experiences are reconstructed using sparse
references in his autobiography *Glory Reflected* and his autobiographical novel *Parole d'Honneur*. The following chapter looks at the inter-war
years when Martin settled down into married life with a family. In 1932
he took over his father's business interests as manager of the International
Psychoanalytical Press (Verlag). This was a period of political unrest in
Vienna, especially throughout the 1930s when Austria experienced men-
acing threats from her neighbour Germany.

By far the most dramatic and dangerous period for the Freud family
came in March 1938 when Hitler annexed Austria in the *Anschluss*.
Sigmund Freud and his family were immediately at risk and that became
apparent when his home and the Verlag Press were raided less than
twenty-four hours after Hitler made his entry into Vienna amidst almost
messianic acclaim. There followed an intense period of just over two
months when diplomatic efforts began from the highest level in Britain
and America to get Freud out of Austria.

Reading of the events at this time, it becomes clear just how close
the family came to peril. Emigration was by no means assured in those
early months. The book follows the narrow escape of Freud with his
family from the clutches of the Nazis to safety in England. Just a couple
of years later, events took an unexpected turn in Britain when both
Martin Freud and his son Walter Freud were interned as 'enemy aliens'
and detained behind barbed wire along with around 30,000 other
German and Austrian internees. Release from internment camps came
for them when they enlisted in the only unit in the British Army open to
enemy aliens: the Auxiliary Military Pioneer Corps. Martin volunteered
in the autumn of 1940; Walter from internment in Australia in 1941.
Correspondence between father and son during this period reveals the
intense frustrations at internment and skills wasted in the army. In 1943
Walter's chance came to contribute something much more direct for the
war when he was approached with a view to undertaking 'special duties'.
After a period of intense training, this turned out to be with Special
Operations Executive. In the spring of 1945, Walter was parachuted

behind enemy lines back into southern Austria in a blind drop. Using extracts from his unpublished memoirs *Before the Anticlimax*, the book reconstructs his lone mission in enemy territory after he was dropped at the wrong height and landed miles away from the intended drop zone without his colleagues. Finally, he made his way to the strategic airfield of Zeltweg and through negotiations with local Nazi dignitaries secured it for British forces.

There was nothing like a hero's welcome for Walter when he finally flew back to England via Paris, even though his escapades behind enemy lines had become legendary amongst the men who met at the Special Forces Club in London. His story does not end there. Not yet demobilised, in August 1945 he was sent to Germany with War Crimes Investigation Unit on the hunt for named Nazi War Criminals and gathering evidence for specific cases for the war crimes tribunals. That period took him to Denmark where he met his future wife Annette Krarup. Her family had been involved in getting Jews out of Copenhagen to Sweden in 1943 and also been actively involved in the Danish Resistance. The book concludes with post-war civilian life in England and how the family adjusted to their new life as British citizens. Walter's son, David, has written a postscript which takes an honest loook at living with the Freud legacy.

The Early Years

In the opening pages of his autobiography Martin Freud writes about being 'happy and content to bask in reflected glory'. As the eldest son of Sigmund Freud, this was no ordinary family to be born into. His life was often defined in relation to being 'the oldest son of Sigmund Freud'. Forging a separate identity and career for any of the Freud children was never going to be easy. Martin was close to his father whom he described as having '*ein froehliches herz*' (a merry heart). Sigmund Freud came from humble roots, his family poor. He was born in Freiberg, Moravia on 6 May 1856, then part of the Austro-Hungarian Empire (now Pribor in the Czech Republic). With the decline of the textile business Sigmund's father Jakob moved the family to Vienna where he hoped to improve his income. A period of severe depression dashed any hopes of faring better. Sigmund was one of seven children by his father's second marriage. On 14 September 1886 Sigmund Freud married Martha Bernays, the granddaughter of the Chief Rabbi of Hamburg. Their eldest son, Jean Martin Freud as he was named at birth, was born at the Suehnhaus in Vienna on 7 December 1889. Named after his father's great teacher, the Parisian Jean Martin Charcot, Martin, as he became known by his family, had a secure and happy childhood. His eldest sister Mathilda and younger brother Oliver were also born at the Suehnhaus (building) which faced the famous Ringstrasse. At the age of two, his parents moved from Suehnhaus to 19 Berggasse in Vienna where they lived for some forty-seven years until the Nazis forced them out in 1938. His youngest siblings, Ernest, Sophie and Anna were born in the flat at 19 Berggasse. His father had already gained a substantial reputation at the General Hospital in Vienna where he worked. Younger doctors often consulted him on medical matters. Visitors to the Freud home were frequent, usually other Jews or members from the upper middle classes. Martin makes a point of stating in his autobiography that none of the Freud children experienced anti-Semitism, unlike his father who had at university. He commented:

> We, father's Jewish children, were never conscious of anything approaching discrimination against us because of our race. Although we were not easily recognised as Jewish, we could not be mistaken for Bavarian or Austrian Gentiles. 'Your children, Frau Professor,' a police German lady once remarked to mother, 'look so Italian'.[1]

Amongst Martin Freud's earliest memories were visits to the paternal grandparents Amalia and Jakob Freud, Sigmund Freud's parents. He described his grandmother Amalia, who was born in East Galicia (now Poland), as having 'a great vitality and much impatience; she had a hunger for life and an indomitable spirit.'[2] It was Amalia's daughter Adolfine, Sigmund Freud's youngest sister, who had the charge of looking after her in her old age. Martin Freud recalled:

> Aunt Dolfi [Adolfine] once took Amalia to buy a new hat – and she was perhaps not wise to recommend what seemed to her 'something suitable.' Studying carefully her image crowned by the hat she had agreed to try on, Amalia, who was on the wrong side of ninety, finally shouted, 'I won't take this one; it makes me look old'.[3]

Although from a Jewish background, Amalia did not observe the Jewish festivals but made a point of organising family gatherings for Christmas Day and New Year's Eve. Food was a feast for the eyes. Martin could not forget these occasions: 'The meals showed opulence; we were usually offered roast goose, candied fruits, cakes and punch.'[4]

The Vienna of Martin Freud's childhood was very much dominated by the power of Emperor Franz Josef. His personality impregnated the city and its people. This was the period known as the Secession in which one of the foremost artists was Klimt. Etiquette and court protocol was the order of the day. Martin recalled his fascination for this era:

> We Freud children were all stout royalists, delighting to hear, or to see, all we could of the Imperial Court. We were always entranced to see a Hofwagen, a coach of the Court, and we could tell with precision the extent of the passenger's importance by the colour of the high wheels and the angle at which the magnificently liveried coachman held his whip. As I see it from this distance of time, the atmosphere of Vienna was a mixture of romance, prosperity and stiffness, mellowed, or softened, by Austrian humour.[5]

In *Glory Reflected* Martin tells a story about the Emperor, which may be apocryphal. Nevertheless it demonstrated the fact that court life was governed around strict rules of etiquette:

> The rules of etiquette governing Court life were extremely rigid, stronger than life perhaps and even able to threaten the law of death, it would seem. During the First World War, when Franz Josef, a very old man, was desperately ill, dying in fact, there came a moment when he lay motionless on his bed, and his attendants, fearing that he had stopped breathing, sent hurriedly for the Emperor's personal physician. Now it was the rule that nobody might approach His majesty unless dressed appropriately – soldiers in parade uniform and civilians in formal evening dress. Since the summons was urgent, the doctor dared not pause to change, and thus he reached the unconscious Imperial patient in ordinary dress. While he was using his stethoscope, the Emperor opened his eyes and glanced in surprise at the doctor, 'Go home!' he ordered 'and dress correctly.' These, it was said in Vienna, were the Emperor's last words. The story may be false in actual fact; but its spreading about suggests the truth that Court etiquette in those days in Vienna had approached the absurd.[6]

Throughout the year the six Freud children saw very little of their father because he was engaged for anything from sixteen to eighteen hours a day with his work. Occasionally they would meet some of his colleagues in the field of psychoanalysis. Martin recalled his impressions of his father's pupil Jung:

Jung had a commanding presence. He was very tall and broad shouldered, holding himself more like a soldier than a man of science and medicine. His head was purely Teutonic with a strong chin, a small moustache, blue eyes and thin close-cropped hair. I met Jung only once. When, later in life, I moved much in psychoanalytical circles, he had already left the Freud-adherents; I cannot flatter myself that he ever noticed me. One of the very few psychoanalysts who showed interest in his host's children at the Berggasse was Dr Sandor Ferenczy of Budapest. He was high in father's favour. A lively, witty and most affectionate man, he found not the slightest difficulty in winning my devoted friendship, a friendship not affected by the fact that I knew he was assuming the role of a mentor in a worthy desire to help me on my way through adolescence to manhood.[7]

Wednesday evenings were often when Sigmund Freud hosted meetings at his home. These occasions figured in Martin's childhood memories:

We were aware of the Wednesday night meetings in the waiting-room of the Berggasse flat where great minds, led by father, strove to bring to the surface knowledge long suspected but still fugitive and still unrecorded with that precision science demands. We heard people arriving, but we seldom saw them. The inevitable curiosity of a boy allowed me to inspect the arrangements in the waiting-room before the guests arrived. Near each chair on the table there was always an ashtray from father's collection. Some of them of Chinese jade. I saw the necessity for this multiplicity of ashtrays one night when, on returning from a dance, I looked into the waiting-room from which the guests had only just withdrawn. The room was still thick with smoke and it seemed to me a wonder that human beings had been able to live in it for hours, let alone to speak in it without choking. I could never understand how father endured it, let alone enjoy it: which he did.[8]

From childhood Martin Freud compiled poems and wrote short stories, something which he continued into adulthood. Sigmund Freud said of him that he lived entirely in his own world of fantasy: 'Martin is a comical creature, sensitive and yet good natured in his personal relationships – completely wrapped up in a humorous world of fantasy of his own.'[9] Even so, Sigmund Freud was somewhat amused by his son's poems and occasionally sent copies to his friends. Of his youngest Anna and sons he wrote: 'Little Anna is positively beautified by naughtiness. The boys are already civilised members of society, able to appreciate things.'[10] As with any family household, the children had their fair share of escapades. Martin recalled one particular incident as a young boy when he was injured at home:

A trapeze was hung on the doorway between the two rooms. My mother was sitting in one of the rooms when we were practising, swinging head-down from the trapeze above the necessary mattress on the floor below us. When my turn came, I lost my grip and fell, not alas fairly on to the mattress but against a piece of furniture. My forehead was cut somewhat seriously and from this incision, several inches long, blood began flowing alarmingly. My mother, who had been quietly sewing, did not drop her work. She merely paused long enough to ask the governess to telephone to the doctor who lived a few doors away from our home and to tell him to call immediately. I was impressed by the amount of blood, but I scrambled to my feet without help, quite surprised that the accident had produced no excitement whatever, not the suspicion of panic, not even one outcry of horror. A few minutes later the doctor, a great big man with a massive black beard, had stitched the wound and adorned me with an impressive white bandage.[11]

The Freud household at 19 Berggasse was run on a strict time schedule, especially the lunchtime meal which always began at 1 p.m. on the dot. Martha Freud was essential to the smooth running of the household. Martin wrote of the domestic arrangements:

My mother ruled her household with great kindness and with an equally great firmness. She believed in punctuality in all things, something then unknown in leisurely Vienna. There was never any waiting for meals: at the stroke of one everybody in the household was seated at the long dining-room table and at the same moment one door opened to let the maid enter with the soup while another door opened to allow my father to walk in from his study to take his place at the head of the table facing my mother at the other end. We had as long as I can remember Herrschaftskoechin, a cook who did no work outside her kitchen; there was a housemaid who waited at table and also received father's patients. There was the governess for the elder children and a nanny for the younger, while a charwoman came each day to do the rough work. My mother knew how to manage servants. They loved and respected her and gave of their best. It is trued that she kept the same servants for years on end: and even in those days this was most exceptional in Vienna. The meal at one o'clock, the Mittagessen, was the principal meal of the day in our home. There was always soup, meat and vegetables, and a sweet: the usual three-course midday dinner, varied during appropriate seasons when, in springtime, we had an additional course in the way of asparagus. Later, in the summer, we night have corn on the cob, or Italian artichokes. My father was not fussy over food but, like most people, he had his likes and dislikes. He was particularly fond of Italian artichokes; but he never touched cauliflower and he was not fond of chicken.[12]

The grandchildren also recorded memories of their famous grandfather. Walter Freud, the eldest child of Martin, wrote in a manuscript entitled *An Austrian Grandfather*: 'After a relaxing and enjoyable evening, grandfather would retire into his study and write his books halfway through the night. One likes to think that the relaxed, friendly and uncritical atmosphere of the people around him, on whom he could rely absolutely, helped him to develop and advance his theories.'[13] The manuscript of *An Austrian Grandfather* was never published. One copy survives amongst family papers and provides a valued firsthand insight into Freud family life from the perspective of the next generation. Walter lived the first seventeen years of his life in Vienna in close proximity to his father's parents. He escaped the Nazis with his parents, leaving approximately two weeks before Sigmund and Martha. He wrote about the pivotal role of his grandmother Martha Freud during his childhood:

> The first star of that court was without doubt grandmother. Not only was she the first, but she was also the catalyst who made the whole court function. I have already mentioned that detractors of Grandfather, unable to attack him on scientific grounds, have imputed sexual malpractices such as cessation of intercourse and a switch of affection from his wife to his sister-in-law. These stories were either malicious inventions or repeated by those who did not have the privilege of knowing my grandparents. According to my personal experience, and my own parents have unfortunately given me plenty of opportunity to recognise an unhappy marriage, my paternal grandparents were a particularly devoted couple; grandmother was terribly proud of

her husband and spoke of him constantly. Grandfather's whole demeanour towards his wife showed his affection … If grandmother had been less than the perfect Hausfrau, her husband might have learned to fix kitchen-shelves, change washers and deal with the butcher, but he would not have had the time to write his 24 volume *Combined Works*. Grandmother's great achievement in life was to provide the time and freedom for Grandfather to pursue his ideas.[14]

Sigmund Freud could be considered to have given his own children an unconventional education for a person of his social standing. In their early youth, his children were educated at home by a governess. For the final year of elementary education Martin Freud was sent to the *Volksschule*, a regular school. Being educated at home had its drawbacks because as he himself admitted in his autobiography, he was not prepared for school life and mixing with other boys.[15] About his unique kind of education, he later wrote:

> The education of Sigmund Freud's children was different from that of other children. I may not say it was better; it was simply of a different pattern. I know that we Freud children did things and said things that other people found strange. Some, like my teacher with the red beard, found them moving. I expect our upbringing might be called 'liberal', if one may use that much abused word. We were never ordered to do this, or not to do that; we were never told not to ask questions. Replies and explanations to all sensible questions were always given by our parents, who treated us as individuals, persons in our own right. I would not presume to advocate this kind of bringing up; it was how Sigmund Freud's children were brought up. But there was no lack of discipline.[16]

From elementary school, Martin attended the Maximilian Gymnasium. He was slow to make good grades, which caused some anxiety. In his autobiography he tells how he would often go after school to an ice rink in the famous Augarten with his sister Mathilde and brother Ernst. One day this enjoyable skating activity was the scene of an unpleasant incident, the memory of which lingered for Martin. It brought to the fore for him issues of justice and honour, a theme which was to crop up again in his adult life when he joined a duelling fraternity. That particular day, he and Ernst had crossed hands, sailing around in wide circles over the ice when they collided with an elderly gentleman with a long white beard. Although they did not knock him over, he was thrown off balance. Ernst reacted by laughing and making an unkind remark about the gentleman, comparing him to an old billy goat. The man became angry, and started shouting and gesticulating. Finally skating past Martin, thinking he was the culprit, he struck him across the face. Martin's reaction turned inwards to his pride:

> Normally, a slap on the face in those days would not mean much to a boy: it would be accepted as part of his education; but, as it happened, that slap on the face was a tragedy to me. In some strange way, or for some quiet reason, I had developed what today might be called a complex about 'honour'. Attached to me in some way was this immaterial element, or whatever you might call it, known to army officers and students of duelling societies as their honour: something which might not be assaulted except at the assaulter's peril.

Consequently he tried to throw himself at the elderly man, but was held back by a crowd of onlookers. The end result was that the man in charge of the rink confiscated Martin's season ticket. This final insult, wrote Martin, 'this act of expulsion, would have trampled my precious honour into the earth if the ground had not been frozen so hard.'[17] The three children returned home where Martin poured out his heart to his father. Sigmund listened with deep interest, and when all the details were laid before him, asked Martin to accompany him into his study. In those sur- roundings, he then asked him to repeat the whole story:

> He listened intently as I told him everything, convincing him, it seemed, that my honour, then so precious to me, had indeed been assaulted and that the very serious view I took of the incident was perfectly natural. I have a good memory for details, and I can recall very little of what he said; but I do know that after a very few minutes what had seemed a soul-destroying tragedy assumed normal proportions; it became only an unpleasant and meaningless trifle. Had father used hypnosis or psychoanalysis on me: I really do not know ... I had been caught in a net of hurt pride, prejudice, fear and humiliation: my father saw that I could not find my way to freedom alone. I expect he removed each cord that held me with the same patience and determination

shown by [a] Bavarian game keeper. He loosened from my disturbed mind all the fetters of fear and humiliation and set me free. As I said above, I could recall little or nothing of what he said to me, and I think this is typical of all similar treatment when a trauma is successfully dealt with: one forgets not only the injury but also the cure. However, I do remember that father did not deny the moral right to hit back when one is hit.[18]

Family summer holidays were something of an expedition, often lasting for several weeks at a time. A significant part of the early chapters of Martin's autobiography narrates in detail those holidays which left such a lasting impression on him. Sigmund Freud's income fluctuated such that during Martin's younger days holidays were often modest and a certain economy was necessary. This sometimes meant that the family travelled third class to the chosen resort. His mother made every effort to ameliorate the conditions:

In Austria in those days a third-class compartment could only offer hard wooden benches; but mother, with the help of rugs, cushions and pillows, soon turned the shabby place into luxurious sleeping-quarters with quite a home atmosphere which did not, however, destroy our feelings of enjoying an adventure. She always calculated precisely how many children could be fitted comfortably along the seats and, if there were surplus children, a hammock or two might be slung. She and the nurse, if any, huddled themselves in corners. My father would have joined us willingly, but what was a victorious battle to my mother would have been, she knew, an ordeal to him: and she always arranged, possibly by subtle means unknown to us, to make him travel alone and in comfort.

Until 1895, the chosen destinations were only two or three hours away from Vienna by train. This included resorts at the foot of the Rax and the Schneeberg, easterly spurs of the alpine chain. But after 1895, Sigmund and Martha took their children farther afield to the Alt-Aussee. This had become a popular location, especially for many of Vienna's middle-class families, many of whom were Jewish.

The house we rented stood on a hill with a magnificent view of the mountains, always a serene joy to those who really love mountains … And within a stone's throw began pine forests stretching, it seemed to us, to the end of the world, over hills and mountains for ever and for ever. These forests were our summer playgrounds.[19]

The high land upon which the rented house stood was called the Obertressen, lying half-way between the market town of Markt-Aussee and the lake nestling amidst forests and mountains. The landscape was dominated by the Dachstein, the highest mountain in the area. Martin recalled that: 'the Dachstein which could always be seen from our windows and balconies in clear weather, exerted a great fascination over me when I was a child, a fascination that never faded even when, in much later years, I crossed it a number of times and climbed not only to its summit but also to several of the less accessible peaks rising from the glacier.'[20] Sigmund Freud organised daily activities for the children in the surrounding area, usually collecting edible fungi. Martin referred to these occasions as 'expeditions':

> The expeditions of young children led by our father, Sigmund Freud, always had a particular purpose: it might be searching for or collecting something, or it might be exploring some particular place. Often it would be the gathering of delicious wild berries of the woods; and since our holidays extended throughout the summer, we could cover the whole range of wild berries, beginning with wild strawberries and ending with the bilberries and black-berries of early autumn. In late summer our subject was the collection of edible fungi; but we never discussed this with local people outside our circle. They would have thought the spending of many hours day after day gathering mushrooms a very dull business.[21]

Over the years, holiday destinations included Lavrana, Styria, Bavaria and the Tyrol. In the summer of 1899, Freud took his family for the first time to Berchtesgaden, long known in Germany as a mountain spa. It was here that year that he wrote his *Interpretation of Dreams*. But Berchtesgaden was to become known just a couple of decades later as the place Adolf Hitler chose for his mountain retreat. At the end of the nineteenth century this spa town attracted both ends of the class structure: from rich clients to less wealthy tourists. Whilst at Berchtesgaden Sigmund preferred to keep away from the fashionable tourist part of the spa and rented a cottage on a quiet hillside. He wrote to one of his friends: 'The cottage is a gem of cleanliness, loneliness and beautiful views; the women and children are happy in it, and look very well.'[22] In a letter written a few weeks later he said: 'Conditions are ideal here, and I feel correspondingly well. I only go out mornings and evenings, and the rest of the time I sit over my work. On one side of the house it is always delightfully shady when the other is blazing hot I can easily imagine what it is like in town.'[23] In spite of long hours of work, what Sigmund Freud gave his children was lasting memories of their family holidays, somewhat carefree and unburdened by life. His friend and psychoanalyst Ernest Jones later commented:

> Freud used to say that there were three things one should never economise on: health, education and travel. Freud saw to it particularly that his children's holidays and travels should not be hampered by any lack of money. He would give them simply all that they wanted, and it speaks well for their characters that none of them ever abused this generosity.[24]

In 1908 Martin finished at the Maximilian Gymnasium, passing with distinction. During that final year he had shown dramatic improvement in his studies, rising from the bottom of the class to the top. As he himself said: 'This transformation was quite inexplicable to my parents and, strangely enough, equally to me.'[25] The time came to choose a direction and career. The strong personality and opinion of his father was a major factor in decisions with all the boys. Sigmund Freud decided that Martin's two younger brothers should follow specific careers; Ernst as an architect and Oliver as a mathematical engineer. In 1908 Martin opted to study commerce at the Export Akademie (Academy of Commerce), starting without the enthusiastic endorsement of his father who had expectations that he would choose a career in law. Martin soon realised that he would never get a highly paid job in the field and would probably end up as an underpaid clerk. Having undertaken just over a year of studies, in 1910 at the age of nineteen, he enlisted in the Imperial Horse Artillery. His mother was instrumental in arranging the purchase of his uniform. He later wrote: 'Mother, who had much experience in looking after father's clothes, took a hand and ordered my uniforms from one of the better military tailors. They fitted beautifully. I had four different outfits, a great contrast to war days when I had one blouse and one pair of breeches, both several sizes too big, which I wore day and night. My parents saw no objection to the custom, followed by most of my comrades, of renting a room near the barracks.'[26] Life in the Horse Artillery was far from dull. Within two to three months of joining, he soon found himself in a scrape which caused concern to his father. The incident brought to the fore his concept of honour:

> It was called an affair of honour, but there was little honour in it. One morning in riding school, I was startled to discover that I had not brought my riding stick, a wooden rod used in training instead of the sabre which, to say the least, could damage a horse's ears if not used expertly. We usually carried these stuck in our boots when dismounted. Without thinking, and without waiting to ask permission, doing something not unusual amongst us, I borrowed a riding stick from a man standing near who had completed his morning's drill. I had chosen badly; this fellow was bad-tempered and disagreeable; and the result was that he promptly punched me. I returned the blow with interest, following this up by flinging the stick in his face. Thus I was again without a stick and risked delaying the beginning of my squadron's exercise. Fortunately for me, a friend, seeing my dilemma, broke ranks and handed me his stick: and I was saved for the moment. I was in so great a hurry to mount my horse to join my squadron that I do not think I thanked this thoughtful friend.[27]

The incident ended with some further repercussions with the military hierarchy which Sigmund Freud dealt with on behalf of his son. Over the years Martin got into many scrapes which his father often sorted out: 'I was always getting myself into some kind of trouble and appearing in the daily press, astonishing it now seems for so completely an unimportant person. Sometimes my troubles were quite serious and, without father's protecting hand, anything might have happened to me.'[28] Sigmund Freud was a pivotal figure in Martin's life and he relied on his father totally for approval throughout his life. He always lived in the shadow of his father's authoritative, but protecting, hand. Imperial power was never far away. In the autumn of 1910, the greater part of the Viennese garrison, including Martin's regiment, was inspected by the Emperor. That day was vividly ensconced in his memory:

This, always a dreadful event, must have cost our troop commanders many sleepless nights as by endless drill they prepared us. As invariably happens there was, when the great day dawned, a long wait of upwards of four hours on the parade ground before the arrival of His Imperial Majesty: and then it was all over in a few minutes. I could not see much of the Emperor because I was in a rear rank and the horse-tail-crowned shako worn by the tall man in front of me blocked my view. But I enjoyed an excellent view of roughly one-half of our tyrannical commander. I could see him plainly from his belt down to his brilliantly polished boots. I am certain that his head, neck and chest remained as rigid as stone when the Emperor drew near; but, much to the malicious joy of his pupils, who so often trembled before his stern gaze, his knees began shaking, not violently but in a sufficiently obvious manner.[29]

Martin's time in the Austrian Horse Artillery was short-lived. It ended abruptly after a skiing accident on the Schneeberg in January 1911 in which he broke his leg.[30] His friend Jaeger stayed with him whilst the other friend went for help. Martin reflects that sadly just a few years later Jaeger died in action during the First World War, shot by a Russian bullet while serving as an artillery observer. Eventually his friend returned with a doctor and a stretcher, having made the arduous ascent in deep snow. It took all night for them to carry Martin by stretcher back to the Hotel Hochschneeberg where hotel staff left him in the passageway with no food or drink. The doctor could not perform surgery on Martin's leg, so it was recommended that he transfer to a Vienna hospital. He recalled: 'my stretcher was therefore placed on a sledge and eight men towed me to the nearest railway station.'[31] According to the rules he should have been taken to a military hospital, but his father intervened to ensure that he was admitted to Vienna hospital. This action saved his leg. If he had gone to a military hospital it would have been just after the doctor's rounds and he would have had to wait another twenty-four hours, thus necessitating an amputation. 'My leg was in a bad way. The men who carried me on a rough stretcher from the scene of the accident to the hotel had done their best, but often the broken leg had hung loosely over the side of the stretcher and thus damage had been added to. My leg had swollen to twice its normal size and bits of my skiing trousers had become embedded in the wound.'[32] In hospital he was well taken care of, but it meant the end of his military service. He had to be invalided out of his regiment.

Serious skiing accidents were not a new experience for Martin. One year, a date not given by him, he and his friends took a skiing trip on Monte Cristello in the Dolomites. He described that trip as 'the most dangerous and saddest':

One of the friends of the Adamello ski-ing trip was lost on Monte and his relatives telegraphed asking me to come to organize a search. His father, a very rich man, the president of one of Vienna's more important banks, had ordered that no expense should be spared and he sent his secretary to arrange with me the financial details. I led a large party of local guides to where it was assumed my friend had left the glacier to climb up an ice-covered rock wall. We found the place where he had fallen. His ice-axe, which I recognised, remained plunged deep into the ice. Very cautiously, we followed the direction of his fall, finding on the way his rucksack and boots which, as is usual in such accidents, had been torn from his feet. It seemed obvious that we would find his body in one of the numerous crevasses in the glacier. I, being the lightest and thinnest of the party, was lowered down into half a dozen crevasses, but there was no sign of the body. And yet had we known it, while we searched so carefully, he was, in fact, lying near us covered with snow. In late summer, when the snow had melted, his body was found perfectly preserved. The loss of this friend was a great blow to me. We both shared the same enthusiasm for alpine climbing, a powerful cement in any friendship and strengthened where there is common respect.[33]

Having been invalided out of the Royal Horse Artillery in 1911, the next three and a half years before the First World War, Martin spent studying law at the University of Vienna. His father supported his decision and paid the first year's fees. At that time the scope of the law studies covered Roman law, old German law and the law of the Catholic Church. Having often become embroiled in public scrapes, Martin made no exception of this tradition during his time at university:

In 1913, I was badly hurt in a brawl between German-Austrian and Jewish students, this case being made more interesting to the newspapers by the fact that the rector of the university, a famous medical man, gave me first-aid. A more serious incident occurred when at a public meeting I made a spirited attack against a crusade whose object was to abolish duelling. In the court proceedings that followed I was fined fifty kronen, but on this occasion father's protecting hand was withheld: I had to pay the fine myself. I am not proud of this affair; for I have long since changed my mind and do not now think duels really necessary. I had many adventures and indulged in plenty of escapades unknown to the press – duels, student brawls, and a quite a number of mountain rescues, some of which were successful. As a young man, neither tennis nor golf interested me; to my mind in those days any sport in which you could not kill yourself had no moral value.

During his years at the university Martin joined the Kadimah, a Jewish duelling fraternity which had first formed in 1883 to defend Jews against anti-Semitism. His father had been a member during his student days there. What provoked Martin to join the Kadimah was an incident which he witnessed one day. The university was cordoned off by police, but the Austrian police were not permitted to enter the grounds, so the fight raged on with no authoritative intervention. The shouts from the fight soon made it clear to anyone listening that the battle was between Austrian students and their Jewish colleagues. What struck Martin was that the Jewish students were striking back fiercely defending themselves: 'this seemed to me out of character, possibly the first time in two thousand years that Jews, accustomed to being beaten up and persecuted, had decided to stand up for themselves. I felt I was witnessing an historic occasion … The idea that Jews might abandon meekness as a defence against humiliating attacks was new and attractive to me.'[34] He watched as the fight began to spill onto the streets outside:

The entrance from the pavement, where the police waited on guard, was formed by two broad sloping approaches and each had balustrades. The Jewish students, I could see, were outnumbered by at least five to one and soon they were being slowly forced down the sloping approaches, both parties fighting fiercely with their fists and sticks. As I watched, I saw the German students concentrating their attention on one Jew, an enormous young man who had the strength of half a dozen of his enemies. They were throwing themselves at him and hanging on his neck.

At this point the police were able to intervene and disperse the fighters. The battle was over, but it left a lasting impression in Martin's mind.

A few days later he decided to visit the headquarters of the Kadimah whose members had taken part in that fight. They were all Zionists, believing in the creation of a Jewish homeland thirty-five years before the foundation of the state of Israel. Martin commented extensively on the Kadimah in his autobiography:

> The Kadimah members I met that first evening appeared to my unsophisticated eyes to be strange and unusual men, entirely different in outlook and manners from the young men I usually mixed with. Without doubt, I in turn seemed the queerest fish that had ever wandered inadvertently into their net. Had I been a young female, they would have decided, judging from my manners and way of talking, that I had been educated in an exclusive convent. Nevertheless, they gave me a hearty welcome. It was about dinner-time when I arrived and, when they discovered that I had not eaten, one of my future brothers took me to a little shop in the same block where an old Jewess sold gherkins and roast goose, cut into small portions, with chunks of black bread. We sat at a bare wooden table innocent of knives and forks and helped ourselves, eating with our fingers. I greatly admired a neighbour at the table who took in his fingers by the tail a large boned herring and slipped this down his throat ... The members of the Kadimah came from all parts of the large Austrian Empire as well as from neighbouring countries like Serbia and even from the Caucasus, the result being that when the First World War broke out these foreign members had to serve with Austria's enemies.[35]

Martin's motivation for joining the Kadimah was 'to teach better manners to those who thought it excellent sport to humiliate and insult Jewish students, girl students not excepted.'[36] Having become a member of the oldest Jewish duelling fraternity, Martin's expectations were soon tempered. His tall, slight build meant that the most he could hope for was to become a champion sabre-fencer. He had to settle for something much less ambitious:

> I had to content myself with joining in brawls when Jews were outnumbered by five to one or even more. As I said earlier, I was wounded in such a brawl by a knife-thrust, and as I was the son of a university professor, the newspapers reported the incident with a wealth of detail. I remember when I got home that night, neatly and expertly bandaged, the family were at dinner with a

guest, the Reverend Oscar Pfister from Zurich. I apologised for my appearance and father threw me a sympathetic glance. The clergyman, however, got up and approached me to shake hands warmly, congratulating me on being wounded in so just and noble a cause. This sympathy and kindliness from a dignified leader of the Christian Church heartened me considerably, making me feel less like a battered ruffian.[37]

On 28 November 1913 Martin graduated from the University of Vienna. Between then and the beginning of the First World War the following summer, he took up a legal apprenticeship doing court work in Salzburg, a position obtained by the direct influence of his father. In a letter dated 23 July 1914 he told his father: 'My life here in Salzburg is reminiscent of the golden age ... I am learning to understand our laws through the trials and especially through the secret consultations.'[38] It would not be long before Martin would be back in military uniform, seeing his duty as fighting for Austria. The European scene was about to irrevocably change and with it the last remnants of the Imperial power of the Hapsburgs. Martin commented: 'One can only judge from one's own experience but for people of my age, the years before 1914 seem a golden age, a time when one could live in tranquility and peace. Nothing like those years has returned for us.'[39] Of those pre-war years he said:

Few guessed that world war was only a few years away and that the game of playing soldiers in beautifully cut uniforms and immaculate boots would eventually turn into a bitter reality of dirt, hunger, wounds, epidemics and, for many officers, a soldier's grave on foreign soil.[40]

The First World War

On 28 June 1914 the heir apparent to the Austro-Hungarian Empire Archduke Franz Ferdinand and his wife Princess Sophie were fatally shot as their carriage drove through the Bosnian streets of Sarajevo. It was just three days before their fourteenth wedding anniversary and fourteen years to the day that Franz Ferdinand had put his signature to a Declaration of Renunciation of Succession Rights, signing away the rights of their children to succeed to the throne on his death. On hearing of the assassination Robert Hollitscher, husband of Mathilde Freud, Sigmund Freud's eldest child, declared: 'That means war and Austria is going to lose it.' His observation was prophetic. The assassination, perpetrated by the Bosnian fanatic Princip, precipitated the outbreak of war. In July 1914 Austria declared war on Serbia. Troops began to mobilise across Europe, with Russia amassing forces at the border. On 4 August 1914, Great Britain declared war on Germany after German troops crossed into Belgium. Sigmund Freud stated: 'I would be with it with all my heart if only I could think England would not be on the wrong side.'[1] Nothing prepared either side for four years of utter carnage and devastation which was to characterise one of the bloodiest European wars thus far. The dreadful conditions in the trenches, soldiers wallowing in deep mud, wholesale massacres and the slaughter of millions of young lives were to become lasting images of the First World War. Over the course of the next four years the Austrian army would fight against

Great Britain, Russia, Belgium and later Italy on three fronts: Russian, Serbian and Italian.

During that August Sigmund Freud's youngest daughter Anna was visiting England. Now she faced internment there as an enemy alien. Fortunately by the end of the month in the third week of August she was able to return to Vienna via Gibraltar and Genoa under escort of the Austrian Ambassador. Three of Sigmund Freud's sons were caught up in the events of the First World War, enlisting in various regiments of the Austrian army. His eldest son Martin enlisted in the Austrian Field Artillery. His middle son Oliver (b.1891) served in the *Eisenbahnregiment* (Railway Regiment) as a fully qualified engineer. He spent most of the war devising engineering work first at a hospital outside Vienna, then on camp construction at Purgstall which lay halfway between Linz to the west and Krems to the north east. Purgstall was a useful position for troops advancing south to the Trentino. From 1915 he spent around eighteen months building a tunnel of strategic and military importance under the Jablunka Pass in Silesia, now in Poland. Towards the end of 1916 he joined a battalion of sappers, stationed in Cracow, then an independent city under Austrian protection. Later he moved to Krems on the river Danube. In June 1918, Oliver Freud was transferred to the Italian front line. He was based at Conegliano, an industrial town south of Vittorio Veneto on the River Piave. The location, in the province of Veneto, would be the scene of bitter fighting. The prize to the victor would be the sovereignty of the Trentino region on the Adriatic between Venice and Trieste. Italy stood to gain this territory under the 'Secret Treaty' from the Austro-Hungarian Empire. Oliver returned to Vienna in October 1918 after the disintegration of the Austro-Hungarian army.

Sigmund Freud's youngest son Ernst (b.1892) served in the *Feldkanonenregiment* Number 8 (Royal & Imperial Field Artillery Regiment). Of the three brothers, he reputedly had the easiest war. He enlisted in October 1914, spending that winter at Klagenfurt enjoying a rich social life.[2] From there he was posted to Neunkirchen, a railway junction of strategic importance SSW of Vienna. Italy entered the war in April 1915. That autumn Ernst was transferred to the Bukovina (now Ukraine), crossing onto Russian soil, albeit for only a few hours. From there he moved with his regiment to the Karst in Istria where he served until the end of the war. He was decorated for bravery after escaping when the rest of his platoon was killed. He served for two years on the front line before being invalided out with a duodenal ulcer and tuberculosis. Like his younger brother Oliver, he returned home to Vienna in October 1918.

Only the fate of Sigmund Freud's eldest son Martin remained of concern. It turned out that he had had a colourful and adventurous war, mostly spent on the Italian front line. He had already served a short time in the Field Artillery in the days of the great Imperial power of Austria. During the second week of August he volunteered to join his old regiment with whom he had already completed a brief period of military service in 1910–11. Now at the age of twenty-four he served in the war as a gunner in the rank of first lieutenant in the Royal & Imperial Austrian Field Artillery Regiment 41. He was twice awarded honours for bravery in the field 'before the enemy'. The first, dated 6 October 1916, was the Military Cross in Bronze. The second Military Cross in Silver was dated 18 April 1918. By the end of the war he was entitled to wear seven medals given for particular campaigns and service during the war, two of which were the Military Crosses mentioned above. He was wounded once in action in 1918 when he was shot through the thigh, exactly where this happened is not recorded but it necessitated a period in hospital.[3] Of his wartime experience he commented to Ernest Jones, psychoanalyst and his father's biographer: 'You got a bullet through your cap every time you showed your head above the trenches.'[4] It is possible to reconstruct Martin's wartime experiences from several sources: sparse references in his autobiography *Glory Reflected*, his novel *Parole d'Honneur*, and letters written home to his father at the time. The novel, which was published in English in 1939, is largely an autobiographical story in which Martin casts himself as the main character Baron Christian Neustätten. It gives an in-depth account of daily life as a first lieutenant in the Austrian Field Artillery on the front line in 1917 and 1918 until his eventual capture by Italian forces at the end of the war. It mirrors exactly Martin's own military service. He dedicated the book to Princess Marie Bonaparte of Greece, a long-standing family friend and one-time pupil of Sigmund Freud, who was later to aid the Freuds' escape from Nazi-occupied Austria in 1938.

In a brief letter of 24 August 1914 Martin informed his father that he was now moving in the field with two artillery batteries under Lieutenant Esener and 'in good spirits'. On 26 August Sigmund Freud wrote to his son, although it not clear whether he had yet received Martin's letter of two days earlier:

> We now know that you have been moved, but not in which direction. We are hoping to have your feldpost number so that we can send you what you may need. The great news of the day is that Annerl [my sister Anna] arrived here surprisingly after ten days' journey via Gibraltar, Genoa, Pontebba, travelling with the Austrian Ambassador. She is very well and behaved bravely. I hope you are well: you are playing your part in a good cause. I hope that you will write to us as often as you can. Some victories in Russia begin to appear more important together with the German victories. Most cordial greetings, Your father.[5]

While he was away with his regiment Martin kept his main luggage in Salzburg with a Dr Zinke and his family where he had been lodging. Three days later on 27 August he wrote a single letter from Innsbruck where he was in training with his regiment. He received a visit from his father there during the first week in September. The Austrian Command had moved a few batteries to the Tyrol against the possibility of an attack by Italy, which at the beginning of the war remained in a state of uneasy neutrality. These batteries were staffed by untrained recruits, one of them being Martin himself. They had little military value and their principal purpose was to show their presence in the region. Even so, they were kept on a war footing and not allowed to use the ordinary mail, only the *feldpost*. In unpublished annotations to his autobiography, Martin recalled how he and his comrades were asked to volunteer for special duties:[6]

> One morning the harassed school commander had the whole large school assembled to read to us a communication from the War Office. Volunteers were asked for, to infiltrate into the most North Easterly part of Austria, the Bukovina, then only loosely occupied by the Russians. The task of this force would be to harass the enemies' communications as guerrilla fighters, the name was not used, but it was practically the same. These soldiers, cut off from the regular army, should live on the land and on what booty they could gather. About two score came forward to volunteer, the best and bravest from the school and everybody looked at me who had already gathered some reputation to be fond of adventures. The school commander looked at

me as well. 'What about you, Freud, as you are a war-volunteer? Think of the rich booty you will collect, it will all be yours!' This was definitely not the way to catch me; what else should we do with any booty? Should we, cut off from contact with our fatherland, if we ever found a golden wrist watch on a shot Russian officer, put the article in a parcel and register it to the war office in Vienna? 'Herr Hauptmann,' I said. 'I have been educated as a lawyer and looting does not appeal to me.' With these few words I let my reputation and popularity in the school drop several hundred fathoms, but the case was settled as far as I was concerned. The volunteers marched to the station a few days later, singing of the sad and sentimental Austrian soldier's songs. Nothing was ever heard of them again, and, as far as I known nobody found out where and how they died.

From Innsbruck Martin moved to Mühlau on the north-west outskirts of Chemnitz on the road to Leipzig, where he remained until early September 1914. Between 8 September and 14 October 1914 he was in Bozen-Gries (now Bolzano in Italy) where he was billeted in a barn. During his posting at Bozen, he contracted flu and was sent to Gries reserve hospital. On 6 October he wrote to his father from there:

The autumn influenza, which in civilian life provides a welcome interlude from work, has suddenly and unpleasantly hit me. After several days of feeling really bad, I collapsed and was brought here. I am being looked after very well and can rest a lot ... Medical treatment is diet, i.e. soup and an inedible flour concoction which would make me much worse except I manage to disguise it by secretly buying ham ... The hospital I am in is for lightly injured soldiers.

Just prior to being posted to the Russian front line, Martin was sent back to Salzburg for officer's training. In an undated letter written whilst he was still in Salzburg, Sigmund Freud sent congratulations on his promotion:

First of all – congratulations on your 'star'! Furthermore I had better tell you that I have sent you through my bankers two hundred kronen, which I hope will reach you. I do not think you need my advice about warm clothing, the importance of buying yourself some before you are sent away. I dreamt that I saw you in a thick fur-lined waistcoat. Frankly, so far as you are concerned, I am more afraid of epidemics, whose acquaintance can be made very easily just now, than of enemy bullets. It is not cowardice to protect oneself as far as possible from epidemics. I realize that correspondence between us will become much more difficult when once you have been sent to the front.[7]

Martin's standard uniform issued by the army was clearly inadequate for the harsh climate and terrain of the Russian front. With the two hundred kronen, he fulfilled his father's dream by having a fur-lined waistcoat specially tailored by a local furrier in Salzburg. He wore it for the duration of the war, though it was eventually stolen whilst he was in a POW camp at the end of the war. There is a parallel scene in his novel *Parole d'Honneur* when the central character has his fur waistcoat stolen in an Italian POW camp. The army boots proved totally inadequate for the campaign on the Russian front, so whilst stationed in Salzburg Martin had a pair of substantial boots made by the best mountain boot-maker in the city. The next letter which Sigmund Freud wrote to Martin was dated 20 December 1914. It indicates that he had some idea of the whereabouts of his son:

I am interested to hear that you are to be sent away very soon and I regret not being able to come to see you since you, yourself, will not be given any leave. I would not dare to make the journey just now while my digestive arrange-ments are so badly out of order. I wish you well in your new unit; but I still think you regard the war as a kind of sporting excursion. I know that it is not safe to take with you anything you do not wear or cannot carry yourself: other-wise things are lost or immediately stolen. This is what we civilians understand from soldiers who have returned. For an officer everything is much better in this respect. Let me know how much money you would like for the month of January. Do not forget that I will not be able to send you anything later: the Feldpost is notoriously unreliable. Nor must you forget that in Poland, or Serbia, you will have no opportunities to spend money. It is a matter of adjust-ing yourself to conditions that change momentarily. Christmas will be quiet and sad here as everywhere. It will be sad and quiet with us.

In his autobiography Martin comments on the lack of sentiment and affection in his father's wartime letters. He acknowledged that his father was always focused on practical matters but that did not lessen the concern about the dangers he believed his son was facing and 'the privations he was certain I was exposed to.'[8] By January 1915 Martin had left Bozen-Gries and returned to his regimental base in Salzburg.[9] A letter from Salzburg postmarked 28 January 1915 was the last which he was able to send to his father for just over two years. Letters do not resume again until 21 February 1917 when he was stationed in Linz, Austria. During the two-year silence, Martin was first posted to Galicia (now part of Poland) fighting the Russians as an artillery observer on the Eastern Front. He was also present when the Russians broke through near Lemberg (now Lwów).[10] Of the conditions as soldiers, he wrote: 'When the First World War came, sleeping on hay, on straw, on hard boards and even on the bare earth became an everyday experience for all of us.'[11] The only incidents which he recounts in his autobiography are for 1915 when his regiment crossed the border into Russian 'Poland':

In the spring of 1915 victories had been won by the Austrian and German armies, and because of these we were able to advance into Russian Poland as quickly as soldiers could march. There was no mechanized transport in the Austrian army of 1915. The cavalry had been abandoned as a vital arm and the mobility of advancing troops was somewhat affected. There was no cavalry to fan out in front of our marching troops and each division had to improvise its own mounted patrols. My artillery unit was asked to supply a patrol rider and I was chosen, chiefly because I was twenty-eight pounds lighter than any one else who could ride and, in consequent, a suitable burden for a horse who would thus escape galls and saddle-sores even when forced to make long journeys. I had the advantage, too, of mountaineering experience and a consequent knowledge of map-reading which prevented me from getting lost often.

My orders were simple. I was to advance through no-man's-land in a north-westerly direction until I was shot at and then to pause until I had fixed my position on the map. After that my duty was to return to report. This was my work for many months, at first alone and later with an N.C.O. and two other ranks. I found patrolling more attractive when I was alone. Sometimes a patrol would last two or three days, and then my orders were to ride only in daylight, to seek shelter by night wherever I could find it. My horse, a magnificent chestnut with a broad blaze, had been, like many other army horses, requisitioned and evidently he had come from superior stables. In England he would have been known at once as a first-class hunter. We soon developed a great friendship and I had every confidence that he would warn me of any danger. When forced to sleep in the open, I always chose the shelter of a tree in a meadow, and here I would sleep peacefully with my head on the saddle padding and the halter rope attached to an arm, the horse grazing around me and being very careful not to step on me. There were few villages left standing, the Russians having scorched everything that might help their advancing enemy; but some out-of-the-way places had escaped. In one of these places I shared a peasant's hut with a small Austrian patrol and its owner, a peasant woman with a young daughter. There was only one room and only one bed which, in due course, were occupied by the woman and the pretty, playful daughter. We soldiers slept on the floor. Being on patrol, even the slightest undressing was dangerous, but on these occasions I risked removing the spur from my left boot so that I could cross my legs. Those who wore high boots had seldom much choice since, once put on, they remained on except when a man was wounded, when they were cut off. It was a curious night. With several young soldiers in the bedroom so to speak, and young soldiers who were clearly attracted by the maiden, the good peasant woman felt bound to take what precautions she could. Like all peasant beds, hers was crowded with bulging feather mattresses and pillows. She built a kind of defensive works with these and put the daughter in the middle.[12]

When the regiment emerged from a bitter winter in Russian territory, Martin provides only a glimpse of the harsh conditions: 'In 1915, as a sergeant in the Austrian Horse Artillery, I had crawled out from the dugout at the end of a severe Russian winter to begin cutting my long beard with the only pair of scissors available. Sergeants in the Horse Artillery of any country are closely akin in not being easily shocked, and I was no exception.' Whilst away from home serving on the front line, his father's words came to the fore. Sigmund Freud made a considerable impression on his eldest son and throughout his life, Martin always looked for his father's approval on many matters. That extended to his army career. Martin's outlook on wartime and killing was compared with his father's own attitude:

Father, as long as I knew him, never owned a weapon, not a gun, not a sword nor even a dagger; and I am sure he hated the dress sword he had to wear as part of the uniform of an officer in the medical corps. I cannot say that my attitude was as peaceful as my father's in the years that followed. During the First World War I made a collection of booty swords and guns; and as a soldier I was concerned in killing other soldiers in the usual impersonal way. But when I was invited as an officer to shoot deer in a forest, and a beautiful roebuck appeared at a most convenient distance, I abandoned my rifle and offered the beast a biscuit.[13]

Whilst serving on the front line in 1915, Martin was reminded of what his father had told him about childhood aspirations and dreams: 'My father once said that true happiness comes only when a childhood's wish is fulfilled, the kind of dream-wish, one might call it, which most of us have as we build our castles in Spain. In one of my childhood's dream-wishes, I saw myself mounted on a magnificent war charger riding into a freed city to be welcomed with flowers and kisses from the liberated maidens, all very beautiful. Perhaps this wish is not uncommon with boys, if not so common as driving steam-engines. The reality, as it turned out, was even more colourful and the girls more lovely: and I was, indeed, completely happy.'[14] His childhood vision was soon fulfilled during his triumphant entry on horseback into Lublin. By this time the Austrian army's aim was to take the towns of Lublin and Chelm thus severing the Warsaw–Kiev railway line and gaining control over the road to Brest-Litovsk to threaten Russian positions near Warsaw. Martin recounts the jubilant welcome he received in Lublin:

It happened that, as the victorious Austrian army was marching towards Lublin (now Poland), a patrol was called for to reconnoitre the city, to find out whether or not the retreating Russians had organised any delaying tactics there or perhaps had even arranged temporary resistance. Since the army was only about two days marching distance from the city, I was sent out alone. I pressed on with my patrol and I was, in fact, the first to enter Lublin. As I cantered up to the city's boundaries, I was met by a crowd of local civilians who had waited many hours for what they regarded as a happy event. Church bells began ringing and a company of pretty girls, in their traditional dress and carrying flowers, surrounded me. I promptly surrendered to their leader, a girl of fairy-like beauty who stood on her tiptoes near my charger ready to offer and to accept a kiss from the first Austrian soldier to enter the liberated city. Unfortunately, at this moment things went a little wrong through the well-meaning action of one of the other girls who, in her joy, threw a garland of flowers around the neck of my horse. Unused to such touching treatment, and already a little excited by the enthusiastic crowd, the horse bucked violently in an attempt to rid himself of the garland, and the result was that my kiss landed on the maiden's nose. Happily, steel helmets had not then been introduced; otherwise the poor girl might have suffered a severe bump on her forehead … When, a day or two later, my artillery unit reached Lublin, I learnt that I had been promoted ensign: that, in fact, I had been riding about as a mere cadet when I was a grander person with better pay and the capacity to draw more respect from N.C.O.s. When this became generally known, sergeant-majors and sergeants stopped me to offer congratulations.[15]

During 1915 it looked as if Germany could win the war, having secured victories against the Russian armies. Sigmund Freud wrote optimistically to his friend Max Eitingon: 'It is a consoling thought that perhaps the war cannot last so long again as it has already.'[16] However the situation for the Austrian army was about to change. On 23 May 1915 Italy joined the Allies and declared war on Austria-Hungary after the covert Treaty of London. Great Britain, France and Russia had made a secret pact with Italy offering extra territory in exchange for their support in the war. This had consequences for Martin Freud's wartime service because his regiment was eventually directed towards the Italian front line. In the introduction to his novel *Parole d'Honneur*, meaning 'Word of Honour', Martin confirms that he was involved in the major battles of the Isonzo and Piave against the Italians. Under the command of General Luigi Cardorna, Italian forces had concentrated their efforts on the Isonzo valley. During 1915, several battles took place between the Italian and Austrian armies, known as the Battles of the Isonzo, which cost the Italians no less than 280,000 lives. The losses provoked Sigmund Freud to write to fellow analyst and friend Sándor Ferenczi: 'I don't believe that peace is near.'[17]

The following year in May 1916 the Austrian army began its offensive from the Trentino. There followed a period of several months in which neither side really gained territory. On 30 December 1916 Martin attended the coronation of Charles IV in Budapest, in what was to be the last such investiture of the Hapsburgs. The face of Europe was changing and with it, the remnants of Austro-Hungarian Imperial power. Attending the coronation was an honour and privilege for this lieutenant of the Austrian Field Artillery. The banquet afterwards became quite a party:

> The behaviour of some of the more exotic guests from the Middle East caused a few eyebrows to be raised; they started to throw the bones and other food residues from their plates behind them for the dogs. In order to avoid embarrassing their honoured guests, the hosts too had to start throwing food behind them, only the floor was not covered by the sand of the Arabian desert but by precious Aubusson carpets. At the end of the meal, and in the absence of any dogs, the dining room looked like the proverbial pig-sty, a sad ending to the last coronation.[18]

By 1917 any hope of a German victory had evaporated. That summer Sigmund Freud's favourite sister Rosa lost her only son, Hermann Graf, in battle on the Italian front. With two of Sigmund Freud's sons fighting on the Italian front line, this loss must have heightened his concerns over their safety. Remarkably all three survived the war. During 1917 Martin Freud spent two periods back in Linz. Letters sent to his father that year confirm that he was stationed there from 21 February until 19 July and 16 August until 22 August. On 5 August 1917 he was stationed briefly at Helmstedt, halfway between Magdeburg and Brunswick. During his time in Linz in 1917, he was granted leave to return to Vienna to see his family. It was during one of these visits that he met his future bride, Ernestine [Esti] Drucker, at a dinner party. She was the daughter of a Viennese lawyer Dr Leopold Drucker. Her maternal grandfather Schramek was a rich, self-made businessman, owning the largest coal business in Vienna. Esti had served as a nurse during the early part of the war and became financially independent as a result of a bequest from Schramek's estate on his death in 1914. Esti was stunningly beautiful and on first seeing her, Sigmund Freud is noted to have said, 'much too pretty for our family.'[19] Whatever Sigmund Freud thought, Esti's parents were not enamoured by her choice. The Freuds were known to have little money, in spite of the international reputation of her future father-in-law. Esti's parents expressed concern that once Martin was out of the army he faced six years on a minimal wage as a trainee lawyer.

Martin soon had to return to his regiment. He and Esti faced a period of six months separation during which time Esti regularly wrote to him.

Her wartime letters to him are reproduced by their daughter Sophie
Freud in her book *Living in the Shadow of the Freud Family*. In one of the
first letters written to Martin, Esti told him teasingly: 'Do you absolutely
have to know that I like to sleep late, and that I can be bribed with
chocolates?'[20] From 9 September 1917 until 10 August 1918, Martin was
serving on the front line, sending all letters home to Vienna via the *feldpost* (field post). None of the letters reveal any military details or strategic
positions. He simply expressed the hope that his father was receiving his post and gave reassurance that he was fit and healthy. During
September 1917 his regiment was involved in the Eleventh Battle of
Isonzo which ended with an Austrian victory on 13 September. Over
the next few months very little was achieved by either side. No ter-
ritorial gains resulted in a temporary stalemate. With the collapse of the
Russian front, Austrian forces were able to focus their troops on the
Italian front which traversed through the Alps from Austria in the north
to Italy's coast in the south. The mountainous terrain was a challenge for
both sides. The Austrian army joined with German forces for an assault
on Italian positions in the deep, narrow valleys around the River Isonzo.
They continued their push southwards, gaining a striking and unexpected victory at the Battle of Caporetto in October 1917. They came
within twenty miles of the city of Venice. The Battle of Caporetto was a
temporary milestone for the Austrian army, bringing a crushing defeat
of Italian forces which resulted in the death of 10,000 Italian soldiers,
30,000 casualties and capture of 300,000 Italian POWs. Caporetto also
precipitated the collapse of 350,000 Italian troops whose units were in
complete disarray and dispersed. However, the German–Austrian success
was shortlived.

In June 1918 came the Battle of the Piave in which Martin's regiment
was involved. The circumstances surrounding the Austrian attempts to
cross the river Piave are chronicled in detail by him in *Parole d'Honneur*.
The central character of the baron had assumed command of the battalion as the battle commander and had decided to reconnoitre the forward
trenches himself:

> The day before I crawled about in our own trenches on the banks of the
> Piave and at length came to the conclusion that the only place from which
> one could get a really good view of the enemy machine-gun positions was a

shallow depression in the ground down by the river, close enough to spit into it. I gave orders for a telephone line to be laid to this hollow during the night and in the hollow itself I had a floor constructed of a double layer of planks; after all, I was not a frog or a duck, and I couldn't afford to sit about the whole day with a certain part of my anatomy under water. I had the communication trench leading to the hollow deepened, but that wasn't much use. The enemy positions on the opposite bank were so much higher that the communicating trench, which led steeply downhill, was in full view for the whole of its length, and even a man who crept up or down it on all fours would present a sure target to the enemy marksmen on the opposite bank.

This meant that I should have to occupy the observation post before dawn and remain there the whole day until darkness fell. So long as I had plenty to do I was not bored. The telephone functioned perfectly, my battery answered the moment I lifted the receiver, and I slowly and clearly dictated the firing orders which I had more or less calculated in advance … The enemy must have spotted the position from which they were being observed; probably, too, they had heard my voice, for I have a habit of yelling into the telephone. They therefore directed an incessant rifle and machine-gun fire on my hollow, and I was only just able to keep under cover, for there was only one spot in the hollow deep enough to afford adequate protection. In this spot I lay, once I had finished giving firing orders, without stirring, waiting for night to fall again. The sun was still high in the heavens.[21]

Martin continued to describe the conditions as an observer in the trenches opposite the Italian positions:

When darkness fell the Italians brought a searchlight into position, so as to illuminate the communication trench, and it wasn't safe for me to get out even during the night. Our infantry fired at the searchlight with rifles, machine-guns and a little Minenwerfer [Mine Thrower] in order to put it out of action, for the Italians had been keeping the communication trench under a furious and continuous barrage of machine-gun fire. I waited until one of our mines fell quite close to the searchlight and for a moment it was pitch dark; my instruments stuffed into my pocket and my periscope round my neck, I scuttled out of the hollow and ran crab-wise over the open ground up the slope and into the main trench. A thick barbed-wire entanglement ran in front of it, but a dozen hands reached out to help me through; they tugged me through the barbed wire with so much zeal that two large jagged holes were torn in my breeches. The firing on both sides was very fierce, and those behind the front lines thought the offensive had been prematurely launched. It was nine o'clock by this time and as I wiped the mud of Piave out of my eyes and ears I calculated that my brother officers at the Imperial dinner-table had now reached the dessert stage; most likely they were tucking into compote and Sachertorte.[22]

Conditions around the Piave were as difficult as other battle forces were finding in the Somme in France. The area was not suitable for warfare, moving heavy machinery and horses was virtually impossible:

The whole of the valley of the Piave was a vast swamp, not all of it equally soft and impassable, but all the same there was not a single inch of ground where a man or a horse would not have sunk right up to the knees. In some places men sank up to their necks in the swamp, and what would have happened there to the horses but for the fact that they were cannier, and simply refused to go on when the ground became too soft, does not bear thinking of. Had we been given time and material we might perhaps have built platforms and been able in the course of a few days to fire effectively, but in the haste in which we went into action, with no chance of making preparations, we were completely impotent and useless.[23]

Moving equipment even a few hundred yards took the Austrian artillery hours. As well as constant shelling by the enemy, the soldiers had to contend with thick black mud which they continually wiped out from their eyes. Every time a shell exploded from Italian positions, they were showered with mud. An advance was virtually impossible. Martin wrote:

We tried to bring the guns into position just behind a railway embankment, about three hundred metres away from the river. From the pontoon-bridge to the embankment led a cart-track, along which, cursing and groaning, we did at least manage to move forward step by step, but the moment we left the track, so as to occupy a position behind the embankment, we got hopelessly stuck in the swamp. The horses, moreover, had to be stationed quite close to the embankment, some of them even on the lower part of the slope, for this was the only place where there was any cover for miles around, and it would have been both idiotic and impracticable to place them in the swamp. The horses struggled wildly and frantically against going a step further in the treacherous soft ground and could not be got to budge.

I believe it took us thirty hours to cover the few hundred metres from the pontoon-bridge to the ill-fated spot where we were expected to take up our new position. A ghastly thirty hours in the pouring rain, up to the knees in clammy mud and continually under very heavy fire. A monotonous symphony, the pattering of the rain and the howling of the shells and the panting and snorting of the poor horses, who could hardly keep on their own legs and yet had to be urged again and again to exert all their strength to draw the heavy, sinking vehicles on and on.

Gradually everything lost form and colour and became one vast vista of blackish-grey clouds of clay. Eyes, mouths and noses we kept free by vigorously and continuously wiping the mud out of them. In addition to being wet through we were exhausted. For hours none of us had had a chance of sitting down, and anyone who leant against a horse or a gun even for a moment fell asleep where he stood. I strode incessantly up and down the column, roaring orders in the men's mud-caked ears, rousing the weary ones who were on the point of sinking into sleep and driving the battery forward metre by metre to the place which the artillery Brigadier had marked with a pencilled cross on his large-scale special map as our new position.[24]

Three months later in early September 1918 Martin saw Esti again during a period of leave, but unfortunately the visit was short-lived. He was recalled urgently to his regiment because the Austrian army was about to begin its last offensive south to the Italian coast. Martin and Esti had become close, as is evident in a letter which she wrote in September 1918, replying to his letter dated 9 September:

You taught me to kiss, in those following eight days that we spent together, and to love you in a different way, novel for me, you awoke in me something physical that I had only obscurely guessed at. Since that time there is never a minute, day or night in which I am alone.[25]

When Esti wrote again on 14 September 1918, it is clear that they already considered themselves engaged, although they had not told their respective families. She ended the letter: 'Your Esti, who loves you very, very much.'[26] In another lengthier undated letter that month, Esti formally accepted Martin's offer of marriage, although it did not become official until the following September.[27] On 28 September 1918, Martin wrote to his father from the field: 'I imagine that you are back in Vienna again. I have written after Steinbruck and have not received an answer. Everything is unchanged here. Otherwise I am well.' Austrian forces were virtually at the gates of Venice when British, Canadian and Australian troops halted their advance. The war was entering its final phase. Back in Vienna, people now knew that it would end in an Austrian defeat. On 10 October 1918, Esti wrote to Martin about the situation in Vienna:

> Many people consider already where they should flee … You know, I am absolutely staying in Vienna. As long as the population is halfway decently fed, there is nothing to fear. What will happen to the German emperor? I fear the worst (for him I mean) … Martin, dearest, I am so happy and I love you. I have changed a lot since you left, I am no longer a little girl but a developed mature woman. I think something quieter more goal-orientated has gotten into me, and I am rich with love and kindness, which pleases me and it is right that I have changed that way.[28]

That same month, Austrian forces faced the Italians in the final battle of Vittorio Veneto which ended in a decisive Italian victory. No fresh Austrian troops or reinforcements were being brought to the front line. The grim scene facing the surviving soldiers was one of constant streams of wounded men dying and surviving soldiers carrying their dead in retreat. By the third week of October 1918 the Austrian army had been obliged to retreat back across the River Piave. However, the situation was about to worsen for them. Besides the bodies of the dead and wounded being carried behind the lines passed the retreating armies, the Austrian artillery regiment had lost most of its horses which were its form of transport. Martin describes the scene:

> It was a desolate sight. The two howitzers were standing alone on the embankment, their barrels pointing upwards, each of them in a pool of blood, as though they were living creatures. It wasn't the blood of howitzers, but that of my best men. The fact that the guns were no longer manned but were standing there with their muzzles pointing into the air, was a sign of

the men's utter demoralization. The dead and wounded had been removed from the embankment, the survivors were sitting huddled together at the bottom of the slope in a trench which they had hastily dug after the air attack. The dead they had laid to one side on strips of canvas; the greater part of the battery had been killed, among them the two ensigns, all the N.C.O.s and No. 1 gunner.[29]

During October, the retreat across the plains continued north. The Austrians still just about held the vast expanse of countryside between the Piave and Isonzo but only as long as it was dark. By day they became the target of enemy aeroplanes which flew low over their positions shooting at anything that moved, and they faced further danger from an unexpected quarter:

> The gunners staggered along, drunk with sleep, little knots of them crowded behind the field-kitchen. This was the favourite spot; you could smell the coffee all night long, and when a halt was called you were first at the urn with your mess-tin. But since everything was in league against us, even our good grimy old foster-mother the field-kitchen turned into a murderess. Sparks fell from the stove on to the road, and on the road lay hand-grenades of all descriptions, thrown away only a few hours before by infantry troops. The grenades ignited and exploded and a whole unit of weary sleep-walkers was blown to bloody bits. The men did not at first grasp the connection between the field-kitchen and the explosions, and thought that civilians were hurling bombs from the houses.[30]

Morale had plummeted, soon resulting in the disintegration of the Austrian army. Martin comments: 'We were no longer an army, but a heterogeneous assortment of regiments, companies and batteries of various nationalities and varied outlook.'[31] Martin's regiment finally settled in a remote house and faced the task of burying some of the dead. One of the funeral scenes is narrated in *Parole d'Honneur*. The baron has the task of burying his comrades, including Hermann Kohn, whom he had sent to the front line. In the trenches the baron had promised Kohn that in the event of his death, he would ensure that he had a Jewish funeral. The baron (alias Martin Freud) kept his promise and buried his Jewish comrade:

Going up to the coffin, there was dead silence now. I said, in a not over-loud but perfectly audible voice: 'I am now going to read a Jewish prayer. I promised my signaller, Corporal Hermann Kohn, who died in the fulfillment of his military duties, to give him a funeral according to the rites of his religion. We have recited the Lord's Prayer for our fallen Christian comrades, and I regard it as only just that we should pay the fallen Jew a corresponding honour. Let those of you who wish to join with me in reciting this prayer replace their helmets like myself, for the Jewish religion prescribes that the head shall be covered on such occasions.' Whilst I myself replaced my helmet and took the paper out of my tunic pocket, my brother officers likewise, one after the other, covered their heads – the last to do so was the General ... 'Jiskadal wejiskaddasch scheme rabo,' [the Kaddish] I began to read, and after the Amen I made a sign on my chest; just as one makes the sign of the cross in Church, so I now traced out the Star of David, the Magen David, in the air and then stepped back into my place.[32]

Martin wrote extensively about the final days of the war and the disintegration of the Austrian Empire. It is worth quoting part of it here:

The Austrian army, still deep in Italian territory, fell to pieces. The different nationalities – Czechs, Hungarians, Poles and others – formed themselves into independent bodies and, with their arms and equipment, marched off to their native countries to enjoy newly won freedom from Austrian domination. The German-speaking units remained where they were, awaiting orders from Vienna, orders that never came. Finally, surrounded by British and Italian troops and having been told that an armistice had been arranged, they submitted to disarmament. They were then marched off to captivity. The process was, in fact, neither simple nor straightforward; army movements seldom are, or never seem to be so, under the best circumstances; but the confusion, inevitable in view of our nation's collapse, produced much that was sometimes tragic and occasionally comic for individual soldiers. I know that I, one of the victims of the downfall of an ancient empire, went through weeks and months of hair-raising adventures before, like a bad penny, I turned up at a small officers' prisoner-of-war camp on the Italian Riviera to enjoy an early spring in pleasant and comfortable surroundings.[33]

Of those last days Martin also commented: 'It was a ghastly retreat. No one had his heart in his job, and each one asked himself for whose sake he was sweating away like this? The department in Vienna responsible for awarding decorations had already closed down. To most of the soldiers the immediate future was something uncertain and vague, no one knew what his place would be in the post-war world.' This same sentiment is reflected by Martin in his final letters sent home from the battlefield before becoming a POW. On 11 October, exactly a month before the Armistice was signed, he expressed his concern about re-adjusting to civilian life after four years at war:

> I haven't been able to write to you lately, not because I am too busy but I'm not in a very good mood which I wouldn't want to tell you about. After all that has happened to me in the last four years, I'm very worried about my matura [exams] ... Oli [brother Oliver] and Ernst will be better than me when peace comes. It will be a very bitter peace with no reason to be happy. Otherwise I feel alright. I am absolutely healthy ... and after all I have got no worries. My rehabilitation has been a very lazy time, not physically but mentally ... My officer thought I would get a medal but I would not be very happy with it in any case. I read in the local papers about your congress. The congress I hear was very good. Ernst wrote to me about my future. I should think about Hungary but I have not taken any measures yet. Everything is very uncertain at the moment. I hope that none of you caught the Spanish flu. We've got a lot of it here. I hope to hear from you soon.[34]

On 25 October 1918, he sent another letter to Sigmund Freud from the *feldpost*. Talking about his wartime experiences would not be easy:

> Thank you very much for your long letter. You are right when you say I have become hard and can't talk about things ... I am frightened that when I get home I won't be able to function anymore ... I am not afraid of it. I look at it correctly. I understand that the war for us officers is finished and therefore we have to make the best of it. Until now everything has been fine. I have learned a lot, without any problems ... but I can't get used to what is happening. A few days ago we had the Spanish flu here and I was busy from morning to night. On the other hand, I myself felt quite well. In the meantime I am healthy. As usual things carry on as normal. In the next few days I and others in my battalion will be sending surplus luggage home.[35]

On 3 November the Austro-Hungarian forces signed an Armistice, bringing an end to their part in the war. In the south the Austrian army surrendered to the Italians. They were ordered to give up their arms which they were informed would be returned at the border. This in fact did not happen. Meanwhile their commander tried to negotiate with the Italians their safe retreat back to the Austrian border. It was now early November 1918. Martin and his battery were taken POW and within twenty-four hours they were surrounded by the Scottish Highlanders whom Martin referred to as English officers:

> We had to walk in single file past an English N.C.O., who was sitting under a tree with an enormous heap of revolvers and bayonets already piled up in front of him, and every man who went by unbuckled his belt and threw his arms on the pile. Some English officers endeavoured to make us form fours and kept shouting 'Fall in, fall in!', but no one understood what they were saying. I caught one last glimpse of my sorrel [his horse] as he was being led away by an Italian peasant.[36]

On 8 November 1918 Martin sent the first standard POW postcard to his father in Vienna from the temporary camp, which read: 'I am a British prisoner-of-war. I am healthy.' He had his first taste of British military organisational skills as they were marched to the camp. En route the Italian population vented their anger on the defeated troops:

> The march through the Italian villages was a grim business; the inhabitants, in particular the old men, came out of the houses armed with every imaginable kind of museum-piece and hurled themselves at us; they knew that scattered throughout the column were officers, and against these they had a particular animus. One elderly adjutant they beat on the head with rusty halberds until he was stone dead before ever the English guard could intervene.[37]

The locations of the POWs cited in *Parole d'Honneur* match exactly the places from where Martin sent letters home to his father, confirming that the novel is an accurate placement of Martin's own experience. He speaks highly of their treatment by the British soldiers. In the temporary barbed wire camp, they were housed under canvas where outbreaks of Spanish flu occurred amongst the men:

The English marched in a humane and sensible manner, calling frequent halts for rests, in the sun so long as it was cool, and in the shade when it grew too hot. We were allowed to take a drink at every fountain we passed, and eventually were even allowed to load our packs on to the baggage wagon. After the first half a most unexpected thing happened. When the order was given to fall in, several men stayed lying where they were on the ground with flushed, bloated features and swollen, sorrowful eyes, their teeth chattering with ague. We knew at once that this was influenza; one or two of our men had gone down with it some days before, although we had had no severe cases. The new victims were all seriously ill, none of them wholly conscious. The English brought a transport wagon up to the head of the column and we put the sick men into it. After another hour's march more men succumbed, and the first deaths occurred.[38]

None knew who would be the next victim of the epidemic. Martin's sister Sophie was to die of influenza in 1920. Luckily Martin escaped the disease, but in his autobiographical novel he fakes the symptoms to protect the woman he loves who has contracted it. The central character, Baron Neustätten, had come across his girlfriend Marcella in the unnamed town where the commander was trying to negotiate the troop's safe return to Austria. Not content to leave her in the hands of Italians or British troops, he disguises Marcella in a dead soldier's uniform and she joins the other soldiers as they march into captivity. Her identity passes unnoticed for several weeks until she contracts Spanish flu whilst in an Italian POW camp. They continue the daily march with the baron carrying his 'comrade' [Marcella] who is too weak to walk. He protects her until she is taken by ambulance to an Italian hospital. He fakes the flu symptoms to be admitted with her and he cares for her throughout the ordeal. Later they are both transferred with other POWs to an isolated monastery for a few days in Teramo in the Abruzzi mountains, ENE of Rome. Was Marcella a fictitious character created by Martin, or did he really save the life of a woman he loved? There is an interesting parallel between reality and fiction in the letters which Martin sent to his father whilst a POW. All the letters, written in German, now survive in the Freud Museum. Martin sent a POW card to his father from an Italian hospital, paralleling such scenes in the novel. Maybe Marcella was no creation but the thread of lost love. In the novel the relationship finally ends in the Italian POW camp San Benigno near Genoa, the same camp where Martin himself spent nine months as a POW.

On 14 November 1918, Martin sent a postcard to his father, saying: 'am still in the field hospital. I feel much better and only have the pain of my broken leg. I hope I will soon be transferred to somewhere and will let you know my new address. What is going on in the world doesn't concern me. Once there is a new order in Vienna and I have contact with everyone again, I hope to have help from your friends in a neutral country.' Correspondence from Martin to his family back in Vienna took several months to reach them. It was some time before Sigmund Freud could establish the safety of his eldest son. Sigmund's concern was evident in a letter which he wrote on 18 November to his half-brother Alexander, who had some kind of connection with the Austrian war office:

> Martin is still missing. It is time to start making enquiries. 9 days ago I sent an urgent telegram to the headquarters of his regiment in Linz, no reaction. I am now waiting an answer to a registered letter, probably with the same result. I had a non-Jewish patient whose father, the director of a bank, I have asked to make enquiries. No answer could yet be expected from this. Could you please send somebody to the war-office in order to find out if there exists an information-desk which knows anything about the fate of the Heavy Artillery Regiment Nr. 44, Fieldpost Nr, 646, or which may be able to tell us from where to get information. Possibly the Headquarter has moved from Linz. It cannot have disappeared altogether like our precious fatherland and if anything still exits then this remainder should be interested in the fate of the regiment. Whether we can in this way any news of Martin's own fate is doubtful; he was stationed with his battery. Sincerely, yours Sigm.[39]

A couple of months later, Sigmund would write to his friend Ernest Jones about Martin and reflect on the immediate aftermath of war:

> These last months are becoming the worst we have had to endure while this war lasted. My eldest son is still a prisoner in Italy. We are all of us slowly failing in health and bulk, not alone so in the town I assure you. Prospects are dark. I am ready to confess that fate has not shown injustice and that a German victory might have proved harder blow to the interests of mankind

in general. But it is no relief to have one's sympathy on the winning side when one's well-being is at stake on the losing one.[40]

On 24 December 1918, Martin wrote to his father from the POW camp at Teramo, the last surviving correspondence to him from there: 'Today I try another attempt to give you my news. I have not received any post whatsoever. I live here in anticipation. I will soon be transported to a prison camp. I am absolutely healthy and quite strong. I have got very friendly comrades. The life is very boring, the weather is occasionally mild with plenty of sun. There is a possibility of being sent to Genoa.' Finally Martin was taken to San Benigno POW camp, a fortification overlooking the harbour of Genoa. He describes it in detail in *Parole d'Honneur*:

> The path from Genoa station rose very steeply; we were being taken to the old barracks of San Benigno, a large and straggling fortress perched on a crag above the town and commanding a full view of the whole harbour. With the best will in the world no one could have called it a pleasant spot. The Italians had at long last decided to gather together in one place all the Austrian prisoners of war of commissioned rank who had formerly been scattered in military hospitals throughout the country and who had, of course, long ceased to be ill. The barracks of San Benigno were selected for this purpose. The fortress contained enormous barrack-rooms, an endless row of them on each of the three floors; they were all bleakly monotonous and in an extremely neglected condition. Accommodation was found for the whole of our batch of prisoners in these rooms; this meant that each man had his own bed, a locker above the bed for his things and a place on the wooden bench round the big table for writing and doing odd jobs. No room was left for later batches of prisoners, and so they had to sleep on improvised beds in the corridors. Whenever any one of us wished to leave the room on a certain errand, he had to clamber over them – and this went on all day and all night.[41]

Once ensconced in the barracks, the prisoners were left to their own devices. They were fed on ample quantities of insipid macaroni and spaghetti. To pass the time they organised various study groups on a number of subjects, formed an orchestra, a sports club and accumulated a large lending library. They started debating clubs and held political meetings. Their guards escorted them to the harbour for a daily swim in the grimy water. They now received their post and pay on a regular basis. At this time Martin was sending POW postcards to his fiancée Esti. She wrote to him regularly even though she often did not hear from him for months at a time. On 23 March 1919 she told him: 'Now I am happy I have your card, know that you almost lack for nothing except freedom and myself.'[42]

Whilst Martin spent nine months in the POW camp, the Allied powers were reshaping post-war Europe. The borders had disintegrated with the defeat of the German, Austrian and Hungarian armies. The Czechs no longer wished to be part of the Austrian Empire and declared independence as the new Czechoslovakia. The Treaty of Versailles set out the terms of reparations to be exacted from Germany for war. As a preventative measure against future aggression, Germany was forbidden to re-arm. In the immediate aftermath of the First World War, conditions for the civilian populations in Austria and Germany deteriorated. Sigmund Freud wrote to Ferenczi: 'all the four years of the war were a joke compared with the bitter grimness of these months and doubtless also of the ones to come.'[43] The consequences of such a heavy hand by the Allied powers on Germany would have repercussions for the next two decades. Shortage of food supplies, coupled with hyper-inflation would affect Europe at every level, physically and politically. Austria was not immune from all this. The country would see periods of political instability which threatened to break out into full-blown civil war in Austria.

In August 1919, Martin was finally released from the POW camp to return to Vienna, still recovering from the collapse of the Austrian Empire. Esti was overjoyed at the news; it was what she had been waiting for for nine long months. At the time she was on holiday with her family in Puchenstuben, a resort in lower Austria, and excitedly wrote to him:

About an hour ago at 7.30.p.m I received your telegram. You are here, finally here, it is like a dream, I cannot believe, I am stunned, am frantic wondering whether someone is playing me a dirty trick. I shall call you right away tomorrow morning hoping to still get a letter from you ... You don't need to bring along food, you get very good food here and much less expensive than in Vienna. Please be sure to take along some very warm clothing, it is very chilly and you will come from a warmer climate ... Martin, I cannot

continue to write, my head is in turmoil and my hands are trembling. I welcome you home most affectionately and wish you a wonderful time. I love
and long for you, am so very happy about your return, kiss you many many
times and cannot wait for the reunion and your visit. Your Esti.

The war was over. Martin was a free man at last but the reality of post-war
life was to have its own problems, as he himself wrote in *Glory Reflected*:

I returned to Vienna, no longer a tall thin young man but somewhat plump
as the result of a diet of spaghetti and risotto. On the other hand, my usually
fulsome and gay spirits had thinned out, dropping to something very low
indeed. Also, I was very poor. Some thousands of kronen I had saved during
four years of service, together with extra war grants, were not enough to pay
for the re-soling of one pair of civilian shoes. This inflation, so devastating to
the foundations of middle-class life, was bad enough; but the sense of insecurity, caused by an absence of discipline which permitted the mob to get
out of hand, was hardest to bear. At my return one could still hear hooligans
fearlessly singing in the Vienna streets, 'Who will now sweep the streets? The
noble gentlemen with the golden stars will now sweep the streets.' Ex officers
like myself found it wisest to wear a scarf over their golden stars or risk having
them torn off, and not too gently.[44]

Three months later on 7 December 1919, his thirtieth birthday, Martin
married Esti Drucker in the Pazmaniten Temple on Pazmanitengasse,
the synagogue which her grandfather Schramek had built from his own
wealth. The wedding ceremony was followed by a modest tea at Esti's
parents' home. Martin then took Esti off for a three-day honeymoon in
Baden bei Wien, just outside Vienna. Their first-born child, Walter, later
commented about his father's wartime service:

I think my father can be rightfully proud of his war-time record and it is to
Austria's shame that he and thousands like him were either hounded out or
met the Holocaust some 20 years later.[45]

The Inter-War Years

Martin and Esti Freud began to settle into married life. Having spent so long in the army, there was concern about how Martin could support his wife and their new situation. They moved into a small apartment on the second floor of the same block where Esti's parents lived at 65 Franz-Josefs-Kai on the corner of the Schottenring. Money was tight and Dr Drucker, Martin's new father-in-law, paid the rent on their flat. He was also instrumental in securing Martin's first job as an assistant to the general manager of Weiner Bank A.G where he worked for a year until 1920. Esti also had adjustments to make to her new life, not being used to cooking and housework. Her parents gave the new couple an open invitation to lunch at their home every day, which Esti enjoyed. This may not have helped them adjust to married life because Martin declared that he would eat lunch every day with his parents at 19 Berggasse. Further friction soon surfaced in the marriage when Martin gambled most of Esti's money on the Stock Exchange and lost it. In 1920 Martin changed jobs and worked as Assistant Manager and Head of the Credit Department at Treuga, a finance company under government control. In 1920, Esti found that she was expecting their first child. What should have been a joyous time was fraught with concerns. Their financial situation meant that they could not support another mouth to feed. Martin notified his father-in-law's friend Lampl who recommended a doctor to carry out an abortion. The young Esti was too insecure to raise any objections and obediently aborted their first child. Martin had not bargained on the physical trauma that this would have on his wife who needed several months away from home to recuperate. The rest of the family was never told about the abortion until it came to light in Esti Freud's privately published memoirs *Vignettes of My Life*, now reproduced in Sophie Freud's book *Living in the Shadow of the Freud Family*. A short time later, Esti conceived again and on 3 April 1921 their son Anton Walter was born. By the end of 1921 Esti was expecting another child, this time a suspected extra-uterine pregnancy which potentially risked her life. Two physicians gave their professional opinion, one recommending an abortion. Esti underwent a second abortion, although it turned out not to be an ectopic pregnancy. Three years later on 6 August 1924 she gave birth to a daughter, Miriam Sophie Freud, known to everyone as Sophie. That same year Martin changed employment due to the economic instability in Austria. Hyperinflation had caused the crisis, necessitating government intervention by changing the Austrian currency from Krone to the Schilling. The finance company Treuga, Martin's employers, lost huge sums of money in the upheaval and consequently he was forced to find alternative employment. From 1924 until 1927 he worked as Assistant Manager, Head of the Credit Department of Fides Treuhand Bank in Vienna.

A year or two after Sophie Freud's birth, the young Walter was displaying signs of a normal active toddler and taking risks. One day during a regular Sunday morning visit to the Freud grandparents and extended family, the young Walter disappeared from the apartment. He made his way down the stairs and out into the main street. His father Martin recalled the incident in *Glory Reflected*:

Evidently, my boy, who already displayed great independence of character, found the company of so many older people rather boring and, without taking anybody into his confidence, he decided to explore the staircase and finally the street. There was so much in the street that could be inspected, studied and experimented with. The street outside grandmother's flat was usually deserted by traffic on a Sunday morning and remained peacefully quiet. But on this morning I became suddenly aware that Sunday's usual peace was being disturbed by somebody's vain attempt to crank up a heavy motor-vehicle. Perhaps instinct, possibly some knowledge of my young son

Walter's deep interest in machinery, made me ask myself 'Where is Walter?'
Without answering this question, and now fearing the worst, I rushed out
of the flat and down the stairs to the street followed by a crowd of elderly
ladies. We arrived at the moment of Walter's triumph. After many trials, it
appeared that he had at last succeeded in starting the engine of a heavy lorry,
and I found him standing in triumph at his full height of about three feet and
apparently expecting applause. Instead of applause, he was promptly deprived
of his magnificent toy, carried upstairs and forced to listen to a full and hostile
account of his shocking exploit.[1]

This was not the only escapade that was to worry Walter's parents. In
Walter's own memoirs of his grandfather, he narrated another close shave:

My father exercised his prerogative of chastising his son only once, when
I was about 7 years old. We lived on the 3rd floor of a solid and large town-
house. The windows of our play-room were of course secured by bars to
prevent us falling out, but these bars did not reach right to the top of the
window frame but left a gap of about 12 inches, just wide enough for an agile
little boy or girl to wriggle through. And this was exactly what I did; I piled
on the children's furniture onto the inner windowsill, ably assisted by my
little sister, and climbed up on it and over the bars to the outer windowsill.
From there I happily waved down to the traffic some 40 feet below; I feel
quite giddy even now when I think about it. Luckily, a policeman spotted me
and came running up to warn the family. After my return to the right side of
the bars, I got the only hiding I ever had from my family.[2]

Holidays away from Vienna were something of an adventure. During
the summer Esti took her children first to Grado, a resort facing south
on the Gulf of Trieste, and then the Tyrolean mountains. Martin usually
joined them later for part of the time but this was perhaps the first sign
that cracks were beginning to show in the marriage. In spite of the tension between the parents, Walter recalls a sometimes-happy childhood.
His vivid memories of Grado display typical boyhood jealousy when his
mother's attention was distracted elsewhere:

I loved Grado and thought of it as my second house. It was surrounded by
lagoons, which made it ideal for bathing; even toddlers could safely splash

about in the warm water. Grado had everything a child could wish for in a holiday: clean fine hot sand, protected bathing and lots of other children to play with. My mother too enjoyed herself. She was a good looking woman and did not mind the attention of male admirers, including Italian pilots stationed nearby. When I thought that such flirtation had gone on long enough, I saved my mother's honour by charging up the beach with lungs at full blast, screaming 'mother, mother'. At the sight and sound of a screaming and obnoxious young boy, even the most ardent admirers made their quick excuses.

Memories of his mother's tempestuous moods remained with him all his life. He later wrote:

She was one of the least accomplished persons I know when it came to human relationships. At times she would be very pleasant but on other occasions she would rage, and on hindsight it seems to me that she probably suffered very badly from P.M.T., pre-menstrual tension, only this was not recognized at that time nor was there any cure or alleviation available. During her periodic displeasures she managed, seemingly by trying very hard, to spoil her relationships with her family and with all her friends and acquaintances. It was my father and I who bore the brunt of her outbursts, my sister escaped more lightly. When I was old enough to understand that my mother was not quite normal at times, I asked my father whether Grandfather [Sigmund Freud] could not help, but I was told that psychoanalytical treatment would not cure her particular affliction. Although she greatly admired Grandfather, she did not have a good personal relationship with him either, and she did not visit her in-laws very frequently. My mother died in New York City in 1980, working to the last, a lonely but tough and independent woman.[3]

Part of the long summer holidays was sometimes spent with his father. Martin would take Walter off to enjoy outdoor activities, away from the bustle of city life:

In summer, my father went canoeing on the fast Alpine rivers of Austria. He had a collapsible boat (Faltboot), which, when not in use could be packed into 3 or 4 rucksacks which were easily portable. On assembly, the boat resembles an Eskimo Kajak, i.e. it was integral with the jacket of the rower and hence quite water-proof. I had the pleasure of going with him on a few occasions;

not on wild waters but on the very placid Danube. I recall the little islands on the Danube occupied by completely nude people of both sexes, which a teenager like myself found very interesting.[4]

Walter followed in his father's footsteps in the love of outdoor pursuits, especially skiing. Again he fondly recalled his father's special holidays:

Another holiday occupation of my father was rock-climbing and he was particularly attracted by a mountain called Tre Cime di Lavaredo (Drei Zinnen) now in the Italian Dolomites, formerly in Austria. This is a spectacular mountain with 3 merlon-like peaks. He claimed to have accomplished a number of 'firsts', i.e. being the first person on a particularly difficult mountain top.[5]

During his youth, Walter was not subjected to any anti-Semitism, unlike his grandfather Sigmund who had experienced anti-Semitism at university. The Freud family moved almost exclusively within Jewish circles. All Walter's friends, and especially those of his grandfather, were predominantly Jewish. Walter was educated in a mixed school for boys and girls called Schwarzwald Schule until the age of ten, after which he went to a Gymnasium (Grammar School). He and his family were forced to flee Vienna in 1938 when he was seventeen and so did not sit his final examinations there, completing his education in England the following year. Later reflecting on his two very different experiences of youth in Vienna and England, he wrote:

If I were to be asked about the main differences between my youth in Vienna and my later life in England I would stress the influence of Geography. In Vienna, my life revolved within a circle of 20 walking minutes, like in a village. My maternal grandparents live literally next door to us, the other grandparents not five minutes walk away. My father's office was just round the corner, and he would daily visit his parents on his way home for lunch. The schools were within ten or fifteen minutes walk, and all one's friends would also live within that circle. One could see them daily if one wished; we were after all nearly neighbours. The idea of taking a train to work, for a journey of one hour or more, did not belong to the life-style of pre-war Austria. A train-journey was not undertaken lightly, or frequently, For the annual summer sojourn, my mother would prepare trunks and large wicker baskets days, if not weeks, in advance, and she would take as much care in selecting her packing as I did for my parachute jump. Indeed, the preparation for our summer holidays were not all that much different from the logistics of Special Force. Both required careful planning, weeks of preparation and much expenditure of money and nervous energy.[6]

From childhood Walter was always conscious of the fame of his grandfather. His mother made sure that he knew about Sigmund Freud's work and international reputation. Walter was taken to visit Sigmund and Martha Freud regularly. It was customary to call on them every Sunday afternoon, just a short walk away from their home. He recalled:

The living room doubled as dining-room at meal times, and shortly before one o'clock the table would be laid. At the stroke of the hour Grandfather would emerge from his study and at the same instant, similar to a cue in a theatre, the door opposite would also open and the maid, Paula, would bring in the soup. A rich hot soup at lunchtime was obligatory in a bourgeois Viennese household; a meal without soup was just a snack. Lunch was served only for the four residents of Berggasse [Sigmund, Martha and two sisters]; it was very rare indeed for any outsider to be invited and my sister and I never had meals there. This was not a lack of hospitality but due to Grandfather's increasing difficulties with eating. After his many operations, there was hardly anything left of his jaws and palate and it is hard to imagine the discomfort and pain which eating and even talking caused him. Naturally, he did not want too many witnesses at the table. We children would discreetly stand or sit around in the background; when I was old enough to understand why Grandfather ate so messily, I felt terribly sorry for him. It seemed to me that Grandfather was not so much a Moses leading his people to the promised land of enlightenment, but a Prometheus who, having given mankind the knowledge of fire, was punished by being eaten up piecemeal. After the soup, Grandfather would visibly relax and talk to us. There would be pocket-money, also for our Fraulein if she was there, acknowledged with a beautiful curtsy. Grandmother would give me some chocolate with the strict rejoinder not to eat it until after lunch.[7]

In 1923 Sigmund Freud was diagnosed with cancer of the palate which necessitated various operations and the fitting of a prosthesis. His dignified,

but protracted misery is well told by his biographer and friend Ernest
Jones. The cancer of Sigmund Freud's jaw, caused by cigar tobacco,
required many operations, mostly under local anaesthetics, throughout
the 1920s until his death sixteen years later. Anaesthetics were not as
advanced then as they are nowadays and the operation site was often
exceedingly difficult to access. Walter Freud wrote about the almost
mythical status which his grandfather's operations had acquired:

> Hajek operated on Grandfather as an ambulatory outpatient, and Grandfather,
> then sixty-seven years old, did not inform his family that he was going to be
> operated on. But instead of being able to return home immediately after
> the operation as planned, he lost a lot of blood and had to rest on a cot in a
> room shared with an imbecilic dwarf. While everybody was out having lunch,
> Grandfather started to bleed profusely from his wound. The bell in the room
> was out of order and Grandfather could neither call nor speak. It was up to
> the dwarf to go scurrying for help which came just in time. Eventually, the
> bleeding was arrested with difficulties, the family was informed and they came
> post-haste. Anna did not leave him again but insisted on staying the night
> with him in the hospital. Next morning, Hajek demonstrated the case to a
> crowd of students and finally Grandfather was allowed home. In my youth,
> this story of Grandfather's first operation replaced the fairy-tales of Grimm
> and Andersen, I heard it over and over again with all the sordid details. It had
> many of the ingredients of a fairy-story; a dwarf, a near death, much blood
> and an indifferent doctor.[8]

Sigmund Freud's health continued to plague him, in spite of which he
continued to work on his books and see patients. Walter recalled:

> He suffered from his ever-spreading cancer, a constant reminder to him of
> the transience of life. He wished to complete his work in the short span
> which remained and therefore he could spare but little time for frivolities
> like playing with his grandson. The constant pain and the shadow of death
> made him a sombre person, I never heard him laugh and only rarely did he
> joke. Because speaking was painful, he used a 'shorthand' type of speech; a
> few keywords would express his views, which would take the place of long
> discourses by people with healthy mouths. He was not a Grandfather one felt
> like arguing with, one was much too awe-struck.[9]

In 1925, Sigmund Freud received a visit from Princess Marie Bonaparte, HRH the Princess George of Greece, who wanted to undergo analysis by him. That first meeting changed her. She became Freud's pupil and friend, little realising then just how vital she would be to the family during the Nazi period in Austria. She visited Freud regularly in Vienna and later in London until his death in 1939. She became a key figure in the psychoanalytical movement. She also supported Martin Freud and the two of them kept in contact for over thirty years.

In 1927 Martin Freud became a partner in a private bank, Walter & Co. The following year he began to write regularly on economic, financial and transport problems for daily newspapers and technical journals. By now his wife Esti was also branching out and had decided to pursue her own career, even though Walter and Sophie were still young. She hired a nanny and in 1932 took up a post as a lecturer in speech and voice therapy at Vienna University. The marriage was now severely strained such that by the early 1930s, Martin and Esti were sleeping in separate bedrooms at opposite ends of the flat. The few occasions when they were in each other's company usually ended in terrible arguments. Both eventually were known to have taken lovers. Walter commented: 'After my puberty it became apparent to me that my father must have company outside the marital home, but if so, it was done very discreetly.'[10] Politically, the late 1920s were turbulent times. Walter records in his unpublished manuscript *An Austrian Grandfather*:

> It was in July 1927 when I was six years old, just prior to my first year at school. (In Austria, school starts at that late age). I was staying at a children's camp at the Semmering, a spa near Vienna, when all of a sudden my father's cousin Harry, (the son of Alexander) drove up in his – or his father's – Graef and Stift, Austria's Rolls-Royce. 'Hurry up, Walter, we have to leave for Vienna at once!' and I remember packing and carrying my little suitcase and throwing it into the car with a grand gesture. I do not propose to into the ins and outs of that particular disturbance, but a mob had set on fire the Palace of Justice in Vienna and a Red revolution was expected, but did not in the event materialise. Harry was the only member of the family who owned a motorcar, so it had been his duty to collect me.[11]

Two years later there was further social unrest. The week of 7 November 1929 saw anti-Semitic disturbances in Austria when Nazi students interrupted classes of the Jewish professor Julius Tandler at the Anatomical Institute. The demonstration spilled onto the streets. In the ensuing years, sporadic disorder broke out. On 13 September 1931 the Austrian fascist group Die Heimwehr headed by Dr Pfrimer made an attempted Putsch. They marched on Vienna in an attempt to overthrow the government, succeeding in temporarily taking over the city. They were eventually defeated, but it was a worrying sign of worse to come. That same year the first attempts were made to install Martin Freud as manager of the International Psychoanalytical Verlag (Press) which published his father's works. Sigmund Freud sought to raise funds for the struggling company by embarking on another book entitled *New Introductory Lectures on Psycho-Analysis*. The existence of the press was crucial for disseminating his ideas at a time when his theories were still controversial and not accepted by the established medical profession. Over two consecutive years Sigmund Freud was dismissed for a Nobel Prize. He is arguably the greatest man never to have received a Nobel Prize. His diary entries for 31 October 1929 and 6 November 1930 make reference to this. In the latter entry he wrote: 'conclusively passed over for a Nobel Prize.' However earlier in the summer of 1930 he received recognition when he was awarded the Goethe Prize, the first step towards mainstream acceptance.

On a personal level his health was still not good. During 1930 he tried to give up smoking cigars, something he had done for fifty years. Like collecting antiquities, he claimed he needed them as one of the few pleasures in life. His grandson Walter commented: 'Grandfather was, by his own account, very much dependent on his cigars and claimed that without them he could not produce creative work.'[12] The cigars were the main cause of his illness and he was aware of that.

In January 1932 Martin travelled to Berlin to meet his father's friend and psychoanalyst Max Eitingon to finalize arrangements for taking over the business. The main stumbling block to the appointment of Martin as manager of the Verlag was Sigmund Freud himself. He took a long time to agree and on 19 January 1932 wrote to Eitingon about his son: 'My poor boy is walking around with a careworn expression, but has taken up his duties seriously.' He also made an appeal for funds from the wider international community of psychoanalysists to make the Verlag into an institution for the benefit of the field.

During 1932 Martin left Walter & Co to finally take over as Manager of the Verlag. The following year he successfully passed his bar examinations and was admitted to the Bar Association of Vienna. His legal knowledge was to be a vital asset. Through his work at the Verlag he met people engaged in the psychoanalytical field and was able to advise his father's clients on business affairs. He received much respect as the son of the founder of the movement and 'basked in this reflected light and thoroughly enjoyed a social distinction to which I had little claim in my own right.'[13] The first urgent task which faced him was to stall the creditors. He asked for a reprieve until the summer. He commented:

> I found the business side of the Press in a shocking state, and I doubt if it would ever have climbed to a sound business basis and avoided bankruptcy without the valuable help given by the International Psychoanalytical Association and its president, Dr Ernest Jones. As it turned out, the Nazis eventually had the doubtful privilege of taking over something of substance and value and then destroying it utterly.[14]

It was whilst he was sorting out the Verlag that he came in contact with Princess Marie Bonaparte, whom he also met during private family situations. She commented later about Martin and this period: 'I could then appreciate fully his lively personality, his youthful humour, which never deserted him in the most difficult circumstances, and which the passage of time has not dimmed in the least.'[15] The offices of the Verlag were just a short walk from Martin's parents' home at 19 Berggasse, first located in the Börse, the Stock Exchange Building. He visited his father daily for lunch which was set promptly at 1 p.m.. But in August of 1932, Martin became ill with kidney trouble, necessitating a period in hospital. He had become indispensable to the Verlag and was absent until September.

Within the Freud family, and with Martin in particular, there was a great pride in being Austrian. This much his son Walter emphasised in *An Austrian Grandfather*:

> After the war, the Habsburgs had gone but they were certainly not forgotten. Both my parents always expressed their greatest regard for the late old Emperor. My father was a reserve officer. As such, particularly after 1932 in the Dollfuss era, he was permitted to wear his former uniform. He

would don this on many a sunny spring Sunday, together with his medals, sword, spurs and other regalia. He would proudly march up and down the Ringstrasse together with me and my little sister, exchanging exaggerated salutes with others like him and probably ending up in the Berggasse. These dressing-up exercises must have recalled nostalgically the pre-war days of the K. & K. Monarchy, when it was said that the Austrian army was the best dressed, best dancing, but worst fighting one in Europe. He took his ceremonial sword with him to England, but in the next war he made it only to Private in the (Auxiliary Military Alien) Pioneer Corps and his days of glory had gone for ever.[16]

All that was about to change by the dramatic turn of events in Austria's neighbour, Germany. On 31 January 1933 Adolf Hitler became Chancellor of Germany. The following day, Sigmund Freud wrote to Jeanne Lampl de Groot in Berlin, a psychoanalyst and childhood friend of his son Martin: 'We are all curious what will come of the programme of Reichs Chancellor Hitler, whose only political theme is pogroms.'[17] Austria would not be immune from the consequences, and a month later Sigmund wrote to her again: 'Something uncanny is happening to our little Austrian state; naturally one does not know what.'[18] Hitler's new power in Germany set Europe on a path that would lead six years later to the outbreak of a Second World War and the annihilation of two-thirds of European Jewry. Austria's independence was threatened several times in the interim years, with episodes of political instability and civil unrest. Hitler's hatred for the Jews had already been voiced in his book *Mein Kampf* (1925). In Germany he began to impose by legal means the culture of a pure 'Aryan' race. That excluded legal rights and public roles for Jews, homosexuals, 'degenerate artists' and political opponents. Any excuse was sought to suppress the 'enemies' of the state. During the early hours of 28 February 1933 the Reichstag, the Berlin parliament, was set on fire. It was rumoured to have been a deliberate plot by Hermann Goering to provide Hitler with an excuse to round up political opponents and ban the Communist Press. That day Sigmund Freud entered in his diary: 'Berlin parliament on fire.' Ten thousand left-wingers were arrested and sent to a concentration camp, most to Dachau, which had been opened for the incarceration of political prisoners, initially housing socialists and communists.

Although the entries in Sigmund's diary only consist of a single sentence for each day over a ten-year period, he mentions every significant political event. He followed developments in Germany closely. On 5 March 1933 he noted: 'Election of Hitler in Germany.' That day communist votes were annulled to give Hitler a two-thirds majority in the German parliament. Hitler was now officially installed as Chancellor of Germany with Goering as Air Minister. The political developments in Germany obviously raised concerns in Sigmund Freud's mind about his own situation and possible emigration should Austria be invaded. He remained cautious about over-reacting. In March 1933, immediately after Hitler's accession in Germany, he wrote to Princess Marie Bonaparte: 'I have even been advised to flee to Switzerland or France. This is nonsense; I do not believe there is any danger here.'[19] The following month he wrote to friend and analyst Max Eitingon: 'Nobody here understands our political situation, people think it unlikely that it will develop as it has in your country ... I will only pack up and leave the place at the very last moment and probably not even then'.[20] From April 1933 the situation for Germany's Jews deteriorated dramatically when Jewish intellectuals were deprived of holding public office. Professionals began to leave the country, amongst them doctors, surgeons, lawyers, university professors, architects, scientists, musicians and businessmen. On 8 April 1933 Sigmund Freud wrote about the situation to Jeanne Lampl de Groot in Berlin:

> We hold fast to two points, to the determination not to move out and to the expectation that what happens here [in Austria] will be markedly different from Germany. We are on the way to a dictatorship of the right-wing parties who will ally themselves with the Nazis. This is far from good, but discriminatory laws against a minority are expressly forbidden in the peace declaration, the victorious powers will never permit annexation to Germany and our rabble is a bit less brutal than its German brethren.[21]

Sigmund Freud was wrong on all accounts. The Treaty of Versailles, drawn up at the end of First World War, was no ultimate protection for Austria. Regarding the Jewish population, Austrian Nazis turned out to be far more brutal and anti-Semitic than the Germans. By the autumn, Jews in Germany were excluded from journalism and the arts. German culture was disintegrating at an alarming rate, a formidable indicator of worse to come. The anti-Jewish laws affected Sigmund Freud's two sons living in Berlin. Oliver Freud left for the south of France. Ernst Freud, an eminent architect, was forced to leave the country in November 1933 to settle in England, his wife Lucie and their three sons having already fled that summer.[22] Sigmund's friends in Germany were also preparing to emigrate. Two of them, the writer Arnold Zweig and psychoanalyst Max Eitingon, left for Palestine.

Economic factors and high inflation affected Austria as much as Germany. It did not take Hitler to destroy Austrian democracy – that was the forte of Austrian Chancellor Engelbert Dollfuss who on 4 March 1933, less than a year after being in office, suspended parliament and ran the country under a self-style dictatorship.[23] Dollfuss banned the Nazis and Communist parties, provoking a backlash which led to a printer's strike on 25 March 1933. Less than two months later, on 1 May, the centre of Vienna was brought to a standstill with planned demonstrations by Nazis and Communists. Dollfuss was taking no chances and the city was sealed off to demonstrators. Their march did not go ahead, although sufficient disruption had been caused to make a point. Sigmund Freud reluctantly supported Dollfuss as a safe alternative to German designs on his country and the Nazi party taking a hold in Austria. Five days later was Sigmund Freud's seventy-seventh birthday during which he suffered an attack of dizziness which his doctor put down to too much nicotine. Freud wrote to Princess Marie Bonaparte: 'since then I have been restricted to three cigars'.

Events in Germany were taking an alarming turn. On 10 May 1933, Goebbels ordered the burning of 'undesirable' books which included those of Sigmund Freud. In Berlin's university square, academics including professors and students gathered late that evening to begin an action of sacrilegious symbolism. Groups of SS and SA men paraded with flags and torchlights, chanting to the sound of band music. That night it is estimated that some 20,000 books were burned, including those of Karl Marx and anyone with a Jewish name. Many of those who took part in the action had little or no knowledge of the contents of the books. Sigmund Freud's own works were hurled into the flames to the words:

> Against soul-disintegrating exaggeration of the instinctual life for the nobility of the human soul, I commit to the flames the writings of Sigmund Freud.

This action was shocking enough if committed by the general public, but the fact that it was done by the leading German intellectuals was a betrayal of everything they stood for. Their act was a betrayal of the freedom of thought, upheld and cherished by universities and intellectuals. Freud noted the tragic turn of events in his diary the following day. He also commented: 'What progress we are making. In the Middle Ages they would have burnt me: nowadays they are content with burning my books.' How wrong he was proved to be. The Nazis were not ultimately content to burn books. The prophetic words of the Jewish poet Heinrich Heine fifty years earlier: 'Where one burns books, one will, in the end, burn people' would become a reality in the concentration camps in Germany, Poland and other parts of Eastern Europe. The following month, June 1933, the Nazis took control of the German Society for Psychotherapy, using it to promote Aryan ideals and obliterate any concepts deemed to have derived from Jewish psychology. Each member of the society had to embrace the principles of *Mein Kampf* as the basis for their work. Over the course of the coming year Jewish analysts left Germany. Psychoanalysis, and in particular the work of Freud, had no future in the country.

The events in Germany of 1933 played on Sigmund Freud's mind. Although he was not a practising Jew, the persecution of Jews in Germany sparked a personal quest for answers to the roots of his own identity and the cause of anti-Semitism. Freud located everything in the founding figure of Judaism: namely Moses. His inner struggle sparked the beginning of his final seminal work which was eventually titled *Moses and Monotheism*. It took a number of years to compete; he started it in 1933 and finally published it in 1939. In a letter to writer Arnold Zweig, he told him about the argument underpinning the new work. Moses was to blame: 'Faced with new persecution, one asks oneself again how the Jews have come to be what they are and why they have attracted this undying hatred. I soon discovered the formula: Moses created the Jews.'[24]

That summer of 1933 Martin Freud was in hospital again, this time with symptoms caused by possible blood poisoning. His father's diary entry for 8 July 1933 read, 'Martin's furunculosis.' The family doctor was unable to treat the condition by the usual method of lancing boils, so Martin was admitted to hospital. That year Sigmund Freud also suffered from a period of prolonged ill-health. In writing to Ernest Jones, he said:

'I am out of bed, have already been making a modest start at work for a week, feel "moderately" well but the consequences of the thrombosis have not yet been overcome and I paid for a first attempt to climb the stairs with a hefty relapse.'[25]

In October 1933, having recovered his health, Martin passed his bar exams. That same month on 3 October, Rudolf Drtil, a Nazi sympathiser, made an attempt on Chancellor Dollfuss's life. Although he was unsuccessful, tensions remained under the surface of Austrian life, only to break out the following year. At the end of 1933 Martin Freud took his son Walter on a skiing holiday. Whilst they were there Martin was taken ill, this time with kidney trouble. After three days he was rushed into the Rothschild hospital and operated on to remove a kidney stone. High fever followed the operation and his situation remained grave. The crisis passed, but by the end of January 1934 the wound still had not healed, necessitating a six-week recovery period at Sanatorium Gutenbrunn in Baden.

Political tensions continued to ferment under the surface of Austrian society, breaking out again in the spring of 1934. Sigmund Freud noted them all in his diary. On 11 February socialists attacked the provincial party headquarters of Dollfuss, leading to a general strike and civil war. Dollfuss imposed a curfew and crushed the civil unrest within a matter of days, but in so doing he had destroyed any possible effective opposition to Nazism within Austria. Dollfuss's days were numbered. On 25 July a group of Nazis broke into his offices on the Ballhausplatz and assassinated him. Although the uprising was successfully quelled, a Nazi invasion of Austria appeared imminent. It was stalled by the intervention of Italian leader Mussolini who mobilised Italian troops across the Brenner Pass. Mussolini had already signed a treaty with Great Britain and France asserting and protecting Austrian independence from Germany. A few days later Martin Freud decided to attend Dollfuss's funeral in full military regalia, proudly donning his First World War uniform, polishing the medals and attaching his dress sword. He described the occasion in his autobiography:

I arrived in good time for the funeral ceremony, being allowed through the cordon of police and troops surrounding the imposing Gothic building where the funeral service was to be held, and being honoured with the usual salute. Few Viennese people attended the funeral. The majority of the Viennese population were now Socialists who had become hostile to the Dolfuss regime after their defeat in the first civil war. A fair proportion were Nazis who regretted that the coup designed to bring down the Government had failed. However, there were many foreign correspondents present taking the usual photographs for their papers. If some of these photographs survive, they may show a lonely artillery officer standing at the foot of the small coffin, one obviously not at ease in his unaccustomed high stiff collar. The service was soon over and the coffin carried out with military honours. The cordon around the Town Hall marched off and now I stood isolated at the great entrance with only the foreign correspondents to keep me company. They were busy packing their equipment. I tried to get into conversation with one or two of them, hoping to see a foreign and detached view of Austria's chances of maintaining her independence, a subject dear to my heart; but they showed not the slightest inclination to say anything to one they probably took for a mere low-browed artillery Lieutenant. I consoled myself with the thought that they would not have been able to enlighten me very much. I had to continue asking myself how long Austria would be able to defend her independence.[26]

It was a year of assassinations. On 9 October 1934, King Alexander I of Yugoslavia and French Foreign Minister Jean Barthou were murdered by Macedonian and Croat terrorists in Marseilles. Europe was becoming increasingly unstable as socialists, nationalist groups and Nazis vied for power and influence.

Throughout 1934, Sigmund Freud continued to suffer from the effects of cancer as well as circulatory and cardiac disorders and spells of dizziness. His cancer was kept under control with X-ray and radium treatment such that no operations were necessary that year. The following year saw four operations and the fitting of a new prosthesis. On 2 August 1934 German President Hindenburg died at the age of eighty-six, paving the way for Adolf Hitler to grasp a tighter hold on power. Hitler was proclaimed 'Führer and Reichskanzler' [Chancellor]. Hindenburg's death prompted Sigmund Freud to write to American Smith Ely Jelliffe: 'This very day the news of the death of the German President Hindenburg has come and nobody can guess what consequences developments in Germany may have for our poor Austria.

We would be enjoying beautiful summer peace in a delightful suburb of Vienna if the political situation allowed it.'[27]

There was more to come the following year. In Germany, Hitler was actively re-arming his forces in contravention of the Treaty of Versailles. In March 1935 he formed the *Luftwaffe*, the German air force, and on 16 March introduced conscription for men between eighteen and forty-five. There was worse news for Germany's Jews when in the summer of 1935 he passed the Nuremberg Laws, effectively outcasting Jews. In April 1935 Martin Freud returned from Zurich, having been there on business, taking the opportunity to move his father's assets around, something which ultimately was to save a large part of his father's fortune. Abroad his father's pioneering work in psychoanalysis received recognition in Britain when Sigmund Freud was nominated as an honorary member of the Royal Society of Medicine. He was suitably impressed by this significant development and wrote to the Society: 'For many years my scientific work found no recognition among physicians. In the honour I am receiving from the Royal Society of Medicine I see a sign that psychoanalysis, which I have practiced and recommended, can no longer escape recognition by the medical world.'[28]

In the interim years between the assassination of Dolfuss and the annexing of Austria by Hitler in 1938, Martin Freud continued as Director of International Psychoanalytical Press [Verlag]. The offices of the Verlag had moved to 7 Berggasse in January 1936. The building now housed both the Verlag and the Vienna Psychoanalytical Society. The Verlag also had outlets in Germany, but on 25 March 1936 its stock of books in Leipzig was impounded by the Nazis. Sigmund Freud immediately penned a letter to Princess Marie Bonaparte: 'From Leipzig comes the news that the Gestapo has confiscated a large proportion of the psychoanalytic books in stock at Volkmar's, almost a catastrophe for the poor Verlag.'[29] Six weeks later on 6 May Sigmund celebrated his eightieth birthday. Letters of congratulations and best wishes flooded in from eminent friends and public figures around the world. These included H.G Wells, Albert Einstein, Thomas Mann and Albert Schweitzer. A congratulatory address from 200 prominent writers was printed in *The Times*. It highlighted the huge esteem and respect felt for this giant pioneering figure:

The eightieth birthday of Sigmund Freud gives us the welcome opportunity of offering our congratulations and homage to the master whose
discoveries have opened up the way to a new and profounder understanding
of mankind. He has made eminent contributions to medicine, psychology, philosophy and art, and has been for two generations the pioneer in
exploring hitherto unknown regions of the mind ... The most memorable
achievement of our generation will be, beyond doubt, the psychological
achievement of Sigmund Freud. We cannot picture the intellectual world
today without his work.[30]

The following month the scientific community in Britain honoured
him again; this time with membership of The Royal Society. The political scene was never far away though. In July 1936 Hitler reoccupied
the Rhineland in a further erosion of the Treaty of Versailles. Austrian
Chancellor Schuschnigg was forced to take two Nazi sympathisers into
his government and lift the ban on Nazi newspapers. In December 1936
Britain was rocked by the abdication of King Edward VIII, recorded by
Sigmund Freud in his diary. He always took a keen interest in British
affairs, telling his son Ernst two years earlier: 'I regularly read English
novels for an hour before going to sleep and in this way I am becoming
initiated into the charm of English landscapes.'[31] His assessment of the
abdication is clear in a letter to Marie Bonaparte:

What is going on with the King? I think he is a poor fellow, no intellectual,
none too bright, probably a latent homosexual who came to this woman by
way of a friend and found his potency with her and therefore cannot get by
without her.

Sigmund Freud's eightieth year had been characterised by celebrations,
including his golden wedding anniversary on 14 September, but it was
also one of ill-health and periods of pain. That continued into 1937 and
on 22 April he underwent an operation to remove a non-malignant
growth. His closest friend Marie Bonaparte sensed that things in Europe
were coming to a climax and commented: 'The greatest happiness of my
life is to have met you, to have been your contemporary.'[32] His grandson
Walter recalled the last years in Vienna with his grandfather:

In all the years I knew Grandfather, not once did I witness him losing his temper, making a scene or behaving otherwise than calmly and collectedly. The hysterical and unstable temperament of his patients had definitely not rubbed off on him; he was the antithesis of being highly-strung. But the most prominent impression I had of him was his helpfulness and the feeling that he would look after one. He was a leader type of biblical proportions. It was only in my last years in Vienna, when I was sixteen years and over, that I was treated as an adult and given the opportunity to have meaningful discussions with Grandfather. He would ask me into his study, a most impressive room by any standard, and the conversation would range outside and above my efforts at school.[33]

In the summer of 1937, Esti Freud took her children Walter and Sophie to Grado for what would be their last holiday together. This was followed by a month in the Tyrolean mountains. The days of Austrian independence were numbered. In the opening page of *Mein Kampf*, first published in 1925, Adolf Hitler had made his designs on Austria very clear:

> German-Austria must return to the great German mother country, and not because of any economic considerations. No, and again no; even if such a union were unimportant from an economic point of view; yes even if it were harmful, it must nevertheless take place. One blood demands one Reich.

In March 1938 the situation for Austrian Jews, the Freuds being no exception, was about to change irrevocably. When Hitler first became Chancellor of Germany in 1933, Sigmund Freud's son-in-law Robert Hollitscher had prophesied: 'He will annex Austria and drive out the Jews.' Sigmund Freud commented to his grandson Walter: 'Don't we live in a dreadful world where Uncle Robert is always right.'[34]

4

Finis Austriae

During the night and early hours of 12 March 1938, Hitler ordered his troops over the border into Austria in what became known as the *Anschluss*. That fateful day Sigmund Freud responded to the news by writing in his diary the dramatic words: 'Finis Austriae'. His life and that of his extended family was about to be turned upside-down by the Nazis. The year had not started well for Freud. His severe facial pain reoccurred and on 22 January Pichler operated again to remove a malignant tumour close to the right eye socket. There was also the worrying news of political developments in neighbouring Germany. Changes were being introduced to strengthen Hitler's powerbase and dictatorship and on 4 February Hitler dismissed his generals and appointed himself Supreme Commander of the German armed forces. Now the Austrian question was uppermost in his mind. Two days later on 6 February Herr von Papen, the German ambassador to Austria, took a train to the town of Hitler's birth Linz, and was driven to the Berghof at Berchtesgaden, Bavaria to meet the Führer himself. The aim of their meeting was to offer a 'solution' to the Austrian situation. Events then moved swiftly, with Sigmund Freud following them closely and noting them in his diary. Less than a week later on Saturday 12 February, Austrian Chancellor Kurt von Schuschnigg arrived at the Berghof with Dr Guido Schmidt, Minister of State for Foreign Affairs, for talks at Hitler's behest. In an alarming development the Nazi figure Dr Arthur von Seyss-Inquart, who would shortly betray Schuschnigg, was appointed Austrian Minister of the Interior with control over the police force. Schuschnigg and Federal President Wilhelm Miklas were forced to accept the appointment. A Viennese witness to the events in Vienna at that time, George Clare (born Georg Klaar) commented in his autobiography *Last Waltz in Vienna*: 'The one politician, though far from power, who understood what was happening, foresaw the consequences and warned, but of course was not taken seriously, was Winston Churchill.'[1] From the political wilderness on the back benches, Churchill spoke about the grave developments in the House of Commons on 12 February, referring to reoccupation of the Rhineland by Germany which began in 1936:

> Now we know that a firm stand by France and Britain, under the authority of the League of Nations, would have been followed by the immediate evacuation of the Rhineland without the shedding of a drop of blood; and the effects of that might have enabled the more prudent elements in the German army to regain their proper position, and would not have given to the political head in Germany that enormous ascendancy which has enabled him to move forward. Now we are at a moment when a third move is made, but when that opportunity does not present itself in the same favourable manner. Austria has been laid in thrall, and we do not know whether Czechoslovakia will not suffer a similar fate.

For the first time in a new development on Sunday 20 February, the Austrian people could hear Hitler's three-hour radio broadcast from the Reichstag, the German parliament. In it, he spelt out his economic achievements in Germany and his successful industrial growth. For those with an astute ear, they could not have missed his failure to assert Austrian independence. That day Sigmund's daughter Anna Freud wrote to Ernest Jones in England: 'There was an atmosphere of panic in Vienna which has now calmed down a little. We have not joined in the panic. It is too early, one can not yet fully assess the consequences of what has happened.'[2] On 23 February Sigmund Freud wrote to Princess Marie Bonaparte: 'It undeniably looks like the beginning of the end for me. But we have no other choice than to hold out here.' The following day on 24 February Chancellor Schuschnigg responded to recent events with an impassioned appeal to his country, calling for unity with the political

Left. It was to be the most important speech of his career and a last-ditch attempt to defy Hitler and assert Austrian independence. He ended with the patriotic call: 'Red-white-red [the flag] until death! Austria!'

Sigmund Freud followed events closely, noting the speech in his diary. It covered seven pages of the *Neue Freie Presse* the next day. In a further move to guarantee Austrian independence Schuschnigg made an announcement on 9 March that there would be a plebiscite, a referendum, the following week. Austrians would be able to vote for a free independent, Christian and united Austria. In an unusual move, he announced the plebiscite from his hometown of Innsbruck and not Vienna. Sigmund Freud noted this too in his diary. Tensions were mounting in Austria; it was widely expected that Hitler would invade. Now it was not a matter of if, but when. A flurry of international diplomatic moves was afoot to protect Sigmund Freud if the seemingly inevitable happened. On 10 March he received a visit at home from John Wiley, the Chargé d'Affaires at the American Embassy. The situation was grave – Hitler was calling for Schuschnigg's resignation. At 7.45 p.m. the following day, Friday 11 March, Schuschnigg called off the referendum. Sigmund Freud simply entered in his diary: 'Schuschnigg's resignation.' He and his family listened to the resignation speech on the radio that evening. Schuschnigg had no desire to see the shedding of Austrian blood and in a move to protect his people, he urged Austrian forces not to oppose a German invasion. The speech ended with the prayer '*Gott schütze sterreich*' ('God save Austria').

Austria would need it. Annexation was now certain. Austrian Jews knew they had most to fear from its consequences. Through the night of 12 March German forces crossed the border, completing Hitler's dream of a united German-Austria. A massive German military force consisting of tanks, infantry divisions and storm-troopers now occupied Austrian soil. *The Times*, a British newspaper, reported: 'After a day of indescribable nervous tension, the Austria of Dolfuss and Schuschnigg – the Catholic-Fascist Austria that by force suppressed parliament four years ago – collapsed overnight under the threat of force.'[3] Sigmund Freud's words 'Finis Austriae' became a reality. Austria was not just politically finished but also culturally and intellectually. The land of culture, music and famous architecture was about to be desecrated. The new Nazi powers did not view it that way. Dr Goebbels broadcast Hitler's highly-charged jubilant victory speech on the radio in which he said: 'The world must realise that the German people in Austria these days are experiencing utmost bliss and joy. Austria sees in the brothers who have come to her help the saviours from their deepest misery. Long live the National-Socialist German Reich! Long live National-Socialist German Austria!'

The anti-Jewish laws which had gradually restricted the lives of German Jews over at least five years came into immediate force for 200,000 Austrian Jews, 180,000 of whom were living in Vienna. From that moment, the cultural and social fabric of Austrian society began to crumble as its Jewish population was denied its public roles. They sought ways to leave the country. Visa queues outside the British Embassy in Vienna grew daily. Notices appeared on shop windows everywhere with the words 'Jews not wanted here'. A number of Jewish businessmen under house arrest took desperate measures and committed suicide, including Sigmund Freud's friend Friedl Stadlen. Jewish doctors were accused of performing illegal abortions. Ex-Viennese refugee Eric Sanders who later became Walter Freud's closest friend in SOE, commented:

> My parents closed our shop and our major daily activities concentrated on what was necessary to be done and could be done towards the urgent goal of getting out of Austria. I had considered myself a loyal Austrian, a Viennese, whose religion happened to be Jewish. The edifice constructed within my mind whilst growing up, was shattered. The Austrians were rejecting and ejecting me.[4]

Of the *Anschluss* Martin Freud wrote in *Glory Reflected*:

> My father at this time had begun to watch developments with eager interest, often expressing warm admiration for the brave Schuschnigg. Because the *Abend* [newspaper] had been a strong supporter of Austrian independence, he felt the paper that Paula [their maid] would bring back would give a reliable report and reduce the prevailing confusion to simple truth. After gently taking the paper from Paula's hands, he read through the headlines and then, crumpling it in his fist, he threw it into a corner of the room. Such a scene might not be unusual in any happy land not enduring political convulsions; but father's perfect self-control seldom, or never, permitted him to show emotion: and thus all of us remained silent in the living-room, well aware that

a turn of events which would allow him to fling a paper from him in disgust and disappointment must have alarming implications.[5]

The Austrian newspapers immediately began to instil ordinary news items with anti-Semitic propaganda. Martin Freud commented: 'All this, we knew, was bad for Austria, a tragedy indeed: but as I read through the paper, I saw that the tragedy had narrowed down for us: that we, Jews, would be the first victims.'[6] Although things were serious enough, Martin Freud believed that his father had not yet seriously contemplated emigration. The idea was floated, even somewhat casually, but no serious attempt was made to start emigration proceedings. The day after the *Anschluss*, the streets were full of Austrian Nazis, described by Martin Freud:

> Their band-wagons crowded with innumerable turncoats, were in full possession of Vienna. No one had offered resistance; and what resistance could there have been when it was known that the powerful German army was marching towards the capital while German bombers, cruising noisily overhead, were heralding its approach?[7]

Hundreds of German bombers, flying low in formation over the city, were dropping propaganda leaflets on a waiting population. Brown shirts with swastika flags were on the streets chanting '*Juda-verr-recke!*' ('Perish Judah!'). The round-up of Jews began. They were made to scrub the pavements to the sound of jeering onlookers. That same day members of the Vienna Psychoanalytical Society urgently met at Sigmund Freud's home to assess their position. At the meeting Freud made one of his parallels between the history of his people and their present situation:

> After the destruction of the Temple in Jerusalem by Titus, Rabbi Jochanan ben Sakkai asked for permission to open a school at Jabneh for the study of Torah. We are going to do the same. We are, after all, used to persecution by our history, tradition and some of us by personal experience.[8]

It was agreed to disband the Society and start again wherever Freud settled. Their decision was an acknowledgement that Freud would have to emigrate, but it would take two Gestapo raids on his home and the tempo-rary arrest of his daughter Anna for Sigmund Freud to face reality. Martin Freud's thoughts at this time were powerfully expressed in *Glory Reflected*:

> My own feelings, if I may express what I felt, were of horror and a strange perplexity. I, a respectable barrister and the eldest son of a man of world-wide reputation, nurtured in security and not unaffected by father's fame, I could only imagine myself enduring a nightmare, as of an innocent man standing in the dock to be condemned by judges unconcerned with a trial, and sen-tenced to death in dishonour.[9]

The following day, 14 March, Hitler paraded through the streets of Vienna in an open Mercedes, amidst a rapturous welcome from the crowd. Thousands lined the route and cheered the procession of SS officers and SA men which stretched the length of the thoroughfare towards the Hofburg where it was rumoured the Archbishop of Vi-enna Cardinal Innitzer was to give Hitler a blessing, thus procuring the allegiance and support of Austrian Catholics. Hitler spoke from the bal-cony of the Hofburg, ending his proclamation with the words: 'Long live National-Socialist German-Austria!' Austria had never seen such a magnificent display of military power. It was a euphoric moment for the people of Vienna, but one of ominous fear for the city's Jews who hid behind closed doors. Hitler, the man who had once swept the steps of Vienna's Imperial Hotel, now stood in power over all he surveyed. He had returned to scourge the world for the rest of the century. Martin Freud wrote of that dreadful day:

> The population was in the street, even in the quiet Berggasse, where the Freud family lived. Spoiled by devilish propaganda they did not stop shout-ing 'Heil Hitler, Heil unserem Fuehrer!' Paula [their maid] was caught in the midst of the enthusiastic mob, she felt forced to protest. 'My Führer is the professor Freud', she shouted, nearly sacrificing her skin for the man she so deeply venerated. She had to run very fast, but fortunately the entrance door to No. 19 was near.[10]

The day that Hitler marched into Vienna, Winston Churchill was deliv-ering another of his prescient speeches in The House of Commons, warning the government of the situation. Referring to the *Anschluss*, he said:

> The gravity of the event of March 12 cannot be exaggerated. Europe is confronted with a programme of aggression, nicely calculated and timed, unfolding stage by stage, and there is only one choice open, not only to us but to other countries, either to submit like Austria, or else take effective measures while time remains to ward off the danger, and if it cannot be warded off to cope with it ... Where are we going to be two years hence, for instance, when the German army will certainly be much larger than the French army, and when all the small nations will have fled from Geneva to pay homage to the ever-waxing power of the Nazi system and to make the best terms that they can for themselves?

On the strategic importance of Vienna falling into Nazi hands, he added:

> Vienna is the centre of the communications of all the countries which formed the old Austro-Hungarian Empire, and of the countries lying to the south-east of Europe. A long stretch of the Danube is now in German hands. This mastery of Vienna gives to Nazi Germany military and economic control of the whole of the communications of South-Eastern Europe by road, by river, and by rail.

Less than twenty-four hours after Hitler's triumphant, Messianic acclamation the danger for the Freud family became an immediate reality. On 15 March the Gestapo raided Sigmund Freud's home at 19 Berggasse and the offices of the International Psychoanalytical Press [Verlag] at 7 Berggasse. That day Sigmund Freud was still recovering from one of his cancer operations when Gestapo officers barged into his apartment. Martha Freud remained calm throughout the ordeal, defusing the stress by treating the intruders like welcome visitors: '... inviting them to put their rifles in the sections of the hall-stand reserved for umbrellas and even to sit down. And although her invitation was not accepted, her courtesy and courage had had a good effect. Father, too had retained his invincible poise, leaving his sofa where he had been resting to join mother in the dining room, where he had sat calmly in his armchair throughout the raid.'[11] All family passports were confiscated along with 6,000 schillings (about £300) from the safe. A receipt was issued for the items taken away. Sigmund Freud commented: 'I have never taken so much for a single visit.' According to Martin Freud, even at this point his father did not consider his days in Vienna numbered. It is fair to say he was in denial:

> In spite of this trying ordeal, I do not think father had yet any thought of leaving Austria. His intention, so far as I could judge, was to ride out the storm in the belief, shared by many civilised Europeans at this time, that the Nazi eruption was so out of step with the march of civilisation, a civilisation apparently supported by so many powerful democratic countries, that a normal rhythm would soon be restored and honest men permitted to go on their ways without fear.[12]

On the same day that Freud's home was raided, John Wiley sent a telegram to the United States Secretary of State in Washington: 'Fear Freud, despite age and illness, in danger.'[13] The new order in Austria was having ramifications for the whole Freud family. Down the street at 7 Berggasse a second raid was happening that day. The offices of the International Psychoanalytical Press were also being searched by an irregular group of SA men. The ordeal was narrated in detail by Martin Freud who was in his office at the time:

> Although I was held in awkward imprisonment in my office chair, two of my guards keeping their rifles pressed against my stomach for much of that Sunday, the time passed quickly enough. The antics of this crazy gang in possession of my office offered no entertainment, but a great deal happened to keep me interested. The safe had been rifled and the contents of the cash drawers, a considerable amount of money in coins and notes of a number of countries, had been placed in piles on a table, but I had removed the papers I wanted to destroy from the safe and placed them on a shelf where they had not been noticed by the raiders. My chief danger, I soon guessed, lay in the silly mind of the haggard-looking man with the revolver who, unlike the others with rifles, had live ammunition and might be controlled by an hysterical impulse if not treated carefully.[14]

That same day, 15 March, a plane touched down at Vienna airport carrying one of Sigmund Freud's closest friends, Ernest Jones. Direct flights from England to Vienna were not available then, so he flew first to Prague and then took a smaller plane to complete the journey. Concerned for Freud's safety, Jones had arrived to persuade him to leave the country and to find ways of getting other analysts out of Austria. He was not hopeful of persuading Sigmund, as he wrote of his friend:

> On many occasions in his life he had debated taking such a step [emigration], and on many others he had been invited to do so. But something deep in his nature had always striven against such a decision and even at this final and critical moment he was still most unwilling to contemplate it. Knowing how strong was this reluctance, and how often in the last few years he had expressed his determination to stay in Vienna to the end, I was not very hopeful about the outcome.[15]

Jones could not have been prepared for the depressing sight which greeted him at the airport. It graphically underlined the risk that his friend was now in. He wrote: 'The airfield was stacked with German military planes and the air was full of them assiduously intimidating the Viennese. The streets were full of roaring tanks and also of roaring people with their shouts of "Heil Hitler".'[16] Jones turned up at the offices of the International Psychoanalytical Press [Verlag] just as it was being raided. He too was arrested, threatened by the irregular gang, and not allowed to speak to Martin Freud. After an hour he was released and left the premises to visit Sigmund Freud at his home and protest to higher Nazi authorities about the Freuds' treatment. Martin was left alone again with the motley gang. As the raiders gradually thinned out, he remained in the custody of one guard who was somewhat more relaxed. The guard began a tale of woe about recent hardships. Martin took the opportunity to empty his pockets of some gold coins and a roll of notes. The guard was deeply grateful for the generosity, but Martin had an alternative motive. He figured the guard could not now refuse him a visit to the toilet. Over the coming hours he made numerous trips to the toilet along the corridor to surreptitiously dispose of business documents which the Nazis might see as suspect if confiscated. He commented: 'I managed to organise quite a number of journeys across the passage until all the papers were torn up and all had begun a procession along the elaborate Viennese sewer system.'[17] Later in the day the district commander of nearby SS headquarters arrived to give Martin and Anna a *passier-schein* (pass) to call at the authorities the following day without fear of being arrested.[18] Martin was then released to return to 19 Berggasse to check on his parents. He was now barred from practising as a lawyer and his business was eventually confiscated.

Events continued to move swiftly. On the same day as the two raids on the Freud premises, Hitler gave a belligerent speech at the Austrian War Memorial in which he spoke of Austria as 'the bastion of the German Reich in the east, the iron guarantor of the Reich freedom and security.'[19] In a further worrying development, on 16 March the Vienna police paraded before Herr Himmler and each one personally swore allegiance to Hitler. Austrian Jews could no longer rely on state protection. Diplomatic efforts now began in earnest to get Sigmund Freud and his family out of Austria. Appeals were made to the US government as well as the Italian Fascist leader Mussolini, although there is no indication that any action was taken by him. In Paris the German ambassador received a visit from William Bullitt, American Ambassador to France, giving him a stark warning over Sigmund Freud's safety: 'A world scandal would ensue if the Nazis ill-treated Freud.'[20]

Concerned by the turn of events and the Freuds' peril, Princess Marie Bonaparte arrived in Vienna on 17 March, staying at the Greek Legation until 10 April. Every day she took meals at their home and spent a considerable amount of time with them. Realising that the Freuds' emigration to England was now inevitable, she began to sort through family papers with Anna Freud to salvage the most important ones to take to England. She worked tirelessly to secure their safety and Freud's valuable collection of antiquities. Martin Freud said of her: 'Our last sad weeks in Vienna from 11 March until the end of May would have been quite unbearable without the presence of the Princess.'[21] Princess Marie Bonaparte herself described it as 'the terrible days of Hitler's invasion of Austria, when Hitler destroyed the peace and charm of Vienna I had myself known for so many years, full of mirth, music and, for those who lived in Freud's atmosphere, of the serenity of scientific research.'[22]

Having already endured one raid, the Freud family was not yet out of danger. Exactly a week after the first raid, on 22 March they were searched again by the Gestapo. This time Anna Freud was arrested and taken to Gestapo headquarters. Princess Marie Bonaparte offered to be detained with her, but the officers would not risk taking someone with a royal passport. The situation for Anna Freud was precarious. She faced possible deportation to a concentration camp. In the event that Anna and Martin were both interrogated by the Gestapo, the family doctor Dr Schur had given them a sufficient dose of Veronal. That day affected the whole family. Dr Schur later said: 'The hours were endless. It was the only time I ever saw Freud deeply worried. He paced the floor, smoking incessantly.'[23] Jones also described the seriousness of the situation that day: 'It was certainly the blackest day in [Sigmund] Freud's life. The thought that the most precious being in the world, and also the one on whom he so depended, might be in danger of being tortured and deported to a concentration camp, as so commonly happened, was hardly to be borne. Freud spent the whole day pacing up and down and smoking an endless series of cigars to deaden his emotions.'[24] Only now Sigmund Freud began to realise that emigration was the only likely outcome. This much Martin Freud admitted in *Glory Reflected*:

He [Sigmund] began to see the writing on the wall on Tuesday 22 March. At one o'clock on that day, I went as usual to the Berggasse and found the flat swarming with SS men in smart uniforms. After a little consideration, I decided to make my visit as short as possible. There was nothing I could do to help; and the fact that I was not popular with the Nazis might even be harmful. The first was the view I had from the window of Anna being driven off in an open car escorted by four heavily armed SS men. Her situation was perilous; but far from showing fear, or even much interest, she sat in the car as a woman might sit in a taxi on her way to enjoy a shopping expedition. The second scene, quite as clearly outlined, is of mother [Martha Freud], highly indignant with an SS man who, on his way through a passage, paused at a large cupboard, pulled upon its doors and began roughly dragging out her piles of beautifully laundered linen all efficiently arranged in the way dear to her housewifely heart, each package held together with coloured ribbons. Without showing the slightest fear, mother joined the fellow and in highly indignant tones told him precisely what she thought of his shocking behaviour in a lady's house, and ordered him to stop at once. The SS man, a big fellow, jumped back from the cupboard and looked quite terrified, quickly withdrawing and appearing very sheepish indeed as mother rearranged her linen.[25]

Anna was interrogated at Gestapo headquarters, an ordeal during which she successfully persuaded the SS officers that the International Psychoanalytical Association was a non-political organisation and not a subversive anti-Nazi movement. She was eventually released and returned home around 7pm. Martin Freud later commented that she had been in a place where: 'the chance to come out again safe and sound was not greater than 50–50.'[26]

The Freud family knew their days in Vienna were numbered. Sigmund Freud knew that it was not only about him. He was now eighty-two, ill with cancer and may well have stayed in Vienna, but he realised that he had to get out for the sake of the family. Their survival was paramount. Princess Marie Bonaparte and Ernest Jones were instrumental in arranging their emigration papers. They did everything possible to get exit visas for the Freud family and a number of other Viennese analysts who were also at risk. A total of twenty-four permits were required: eighteen adults and six children. Although by 28 March emigration for the Freuds was within sight, there was still a long way to go. Before they were free to leave they were required to pay the *Reichsfluchtsteuer*, the hefty 'fleeing tax' calculated at twenty-five per cent of their assets, something which was required from all Jews leaving Austria. They also needed the *Unbed-enklichkeitserklärung*, the statement of no impediment, confirming that they owed nothing to the State. To enable that to happen, the Press and all Sigmund Freud's assets had to be liquidated. Due to bureaucracy and confusion over new laws, this process took two months to complete. Jones wrote to Sigmund Freud: 'The delay is not our fault, it is connected with the wealth and property transactions and with the peculiarities of this transitional period during which the officials are no longer certain which rules they should be working by.'[27]

The situation for Austria's Jews was deteriorating further. By April 1938, over seven and a half thousand Jews had been arrested by the Gestapo. On 1 April, the first train of political prisoners left for Dachau concentration camp. The following day, Britain officially recognised the German annexation of Austria by Germany. America and France followed suit. Only Chile, China, Mexico and the Soviet Union refused. The following week on 9 April Hitler was back in Vienna to secure results of a referendum in his favour. The people voted overwhelmingly to accept the new order, with the slogan: 'We are Germans and belong to Germany and to the Führer forever.' By now the strain of events around him meant that Sigmund Freud himself could no longer concentrate sufficiently to treat his patients. He told one of his pupils Smiley Blanton: 'When the conscious mind is troubled, one cannot be interested in the unconscious mind.'[28] Instead he focused on writing up his theories about the prophet Moses and completing with Anna a translation of Marie Bonaparte's book *Topsy*. He was frustrated about *Moses and Monotheism*, telling Ernest Jones: 'I work for an hour a day on my *Moses*, which torments me like a "ghost not laid". I wonder if I shall ever complete this third part despite all the outer and inner difficulties. At present I cannot believe it.'[29]

Princess Marie Bonaparte returned to Vienna on 17 April to keep the Freuds under her protection. She made numerous trips to Vienna during this precarious period, often staying for a few days at a time. When she departed, she smuggled out items from Sigmund Freud's valuable collection of antiquities. Martin Freud also sent some of his father's library to Switzerland, but this ultimately did not save the collection of books. He wrote:

> Indeed, the Nazis were not satisfied to destroy the books remaining in Vienna; they arranged to have returned a much larger number which I had sent to Switzerland for safe keeping. The Nazi official who organized this business showed a strange sense of humour when he debited father's account with the quite considerable cost of the books' transportation to their funeral pyre in Vienna.[30]

With Princess Marie Bonaparte now in Vienna keeping an eye on the Freuds, Ernest Jones felt comfortable about returning to England to sort out the visas and permissions for the family to emigrate there. Through a number of contacts at the Royal Society Jones was able to write directly to the Home Secretary Sir Samuel Hoare. The result was astounding and was achieved more easily than he had imagined possible:

> To my great relief, Sir Samuel Hoare without any hesitation displayed his usual philanthropic qualities and gave me carte blanche to fill in permits, including permission to work, for Freud, his family, servants, his personal doctors, and a certain number of his pupils with their families. Refugees at that

time were otherwise less lucky; they had to find someone willing to guarantee their support.[31]

One hurdle had been overcome. Now what remained was to persuade
the Nazis to grant permission for the Freuds to leave. No one was under
any illusion about how difficult this was going to be. It took nearly
three months and delicate negotiations to secure that. In his diary entry
for 5 May 1938, Sigmund Freud penned the words: 'Negotiation with
Gestapo.' The Nazi commissar assigned to winding up the Freud assets
was Dr Anton Sauerwald. Although a Nazi, ironically Sauerwald had studied chemistry under Dr Herzig, one of Sigmund Freud's oldest friends.
This connection was to be crucial. He soon developed a loyalty to the
Freuds that was to be the saving grace in the coming weeks. Freud's last
will and testament had been confiscated, but Dr Sauerwald chose not to
disclose it to the Nazi authorities because it listed all of Freud's foreign
assets. Holding foreign assets was illegal under the new regime and would
have jeopardised Freud's emigration. Without the discretion of Sauerwald,
Freud and his family might never have left Vienna. All negotiations with
the authorities were carried out by Anna Freud with the help of Princess
Marie Bonaparte because Martin was banned from the city:

> It was not thought advisable for me to play anything but a modest part in
> negotiations with the Nazis. They had forced my retirement from the Bar
> and, eventually, I was forbidden to enter the press offices from which they
> had taken away all money and documents with the assurance that everything
> belonging to non-Jewish clients would be returned to them. Finally I was
> ordered out of Vienna, a measure which could possibly have been inspired by
> friends who did not think my temperament sufficiently equable to be trusted:
> a fear I could accept as justified, so intense was my hatred of the Nazis. My
> exile from the city was not hard to bear. There being no supervision of my
> movements, I could go to Vienna nearly every day, to play cards with father,
> to discuss plans with the princess and help where possible in plans for the
> family's emigration.[32]

Sigmund Freud's assets were finally totalled at 125,318 German marks,
necessitating the payment of a 'fleeing tax' of 31,329 German marks.
Since he had been forced to sign over his property to the Nazis and

therefore had no means to pay it, Marie Bonaparte stepped in and loaned him the *Reichsfluchtsteuer*, settling with the Nazi authorities on his behalf. The sum was required by 1 June to secure his emigration papers. As he signed over his property to the Nazis, the statement read, 'I, Professor S. Freud, am leaving my house of my own free will at the request of the SS.' Martin Freud wrote in his autobiography that in a last act of defiance his father added to the statement the comment: 'I would like to recommend the SS to everyone.' This is thought to be apocryphal; Sigmund Freud would not have risked his family's exit to safety with such a sentence in writing. The document has subsequently been published and no such additional words are on it. It is thought that Sigmund may have uttered the words sarcastically under his breathe but there is no independent evidence for this. Sigmund Freud's home at 19 Berggasse for over forty-seven years was finally given over to the Nazis. On 12 May the family's new German passports arrived. Anna Freud commented that in succeeding to obtain visas for all of them, Ernest Jones had achieved 'the near impossible.'[33]

Two days later on 14 May, Martin Freud left Austria for good. His father recorded this in his diary. It appears from what Martin later wrote about his emigration that his wife Esti and the children had already left for Paris:

> During that first Sunday rag-time raid on my offices, a number of incriminating (in Nazi eyes) documents had been found and I had become a certain candidate for a concentration camp, most probably Buchenwald, where a number of my friends actually perished. Happily, the new Vice-President of Police, a man with a criminal record, was a close friend of my cook. Through this contact, I was able to buy back the documents quite cheaply and, during negotiations, I was given timely warning of my projected arrest ... I decided to make for Paris to join my wife and two children who had been sent there some days earlier.[34]

For some of the younger members of the Freud family the ordeal and stress of recent months was over. Martin Freud expressed his feelings of joy at freedom: 'It is impossible to express the relief I felt when, at last, the train crossed the Rhine Bridge at Strasbourg and I had steamed out of Hell into a Heaven which I felt would be entirely happy when mother, father and Anna could join me.'[35] His son Walter recalled of the exodus with mother and sister Sophie: 'The journey from Vienna to Paris on the Orient Express was uneventful and I believe it was in the early morning of the following day that we crossed the Rhine bridge from German Kehl to French Strasbourg and freedom. We stayed with my mother's sister in Paris for two weeks, and then moved to London where grandfather joined us a few days later.'[36]

On 24 May, Sigmund Freud's eldest daughter Mathilde and her husband Robert Hollitscher were also free to leave. They stopped overnight in Paris with Marie Bonaparte before travelling on to England. It would be another week before Sigmund and the rest of the family could leave. On 2 June the final obstacle to emigration was overcome. The *Unbedenklichkeitserklärung*, the statement of no impediment, arrived confirming that Freud's debts had been paid. He was now free to leave Austria. His health was poor, so daughter Anna arranged for their travel tickets and foreign currency through Thomas Cook. Walter Freud wrote of his grandfather's emigration:

> In retrospect, the blindness of the Austrian Jews, including Grandfather, to the impending danger is hard to understand, but at the time they had some good excuses. To leave one's relations, friends, jobs, schools, to pack up one's possessions and move to a strange environment with unfamiliar customs and language needs a lot of courage and enterprise. A stronger incentive was needed to say good-bye to a good and stable existence than threats by a few unhinged politicians. Was not Germany the land of Goethe and Schiller, foremost in European culture and civilisation? Such a land would never do anything dishonourable to its Jewish citizens.[37]

The impact of emigration upon the Freud family lived with them for the rest of their days. For them, as with many refugees in their position, being forced out of their country was the ultimate rejection. Walter Freud commented about this cataclysmic experience in his own writings:

> We were driven out of Austria like mangy dogs and considered ourselves lucky to escape alive. If, at that time, a prophet had forecast that in fifty years the reconstituted Austrian currency (it had turned into Marks by then) would have a picture of grandfather on its 50 Schilling note, one would not have

given much for his crystal ball. And yet, today grandfather features not only on Austrian stamps, has a Viennese park called after him, but the new Austrian banknote, probably the most common one, displays a good likeness of him.[38]

Sigmund Freud's own feelings just prior to leaving Vienna were succinctly summed up in a letter to his son Ernst. In it he likened himself to the Biblical patriarch Jacob: 'Two prospects present themselves in these troubled times – to see you all together once more, and to die in freedom. Sometimes I see myself as a Jacob being taken by his children to Egypt when he was very old. Let us hope that there will not follow an exodus from Egypt. It is time that Ahasvar comes to rest somewhere.'[39] Finally on Saturday 4 June 1938 Sigmund Freud with his wife Martha, daughter Anna, their maid Paula Fichtl and others members of the household left Vienna on the Orient Express for England via Paris. Because of Sigmund Freud's health they were accompanied by Dr Josefine Stross. For diplomatic protection and to save problems at the border checkpoint they were escorted by a member of the United States Legation. As it happened, they were permitted to cross into safety without being searched. As they crossed the border, Sigmund Freud simply uttered the words: 'Now we are free.'

The following day, on Sunday 5 June, the delegation arrived at Gare de l'Est in Paris. Waiting to greet them on the station platform were Sigmund's closest friend and supporter Princess Marie Bonaparte, and his son Ernst Freud with William Bullitt, who was now the American Ambassador to France. The entourage was immediately swamped by journalists eager to photograph and report this momentous occasion. The Paris correspondent for *The Times* reported: 'Professor Sigmund Freud arrived in Paris this morning with his wife and daughter. All the members of his family have now left Austria.'[40] Sigmund Freud's first letter written in freedom was to his friend in Palestine, Max Eitingon:

The welcome at Paris – Gare de l'Est – was cordial, rather noisy with journalists and photographers. From 10am to 10pm we were with Marie at her house. She excelled herself in kindness and thoughtfulness, gave us a portion of our wealth back and would not let me travel further without new Greek terracottas.[41]

Sigmund Freud's reference to 'a portion of our wealth' referred to the gold currency which he had collected in Vienna against inflation. Marie Bonaparte had smuggled the gold coins out of Austria for him in the Greek Legation's diplomatic bag. Now that he was free, she was able to return them to him. Martin Freud later sold the gold coins on 11 April 1939 for approx £1586 and on 23 September 1939 for approx £1012.[42]

The Freud party continued the next stage of their journey by train to the port of Calais where the train was loaded onto the ferry. During the crossing, they stayed on the train, only seeing daylight when they landed at Dover at 9 a.m. the following morning. It was now monday 6 June. The much-loved family dog Lün was taken into quarantine. The party continued by train to London Victoria where they were exempt from customs. Their train was re-routed to another platform to avoid the bevy of journalists waiting for the arrival of this world-renowned figure. On the new platform a small gathering was waiting to greet them: Sigmund's daughter Mathilde and son Martin, with Ernest Jones and his wife. Of his new-found freedom, Sigmund Freud told Ernest Jones: 'I am almost tempted to cry "Heil Hitler".'[43]

Jones drove Freud across London to his new temporary home at 39 Elsworthy Road, near Primrose Hill in north London. The rest of the party followed in two taxis with the luggage. Sigmund Freud's arrival in Britain was reported in all the newspapers. Immediately after his arrival in England, he wrote to his dear Marie Bonaparte: 'The one day in your house in Paris restored our good mood and sense of dignity; after being surrounded by love for twelve hours we left proud and rich under the protection of Athene.'[44] Athene was one of the statuettes that Marie Bonaparte had smuggled out of Vienna and returned to him in Paris. Rather appropriately, Athene was the Goddess of Wisdom.

Without the dedicated loyalty of Bonaparte and Jones, Sigmund Freud and his family might never have escaped the clutches of the Nazis. Freud's other close friends were in his thoughts. From England, he lost no time in writing to Max Eitingon: 'The feeling of triumph at being freed is too strongly mingled with grief since I have always greatly loved the prison from which I have been released.'[45] His grandson Walter commented: 'I believe this truly reflects his real feelings toward Vienna and Austria and must have been echoed by many an emigrant.'[46] In the coming days he was showered with gifts and greetings from members of the public and friends. He wrote to Jeanne Lampl de Groot:

> So now we have really arrived in England, it is very nice and the public, whether friends or strangers, has prepared us a warm welcome ... Of course everything is still uncustomary and as if unreal, a clear sense of alienation.[47]

Martin Freud's marriage had been deteriorating for over ten years. Emigration provided an excuse for him and Esti to separate permanently, although they never divorced. Martin took his seventeen-year-old son Walter to England with him. He found that he was unable to practise as a lawyer in England without undergoing a period of training, the foreign qualifications of lawyers and doctors not being accepted by the British. He struggled to make a living in the early years after emigration and began work on the manuscript for his autobiographical novel *Parole d' Honneur* which was published by Victor Gollancz in the autumn of 1939. He also founded a company, Martin's Preparations Limited (1939), based at 3 Hanover Court, Milton Street in the EC2 area of London, in which he experimented with a new kind of toothpaste. The business venture proved unsuccessful because the outbreak of war meant that the government confiscated certain chemical products.

Walter continued his education at a small private school in Shepperton-on-Thames and then at Faversham School in Kent. The experience at Shepperton brought to the fore the very different class structures in Vienna and England. Both Austrian and British society were class ridden, but it was different. Walter wrote:

> In England, the class to which one belonged was to a large extent determined by the money you could spend, or which your parents spent on you. During my first year in England, I lived with a teacher's family in Shepperton. The two things which surprised me most were, firstly, that I was not allowed to speak to the servants. I found this very odd, because our servants had been part of the family, and I had spent many happy hours sitting in the kitchen and listening and talking to them. The Shepperton servants were like frightened little birds, who would disappear up their own staircase and blush violently when being wished 'Good morning'. The second surprise was the very limited social circle

of my teacher and his family. There existed only one or two other couples with whom he would socialise. Everybody else in Shepperton would either earn £5 a year more, or less, than he did, and social intercourse with his betters or inferiors was not desirable and therefore shunned. He and his family lived very lonely lives. In Austria, the great class chasm was religion and race, Jews and non-Jews, and it was almost unbridgeable ... Before any social or other contact could be established, the question of 'Jew or non-Jew' had to be settled.[48]

It is to Walter's credit that after a year at Faversham he passed all his examinations with grade A in a language that was not his own.

After leaving Austria, Martin's estranged wife Esti Freud remained in Paris with their daughter Sophie, and took up a post at the Sorbonne teaching speech therapy. There they lived for nearly two years until the German invasion in May 1940 forced a hazardous escape across France via Spain to Casablanca. They eventually settled down to a new life in America.[49]

Back in England, the search began for a suitable house for Sigmund Freud to purchase. In the latter part of June, Marie Bonaparte came over from Paris to visit the family for three days. By July 1938 it was clear that Sigmund Freud was mortally ill, but at the age of eighty-two and struggling with the aggressive effects of advanced cancer, he continued to see pupils. In his diary entry for 17 July he noted: '*Moses and Monotheism* finished'. Even so, the subject continued to obsess him and discussions about it frequently came up in conversation with friends. That same day a new will was drawn up naming his children Anna, Martin and Ernst Freud as executors. At the end of the month on 28 July, Sigmund Freud's last residence was purchased, a house at 20 Maresfield Gardens, now the Freud Museum. According to Walter Freud it was 'far superior in beauty, spaciousness and general convenience to the dark and cramped quarters of the Berggasse.'[50] That September Dr Pichler was flown over to England from Vienna at Sigmund Freud's expense. On 8 September he performed another operation. At the end of the month on 30 September his new home at 20 Maresfield Gardens was ready to move into. That same day British Prime Minister Neville Chamberlain raised the hopes of the nation with his radio broadcast promising 'peace in our time.' He had just returned from Munich. War had been averted, but for how long? Sigmund Freud scrawled across his diary that day the word 'peace'. On 4 October he wrote to Marie

Bonaparte: 'Now that the intoxication of peace has subsided, people as well as Parliament are coming back to their senses and facing the painful truth. We too of course are thankful for the bit of peace, but we cannot take any pleasure in it.' At the end of October, Marie Bonaparte visited him again in London bringing with her an addition for his collection of antiquities; this time another statuette. Sigmund Freud described to Eitingon how the Princess's presence was 'always invigorating'.[51]

On 9–10 November 1938 the Nazis unleashed *Kristallnacht*, the Night of Broken Glass, in retaliation for the shooting of their diplomat Ernst von Rath in Paris by a Polish Jew Herschel Grynszpan, whose family had recently been deported. Jews paid a heavy price for the action of Grynszpan. The Nazis brought terror to the Jewish communities in Germany and Austria as Jewish businesses had their windows smashed and synagogues set on fire. The destruction was as yet unparalleled. Thousands of Jewish males were rounded up and sent to concentration camps. It was an ominous sign of worse to come for Europe's Jews. Walter Freud later said of it: 'That night Hitler crossed his Rubicon. Every Jew in the world knew that it was either Hitler or them and that the world did not have room for both.'[52] Sigmund Freud's entry in his diary for 10 November read: 'pogroms in Germany'. Interestingly it was written in English not German as if to distance himself from the language of his birth. He had every reason to be concerned by the turn of events. His four sisters were left behind in Vienna. Although he had made enough financial provision for them, he now heightened efforts to get them out and appealed to Princess Marie Bonaparte:

> To maintain them in England is beyond our powers. The assets we left behind for them on our departure, some 160,000 Austrian shillings, may have been confiscated already, and are certain to be lost if they leave. We have been considering a domicile on the French Riviera, at Nice or somewhere in the neighbourhood.[53]

His own death the following year meant that he never learned of their terrible fate. All died in the Holocaust: Paula and Mitzi [Marie] in Treblinka; Rosa in Auschwitz; and youngest sister Dolfi of starvation in Theresienstadt. *Kristallnacht* was not the only European catastrophe that affected Freud. Civil war was raging in Spain and on 10 November, the same day as *Kristallnacht*, Franco publicly banned the works of over a hundred writers there. That included Sigmund Freud and also his friend H.G. Wells. The events unfolding across Nazi Germany and Austria brought the concern and sympathy of old friends. Sigmund Freud received a letter from Eitingon in Palestine: 'We are also receiving awful news from Germany. A synagogue my father founded in the 1920s has been burnt to the ground and the Jewish Hospital, the Eitingon Foundation, also faces closure. Both chief doctors were arrested.'[54]

By the beginning of 1939, Sigmund Freud's cancer was diagnosed as terminal and inoperable. He was in constant pain, and found it difficult to eat and talk. He received constant nursing care from his daughter Anna. That year there were fewer entries in his diary and fewer visitors to the house. His grandson Walter wrote of this period: 'After every one of the many operations one could note a deterioration of Grandfather's general conditions. He became thinner and thinner because of his difficulties in eating and the post-operative recoveries took longer every time.'[55] On 28 February the results of X-rays showed the extent of a new malignant growth which was too close to the eye to operate. The only good piece of news that month was the publication of his seminal work *Moses and Monotheism* by Allert de Lange in Amsterdam. *The Times* described the book as 'bearing the mark of a genius.'[56] The following month, March 1939, Hitler's forces invaded Czechoslovakia, Bohemia and Moravia. The land of Freud's birth and upbringing were now under Nazi control. It looked as if another world war was inevitable. Ill health now prevented Sigmund Freud from carrying out a number of engagements. He was invited to the opening on 16 March of the Austrian Centre at 124 Westbourne Terrace in London's W2 district.[57] His sons attended in his absence.

That summer of 1939 before world events were turned upside down by war, Walter Freud travelled to France to join his sister Sophie for a holiday in Morzine in the French Alps. He had not seen her since their parents' separation the previous year. Whilst they were in the Alps, war was declared on 3 September. There was every chance that he would be stuck in France, unable to get back to England. Both their passports were being held in the local town for the duration of the holiday and so neither of them could leave. They appealed to the owner of the guest house where they were staying to intervene on their behalf. The passports were successfully retrieved and Sophie returned to Paris, Walter to England to begin his studies in Aeronautical Engineering at Loughborough College. There was an unexpected surprise in store for him on his return. His status and that of his father had changed. They, like other refugees from Nazi oppression who were living in Britain, were classified as 'enemy aliens'. This would have consequences for both of them the following summer. That same month Martin's novel *Parole d'Honneur* was published in English. One reviewer wrote in *The Observer* that the book has 'a ring of classic romance. Whether this is because of the girl's disguise, always a favourite device with picturesque novelists, or whether, as I believe, it is because the narrative is engrossing, I leave readers to determine for themselves. That they will find *Parole d'Honneur* deeply enjoyable I have no doubt whatever. The book is written with great simplicity, is on the whole well translated, and such perceptive humour beneath its attractive manner that it will remain long in memory.'[58]

By now Sigmund Freud's health was deteriorating and he was in considerable pain. He was nearing the end of his long struggle with cancer. One of the last friends to see him was H.G. Wells who visited Sigmund in August 1939 before his trip to Stockholm. H.G. Wells said: 'We talked among other things of the possibility of his being naturalised as an English citizen – a thing he desired greatly. There had been a hitch and I said, "I will come back and tell you all about it when I come back." "You won't find me," he said. "This is goodbye."' Grandson Walter Freud commented on that last difficult month: 'Grandfather could hardly leave his bed any more. Eating was torture and even reading became difficult. The cancer had turned gangrenous and eaten a hole through the cheek like a second mouth which emitted the smell of death.'[59] Walter last saw him a couple of days before his death, saying farewell to the patriarchal figure whose international fame and legacy was now assured:

> I said good-bye to Grandfather Freud two or three days before he died on the
> 23 September 1939, just when I started my first term in an English College.
> His last words to me were: 'Take a good look at me, it is your last'.[60]

The pain became so unbearable that on 21 September Sigmund asked Dr Schur for an overdose of morphine. The end was nigh. He slipped into a coma for two days and died on 23 September 1939; he was eighty-three years old. Three days later on 26 September his funeral took place at Golders Green Crematorium, North London, attended by over 150 people. There was no religious ceremony. In an earlier version of his will dated 31 January 1919, Sigmund Freud had requested a simple funeral:

> The greatest economy should be exercised for my funeral arrangements. The ceremony should be as simple as possible, without funeral oration, and news-release only afterwards. I promise that I shall not be sad because of the absence of reverence. I would prefer cremation if it is more convenient and cheaper. If I should be famous at the time of my death, one never knows, then this should make no difference to the arrangements.[61]

Ernest Jones gave the funeral oration, saying of his friend of thirty years: 'He died surrounded by every loving care in a land that had shown him more courtesy, more esteem and more honour than had his own or any other country, a land which, I think, he himself esteemed beyond all others.' Sigmund Freud's ashes were placed in a black marble column in the Ernest George Columbarium at the crematorium in a window recess where other family ashes have since been placed in their various caskets. After the funeral, Martin Freud was quoted in the *Daily Herald* as saying of his father: 'His spirit was unbroken by his illness and even by events which necessitated his migration from his Vienna home at the age of eighty-two. The splendid hospitality which he received in Britain made his last months as peaceful as they could be.'[62] Martin ended his own autobiography with the words: 'I can add that Ernest Jones was right. Father loved England.'[63]

There is a touching anecdote about Freud's final resting place in Golders Green Crematorium. In the ensuing years, an ex-refugee from Berlin, the late Rabbi Dr Albert Friedlander, frequently conducted funerals at the crematorium. He always visited Sigmund Freud's memorial and placed white flowers at the base of the marble column which holds Freud's ashes. This may be the spray of artificial white flowers which are still there today. The site has become a place of pilgrimage, with several visitors and students each year eager to pay their respects to the man who has, even after death, touched their lives in so many ways. On the 150th anniversary of Freud's birth on 6 May 2006, the city of

Vienna sent an enormous bouquet of flowers to be placed at the base of his black marble column. They too had not forgotten their most famous citizen who spent most of his life in Vienna.

To those closest to Freud, his family, friends and colleagues, his death left a huge void. His charisma no longer part of their lives, his spirit lived on in their memories. Ernest Jones as one of his most respected friends offered his personal reflections on Freud the man:

> He has lost nothing through death, so we cannot truly mourn for his sake. But what of ourselves? A world without Freud! A world without that vivid personality, without that entrancing and benign smile; without whose wise and trenchant comments on the great and small things of life.[64]

Paying tribute to him in *The Spectator*, he said: 'with his death we lose a revered teacher, wise and inspiring companion and a man of enduring friendship.' Such was the impact and fame of Sigmund Freud that obituaries and articles appeared in newspapers and journals worldwide. The accolades came from every corner of the globe. *The Listener* reported: 'With the death of Sigmund Freud there has passed away one of the great figures of our time – perhaps indeed of all time.'[65] Psychoanalyst and friend Max Eitingon wrote in the *Palestine Post*:

> Freud was an explorer of the sombre depths within the human personality and the first to discover some of the laws according to which their apparent chaos is ordered. He found many unknown bridges within the character of man, and examined the boundaries and the conditions under which the conscious ego may maintain its mastery. This was an achievement of immeasurable importance, and it is known by its fruits to all but those who do not wish to see it.[66]

The *British Medical Journal* was equal in its praise, recording that his death 'marks the end of a revolutionary phase in the history of medicine.'[67] On 28 September *The Listener* printed a broadcast tribute to Freud which spoke of his achievements in exceptional terms:

> There are few men of whom it can be said with certainty that their names will live as long as the memory of man endures ... The genius and the achievements of Freud will not only set his name alongside Copernicus, Newton

and Darwin, but have made it a household word ... Freud was, of course, no manufacturer of cheap philosophies of life, but all his work, his researches and discoveries bear witness to his profound belief in the value of truth, of truth however incomplete it may be.

In an obituary in *News Chronicle*, it was written that: 'His work illuminated and modified the whole of modern thought, but his unflattering conclusions about the origin of our motives and beliefs incurred the anathema of orthodox medicine and religion, and made him for years one of the most derided men in Europe.'[68]

The scientific world paid its tribute too. On 25 October 1939 the Secretary of The Royal Society of Medicine wrote a letter to his widow Martha: 'The Society is very sensible of the great services which Professor Freud, during his long and distinguished career, has rendered to Medicine and humanity generally. His continued valuable services and writings have justly given his name a world-wide renown.' At the bottom of the letter was a copy of the resolution which the Council passed which read: 'That the Royal Society of Medicine desires to record its deep sense of the loss which the Society and the medical world have sustained by the death of their esteemed Honorary Fellow, Professor Sigmund Freud, and to express to his family the Council's sympathy with them in their bereavement.' This was passed while all the members stood in silence. It fell to Martin Freud to reply on the family's behalf. On 27 October he wrote to Geoffrey Edwards, the Society's Secretary: 'In answer to your letter of October 25th addressed to my mother Martha Freud, may I express hers and her childrens [sic] sincerest thanks for the sympathy shown to us at the occasion of Professor Sigmund Freud's death.'

Joan Riviere, who had met Sigmund Freud at the first International Congress of Psychanalysis after the First World War, wrote after his death in *The Lancet*:

The long pale face with grey beard and stooping shoulders were those of an intellectual and might have suggested a learned profession, but for two other essential characteristics. There was his lean but broad sturdy figure, the rather stern expression and firm jaw, which bespoke a great reserve of dignity and hidden strength – an indomitable tenacity. He appeared somewhat aloof; in fact he could easily be bored by crowds and gatherings. This most striking feature, however, was the forward thrust of his head and critical exploring gaze of his keenly peering eye. Finally, this rather awe-inspiring appearance was lightened by the glow of an enchanting humour, always latent and constantly irradiating his whole person as he spoke, which reassured one that the Olympian was indeed a mortal too. I knew already from his writings of his astonishing knowledge of literature; of his memory, especially for Shakespeare; and of his other tastes, his love of all antiquities, or Greece and Rome, and the art of earlier cultures.[69]

To the world at large, Sigmund Freud bequeathed his insights into the human mind and became known as the founder of psychoanalysis. Today his books are sold in every country in countless languages and form the basis of psychoanalysis. In their day his theories were often deemed controversial by the established medical profession. His work continues to provoke much scholarly debate; nevertheless he can rightly be characterised as a pioneering genius. His name and Freudian terminology permeate the English language, with phrases and words like 'Freudian slip', 'libido', 'Oedipus complex' and 'death wish'. After his death *The Times* called him 'one of the most challenging figures in modern medicine.'[70] It is to universal disgrace that the Nobel Prize was never awarded to him.

Many influential friends like H.G. Wells tried to persuade the authorities to grant Sigmund Freud British nationality without having to wait for the usual five years. H.G. Wells said at the time:

> Professor Freud's passionate desire was to become a British citizen and a number of us did all we could to satisfy that desire, for it was a great honour to Britain. But we were unable to do it. All that was necessary was a small private Bill which could have been passed in half an hour with the consent of government, but it was not done. I am extraordinarily sorry that that could not be done.[71]

But H.G. Wells was too well known for his anti-royalist stance and his particular efforts failed. In this regard, Walter Freud makes a thoughtful concluding reflection on his grandfather's life:

Grandfather died 'stateless'. His only regret regarding his move to England was that he had not undertaken it fifty years earlier. But he died a free man in a country which he had always admired and which in 1939 had assumed the responsibility for the upkeep of the world's civilisation.[72]

It is indeed a sobering thought that the man who was responsible for transforming the understanding of the human mind died stateless. In a way, it is symbolic of how his theories transcend national boundaries and borders. Maybe it was an apt end for a genius who left an enduring legacy to the world.

His Majesty's Loyal Enemy Aliens

September 1939 marked the end of an era for the Freud family, adjusting to life without its central figure of Sigmund Freud. The declaration of war on 3 September meant that immediate family members, with the exception of Ernst Freud and his sons, were classified as 'enemy aliens'. In October 1939, as with all enemy aliens living in Britain, Martin and Walter Freud both had to appear for questioning before an Aliens Tribunal to assess their security risk to Britain. This must have seemed preposterous to them, coming from an internationally renowned family. Only Ernst Freud and his family escaped this classification because they had come to England in 1933 and by 1939 had already received British nationality. Walter Freud was studying Aeronautical Engineering at Loughborough College when he was summoned to appear before the local Aliens Tribunal that month. Martin Freud tried to intercede on behalf of his son and on 14 October he wrote to the tribunal from his home at 1 Holly Terrace in Highgate, north London:

Anton Walter Freud was included in the invitation issued by the Home Secretary Sir Samuel Hoare to his grandfather, the late professor Sigmund Freud, foreign member of The Royal Society, who has been highly honoured by this country for his scientific work. May I add that my son, as myself, is absolutely loyal to the British Kingdom.[1]

Although classified as 'friendly' enemy aliens, this did not prevent their internment the following summer. On 10 May 1940, Hitler ordered his troops to invade Holland, Luxembourg, Belgium and France. Luxembourg fell immediately with no resistance. The Nazi war machine was sweeping through Europe as far as Norway at an alarming rate. Britain looked to be next, as captured enemy intelligence later proved. But political events were also on the turn in Britain when that same day, 10 May, Winston Churchill was driven to Buckingham Palace to ask George VI for permission to form a new government. Churchill's staunch leadership would prove essential for directing Britain through the critical war years. He later wrote of his becoming Prime Minister: 'I was conscious of a profound sense of relief. At last I had the authority to give direction over the whole scene.' That he certainly did with strong vision, keeping his sight on ultimate victory and raising the morale of the nation through the toughest times, especially through the Blitz and battles in the skies above Britain.

With the fall of the Low Countries in May 1940, the British government was forced to evacuate over 300,000 retreating troops from the beaches around Dunkirk in an epic rescue operation using hundreds of small fishing vessels and pleasure craft to augment the Royal Navy. The weather and conditions were deemed perfect for an invasion of Britain at that time; the refugees from Nazi oppression terming it *Blitzkrieg*, meaning lightning war. In their new country their problem now was not anti-Semitism, but strong anti-German feeling of the populace. This meant that speaking with a German accent in public was potentially dangerous. Walter Freud commented: 'You kept quiet about your background.'

The advance of Hitler's troops across Europe had consequences for enemy aliens living in Britain, and that included the Freud family. The potential risk of Nazi spies and fifth columnists entering Britain and infiltrating refugee groups was considered high. If that happened, the government feared it would be impossible to separate genuine refugees from enemy spies. The only speedy solution deemed appropriate to this dire emergency situation was the mass internment of enemy aliens. The new Prime Minister Winston Churchill swiftly endorsed the policy of 'collar the lot' recommended to him. This led to the internment of nearly 30,000 Germans, Austrians and Italians in camps on the Isle of Man, mainland Britain, Canada and Australia. Neither Martin nor Walter

Freud was immune from this policy. In spite of their name, father and son both found themselves behind barbed wire.

On 29 June 1940, seven weeks after the government order, Martin Freud received a home visit from a police officer who promptly arrested him. He was sent to the Isle of Man and then later a camp at Huyton near Liverpool. Ironically, twenty-one years after being a British POW in Italy in the First World War, he found himself again in British custody behind barbed wire. The first person his sister Anna turned to at this time was Leonard Woolf, husband of Virginia Woolf and Sigmund Freud's publisher. Leonard Woolf and Sigmund Freud had corresponded regularly, sometimes through Martin Freud, but the two men had never met until 28 January 1939 when Leonard and Virginia took tea with the Freuds. Not unsurprisingly Sigmund Freud left an indelible impression on Leonard who wrote in *Downhill all the Way*: 'Nearly all famous men are disappointing or bores, or both. Freud was neither; he had an aura, not of fame but of greatness.' With Martin in internment, Anna appealed to Leonard in a letter: 'After all, it is very clear that we came to England as friends and not enemies.'[2] Leonard proceeded to take the matter to a higher level and to intercede also for Walter Freud. On 24 August 1940 he sent a letter to Clement Attlee, then Leader of the Labour Party group in Churchill's coalition government: 'Freud and his family, when they came here, were welcomed as distinguished guests and victims of the Nazis ...That any of them should now be interned as dangerous and that a grandson of Freud should have been sent off to Australia by the Government seems to me amazing.'

Martin Freud was interned alongside many other German and Austrian intellectuals. The camp at Huyton, like those on the Isle of Man, became a microcosm of German and Austrian cultural and academic life. Martin, himself a highly qualified lawyer, was amongst fellow intellectuals who were never going to idle away their time. A mini university was formed by the internees offering a wide range of lectures on science, medicine, the arts, economics, statistics and mathematics. Artists captured their experience of internment in paintings and drawings, often sketched on makeshift 'canvases' of newspaper or toilet paper. No one knew how long they would be there. Martin fictionalised his experience as an internee in an unpublished short story entitled *The Alien*. It provides an important insight into the emotional instability for many like him and the fears provoked by internment. Rumours were rife as there was no information available to them on the progress of the situation. The summer of 1940 was one of the most critical times in the war. The future of Britain was being decided in the air by Battle of Britain pilots. The leadership of Winston Churchill inspired fortitude and robust defiance in the national morale battle that refused to concede to the enemy. Internees, including Martin, had no idea about the progress of the war. In the early months they were not allowed to read newspapers in the camps. This lack of knowledge increased their insecurity and isolation. All this is reflected in Martin's short story in which the main character (Martin himself) gets onto a trolleybus heading for Hampstead in north London. The author goes to the upper deck to find an unnamed man sitting in his usual seat. He described him as 'a bit shabbily dressed, not too well built with thick spectacles and long, nervous fingers. I remembered those fingers better than the face. This man had played the cello in a musical performance arranged by some society for international co-operation of artists.' The fellow passenger then recounts to Martin his experiences as an enemy alien internee, mirroring precisely Martin's own experiences in internment:

I suffered of course, not so much bodily as mentally. Those of us who came here without money had lived in similar conditions concerning sleeping and feeding. After a short initial time of rather poor improvisation the whole thing ran smoothly and without much friction, like a very cheap holiday camp, males only of course. But as I said, our sufferings were mental. We had no communication with the outside world and no newspapers at all. We did not know what was going on outside and the last things we had heard before we were cut off had been discouraging. I think it was worse than being cut off from the world on a lonely island. We knew that the sentry who looked out from his observation platform over the camp patiently and calmly – nobody ever tried to escape – had read his paper, possibly today's paper early in the morning. We knew that the A.T.S. secretary, who was escorted daily through the camp on her way to the Commander's office, was listening to the BBC every evening. (By the way, there were several female secretaries, none of them ever crossed the camp without escort, but they had different degrees of protection. Very young and attractive blondes had a sentry on each side with bayonet fixed.) The world of the camp was therefore divided into a knowing on one and an ignorant on the other side and it happened of course that information passed from one side to the other in disfigured form. We had to listen to rumours and we started to believe in rumours. The rumours were bad. I remember the 3 July, there were two rumours: the first asserting that there had been a naval battle near Oran between the British and the French fleet. Nobody believed that one, although it happened to be true. The second that the Government had resigned, including Churchill, and that a new Government was being formed, headed by Lord X – I will of course not repeat the name – with the leader of the British Fascist party in a prominent position. We believed the second story and were all very sad. All seemed to be so final and hopeless. When we had suffered from Nazi atrocities there was still somewhere in the background some hope of escape, some hope of retribution, but now it seemed to be all over. It was the end. We expected to be handed over to the Nazis with full records within reasonable time. Nobody touched his supper this evening, not even the greedy ones. I do not remember how many days exactly we lived in such gloom and despair. But it was not long. A new camp commander took over and cancelled the prohibition of news. A loudspeaker was installed and we heard the first glorious news of the air battles, which were later called the Battle of Britain.[3]

Churchill sensed this last sentiment, later saying: 'this is not the beginning of the end, but it is the end of the beginning.' At the end of this short story, the man tells Martin how he joined the British Army's Pioneer Corps from internment. His final comment about the national anthem provides the reader with an important insight into German/Austrian refugee patriotism for the country which had saved their lives:

We started very humbly, as pioneers scrubbing kitchen floors and loading trains, but this was only a beginning; today some of us are already in the real fight. Those who were not strong enough to become soldiers tried to cooperate in others ways. It was a wonderful frame of mind and it affected also those who joined us later from other camps. We had lots of meetings, all on the same theme, to join the fight. On a piano somewhat out of tune the National Anthem was played at the end of every meeting and if someone had dared to move or make a nasty remark while we stood at attention we would have torn him to pieces.[4]

Martin's son Walter was taken into custody the day before his father on 28 June 1940 while sitting a mathematics exam at Loughborough College. A police officer entered into the examination hall and arrested him. Walter's formal education was disrupted for a second time; first in Austria under the Nazis and now by the British authorities. Little did he know that it would be six years before he could take up his studies again. Walter was taken to a local police station where his protests of innocence were to no avail. The policeman replied: 'In war time there are worse criminals than thieves or murderers.' The next day Walter wrote to his father:

> My luck deserted me yesterday. In the morning, just in the middle of my mathematic exam, a very unpleasant policeman came to fetch me. I was just allowed to pack a suitcase and then off we went; every Austrian, German and Italian from the college. I am now at an intermediate station and I shall stay here for only a few days before going to camp. Where are you? I wonder whether you too are interned.[5]

A couple of days later Walter was moved to a racecourse outside York where he joined the company of other German and Austrian internees under canvas. After a few days there, he was transferred to the Isle of Man where he was accommodated in one of the boarding houses. This was just the beginning of what was to be a lengthy ordeal of internment for him. His father knew nothing of his whereabouts and it would be six weeks before he received news of his son's location. The British Government decided to ship some of the younger internees to Canada and Australia. After just a few days on the Isle of Man Walter was taken with two thousand other internees to the docks at Liverpool. At the dockside a huge three-year-old grey liner called the *Dunera* awaited them.[6] Now converted from a passenger vessel to a troopship, it was totally unsuitable to carry so many internees. Its new capacity was a maximum of 1,600 people including the crew. Some 2,000 male internees (originally victims of Nazi oppression) were herded aboard with 251 Nazi POWs and 200 Italian Fascists, all guarded by British soldiers. On 10 July 1940 the Dunera set sail for an unknown destination. None of the internees knew at that point that they were bound for Australia. At 9.20 a.m. on 12 July, less than forty-eight hours after leaving the port of

Liverpool, the ship took a direct hit from a German submarine U-56 off the coast of Ireland. Fortunately the torpedo failed to detonate and no lasting damage occurred. Although they continued the rest of the journey safely, it was to be a harrowing nine-week ordeal in appalling conditions amidst much personal mistreatment. Once on board their entire luggage was confiscated by the British soldiers guarding them and some belongings thrown overboard. Walter wrote:

> Although the most essential medicaments were lacking, vital medicines like insulin were thrown overboard when discovered to be owned by the intern-ees. False teeth were removed, destroyed or thrown overboard ... Religious artifacts – vestments, prayer books, bibles and phylacteries were taken away or torn. Some vestments were returned thanks to the interned Chief Rabbi Lt. Malouy. Some of the vestments had been removed from burning synagogues in Nazi Germany.[7]

The lack of any personal possessions was not the only humiliation suf-fered by the internees. The troopship was dangerously overcrowded. The 12,615-tonne ship was in a precarious position being a thousand men over its capacity. This led to excessive overcrowding and extremely cramped conditions. Not only that, but the internees were confined below deck for twenty-three hours a day with only a maximum of one hour's exercise above deck. The upper part of the ship where it was pos-sible to get fresh air was out of bounds, the access barred by barbed wire and bayonets. Below deck the internees slept in three layers with one group sleeping on the iron floor, another on long tables and benches, and the third on hammocks strung above the tables. Most suffered sea-sickness. Walter Freud commented: 'I was lucky and found myself in a hammock, able to be sick on everybody below me.' Walter has much to say about the conditions that he and his fellow internees endured. In a lengthy unpublished account written whilst in Australia and his later unpublished memoirs *Before the Anticlimax*, he vividly described the nightmare experience:

> On the first evening it was forbidden to leave the decks. Buckets for urine were provided. The buckets were soon overflowing and sewerage flooded the decks as the ship rolled. In the midst of it men were lying on the floor to sleep,

for at first there were neither hammocks nor blankets. For weeks the hatches were kept battened down. Neither daylight nor natural air ever reached the decks. For weeks, one was dependent on electric light and artificial air supply through ventilators. Later the hatches were opened where it was possible. The port holes were closed the whole time. No inoculation against typhoid and cholera was administered in spite of circumstances obviously favouring an epidemic of this kind.[8]

The sanitary arrangements for the whole journey proved to be spartan with only ten toilets for 2,000 men. Walter's mathematical brain calculated that if all ten toilets were in use all the time, then each internee would have just seven minutes a day for their requirements. Such a situation necessitated major managerial creativity. He wrote: 'The organisational talent of some of our co-internees, genuine German-Prussian merchant seamen and similar prisoners, came in very useful. They formed the toilet police, calling up people as vacancies arose. The shout "*Drei Mann rechts ran zum pinkeln*" (three men to the right for peeing) is still clearly audible in my ears.' The arduously long hours below deck were relieved by playing cards. Walter whiled away the time playing bridge and became a skilled player. For the older internees, the conditions were insufferable, likened by the internees to a floating concentration camp.

The *Dunera* docked three times en route: at Takoradi, Capetown and Freemantle in Western Australia. Between North Africa and landing in Australia, fresh water was only supplied two or three times a week. Razors and shaving equipment had been confiscated so the internees grew unkempt beards until they were permitted to shave just before docking in Australia. On 6 September 1940 the Dunera finally reached Sydney. Walter described their arrival: 'We were unceremoniously unloaded, but not before we had thrown out of the port-holes most of the miserable eating utensils with which we had been issued, and which had to serve for three sittings, three times a day.' After nine weeks at sea in horrific conditions, the internees faced a nineteen-hour train journey across Australia to Hay in New South Wales. Their new destination: camps located 750km from Sydney. On arrival they were accommodated in two adjacent camps named Hay 7 and Hay 8, not far from the Murrumbidgee River. Walter was accommodated in Hay 7. A vast expanse of dry barren landscape lay around them with swampy land farther on to the west. The local wildlife occasionally made an appearance, particularly the many colourful birds which flew into the camp. Walter recalled:

> One day I noted that somebody had drawn with black crayon a large, hand-sized spider with eight long hairy legs on the wall of our hut. As we kept our hut very clean, I thought that this was a really silly bit of vandalism and proceeded to wash off the picture. I was rather startled to see it run away. We cleaned our hut thoroughly that night.

Although security by the Australian guards was somewhat relaxed, there was nowhere for any escapee to go had they attempted a break-out. The internees settled into their new life, determined to make the best of it. Accommodation consisted of wooden huts, a luxury compared to conditions aboard the *Dunera*. Food was plentiful, and the guards pretty much left the internees to their own devices. Walter volunteered immediately for kitchen duties which started at 4.30 a.m. by lighting the fires under the large boilers in readiness for cooking porridge for around 800 internees. The internees composed their own camp song:

> Say Hay for Happy,
> and you feel snappy,
> and you don't want to die.
> Even if you sell your overcoat,
> for just the sight
> of one more bite
> of tasty butterbrot.

It was several weeks before the internees were permitted to write letters home, and even then it took these letters three months or more to reach England. At the first opportunity, Walter wrote to his father. He also corresponded with his then girlfriend Jean Adkin from South Woodford in London. He had met her in 1938 during a holiday to Beer in south Devon. He comments that: 'these letters, more than anything else, kept up my spirits during the remainder of my internment. In case I should be accused of not having been grateful to Jean by not marrying her, it was she and not I who declined this opportunity.'[9]

As with the internment camps back in England, the internees in Australia very quickly made use of their professional qualifications and formed a mini university. Walter offered lessons in mathematics and others provided lectures on their specialist subject. It was for him the 'most scholarly institution' with almost every profession represented. He had one regret about that period of his life: 'I now wish that I had used that year in Australia more productively. I could have learned any amount of languages, or higher mathematics, or astronomy, or calligraphy, or almost anything. Instead, I wasted much of it, boiling porridge and playing handball.' His time in Australia passed with only one major incident when he fell against a window. The glass splinters severed the tendons across three fingers of his right hand:

> Luckily, amongst our highly qualified lot, there was also a string of surgeons. We did not have a hospital in the camp, but there was a first-aid room where two of the surgeons managed to sew together the severed tendons. I did not have an anaethsetic, but the hand was almost numb with shock. They did a good job; my hand was soon as good as new again, and only a scar and the incapacity of making a clenched fist remind me now of what could have become a serious disability.

For Walter, life as an unmarried internee was relatively stress free, however that was not the case for many of the older married people. They worried about the families left behind through no choice of their own in either England or Nazi-occupied Europe. Few of them escaped some kind of psychological trauma. News about the progress of the war rarely filtered through to the internees. They had no idea whether or not Britain had been invaded by Hitler. The Australian newspapers appeared to be more interested in sporting events than the campaigns of the war. Walter explained the situation:

> Physically, we were no worse off than millions of soldiers in army camps around the world; indeed probably better than most, because we had good food, an excellent climate and were in no danger to be sent anywhere to fight and die. Mentally however, the strain was considerable. The married men among us had no idea what had happened to their families and whether they were still alive. We had heard that England was being severely bombed,

which did not lessen our anxiety. My sister and mother had emigrated from Vienna to Paris; Paris had fallen to the Nazis just before I was interned and I had no idea of their whereabouts and whether they had been able to avoid the clutches of the Nazis. My father had lived in London; I knew nothing of his fate. I knew nothing of anybody, one was suspended in space-time like being on a far distant asteroid.

In spite of the conditions they endured, Walter was realistic about the benefits of being in Australia. He commented philosophically: 'With hindsight, to transport us away from England was an act of mercy. If Britain had been invaded in the autumn of 1940, as many people anticipated, the Jews, particularly the German and Austrian Jews, could not have expected an easy time ... Alternatively, if Britain had been forced to make a dishonourable peace, she might well have been asked to extradite all the immigrant Jews back to Germany. Far away, in Canada or Australia, outside British jurisdiction, we would be safe from such a fate.'[10] About the whole experience he poignantly concluded:

> For me, the worse thing about my internment was not the physical treatment or the absence from home, or the uncertainty of when I would be released, but the fact that nobody in the whole world seemed to like or want me or mine. We were thrown out of Germany under threat of death and when we thought that we had found a new home, we were again thrown out unceremoniously. The earth did not seem to have a single spot where we could live undisturbed. This insecurity affected many of us.

Whilst Walter was safe in Australia, his father was busy recruiting fellow internees in Huyton for the British Army. The previous year the British government had permitted enemy aliens to join the army, with only one unit open to them: the non-combatant Auxiliary Military Pioneer Corps (AMPC). The first six alien Pioneer Corps companies were formed from German and Austrian refugees in Kitchener Camp near Sandwich in Kent. Five of these companies were sent to France in the spring of 1940 to support the British Expeditionary Force. A sixth alien company was sent from Kitchener Camp on vital coastal defence work around Britain. With the invasion scare from May 1940, the training centre of the alien Auxiliary Military Pioneer Corps was rapidly moved from Kitchener

Camp to Dartmoor in the heart of Devon, and from there to Westward Ho! on the North Devon coast. From the summer of 1940, Parliament debated the internment policy of the enemy aliens and discussed possibilities for their gradual release. One of the few ways to leave the camps early was to enlist in the British Army. That meant only one thing: the Auxiliary Military Pioneers Corps. A drive began in the internment camps to enlist male internees into the Pioneer Corps. Stories vary as to the amount of pressure that was put on them to enlist. Martin Freud was approached as a suitable orator to persuade the men, and his original speech made in Huyton has survived amongst unpublished family papers. It was an impassioned speech in which he addressed their fears and concerns. It also demonstrated the patriotism which many internees felt for the country which saved them from Nazi persecution:

> You know and I know what the real feelings in this camp are: how immense the enmity against Hitler and his Nazis and how great our wish to fight. But we have got to convince our friends by deeds and not by words only of this spirit in our midst ... I think I know what is wrong: it is not fear of the military life nor attempt to evade the hardship or the dangers of service – I have talked to many of you individually and I know that the hitch in most cases lies in a very different direction. You have been free men and you are proud men, and for you that it is not compatible with your honour to enlist behind barbed wire. Some of you even might say that the thankfulness inspired in you by the friendly and hospitable treatment received from the English people has been killed in these last few months by the injustice of internment. Others who are still willing to enlist object to filling the ranks of a labour corps which, only partly armed, might be looked upon by inexperienced critics as a second-grade unit of the British Army.
>
> Would you like to return to Hitler, who may think again whether it would not after all be possible to put to some use what is vermin in his eyes, before destroying it definitely. Is it better to leave this country? If you can get a six months' visa for San Domingo there might be a chance of staying in Panama for a year, and if you are among the lucky ones, the way will lead on to Shanghai. Maybe, there you will meet, coming around the other half of the globe, Hitler again. Do you really prefer going on to be hunted around the world with the rest of the lost and defeated? – Or would you rather that to you, as an upright and striving human, the proudest of all the nations should

say: You can be my soldier! Against the old enemy you can carry on your fight under the protection of the Union Jack! If these words of mine have not fully convinced you that there is no stigma in joining up behind the barbed wire; if you still think there is humiliation in doing this – would you not rather undergo this humiliation if that will serve the right and just cause?

We have got to be confident that this country will not forget but will reward in the hour of victory those who have been fighting with it and for it, and I am absolutely confident that this hour of victory will come... There is no release into the old free life, as we knew it. As the war is becoming more and more embittered, civilian existence will be more and more precarious. In the course of this last year we have gone through very different stages. We have been, at first, a sort of neutral observers, tolerated but somewhat suspect. As for me, I should not like to return to that stage of life. Next, we have been Enemy Alien Internees, and you know all there is to know about this stage. But now we have in front of us the possibility of beginning a third stage. In a few days we can become British soldiers. Do you think we can afford to miss this happy and honourable opportunity?[11]

It is not clear precisely how many internees Martin finally persuaded to join the army; but a letter to Lord Reading as the Commanding Officer of the 'alien' Pioneer Corps indicates that he was very successful. A copy of the typed letter, unsigned by the sender, exists amongst Freud family papers. It was originally dispatched from A Battery, E6 Squad 16, Arborfield in Berkshire and speaks of Martin Freud in glowing terms:

The point about Freud is that when the issue in relation to the AMPC first had to be faced he was the man who in fact persuaded Austrians to join with such success that recruits increased from 50 to 300. I feel therefore that whereas the whole of civilisation may be indebted to many of your other privates, the AMPC owes a special debt to this man.[12]

A total of between 3,000–4,000 internees eventually enlisted from all the internment camps around Britain, as well as those from Canada and Australia. That included Martin himself. Amongst his papers is an undated reference which Ernest Jones, as President of the Institute of Psychoanalysis, wrote in his support, possibly in response to Martin trying for release from internment. In it Jones wrote:

I have known Martin Freud well for thirty years and happened to be an eyewitness of some of the Nazi persecution from which he suffered in Vienna, so I am not surprised that he is now trying to enlist a body of Austrians to fight on our side. He was admitted to this country on the invitation issued by the Home Secretary Sir Samuel Hoare to his grandfather, the late professor Sigmund Freud (whose eldest son he is) and family. I can vouch for his integrity and loyalty.

With the expected arrival of so many extra recruits, the AMPC training centre was moved from the tiny holiday camp at Westward Ho! to the seaside town of Ilfracombe, some twenty miles along the north Devon coast. In its Victorian heyday Ilfracombe was a popular holiday resort which flourished well beyond Edwardian times. The town, set in steep hills and flanked by rugged red cliffs, its old harbour and lifeboat house, possessed many hotels. It was about to be transformed by the arrival of over 3,000 Continental intellectuals in British Army uniform fresh out of internment. The War Office requisitioned a number of the hotels for use by No. 3 Training Centre of the Pioneer Corps. Its headquarters was based in the Osborne Hotel near the seafront. In the summer of 1940 Martin Freud himself volunteered for the Pioneer Corps, little realising just what was in store for him in an untrained manual labour corps. Still as an enemy alien he swore allegiance to George VI and received the King's shilling. At the end of September 1940 he was released from internment in Huyton and sent to Ilfracombe. His army number was 13803060. The first four digits denoted his status as an alien soldier. Martin soon became frustrated with the Pioneer Corps which he deemed a waste of time. He had trained as a lawyer in Vienna, had served as an officer in the First World War and found himself engaged in endless rounds of washing-up duties in the Osborne Hotel. In his autobiography *Glory Reflected* he wrote only briefly about his time in the Pioneer Corps:

My chief occupation was peeling potatoes when I was not scrubbing the kitchen floor. One day, through some kind of disorganisation, the trays filled with sizzling sausages and onions were ready to be carried to the mess-room, but there was no one to carry them. Trying to be helpful, I took up one of the trays and made my way to the door. Here I was met by an indignant corporal who, taking the tray from my hands, barked, 'Who do you think you are – to serve in the Sergeants' Mess?'[13]

Martin was by no means alone as an intellectual in an unskilled labour unit. He was completely in the company of other recruits who were also highly trained professionals. Amongst them were the finest brains in Europe, including surgeons, lawyers, professors, writers, actors, musicians, artists, architects, engineers and businessmen. As with the internment camps, the army training centre at Ilfracombe became a microcosm of German and Austrian intellectual life. After daily army routine and training often carried out on the town's promenade, the men organised lectures on a range of subjects, structured again much like a mini university. Entertainment, concerts and shows were performed in the town's garrison theatre under the organisation of Coco the Clown, alias Lt. Corporal Nicolai Poliakoff. The Continental army orchestra was conducted by Breslau-born violinist Sgt Max Strietzel, already a survivor of Buchenwald concentration camp. Once their army training was complete the men were allocated to new 'alien' companies and sent around the country with their Pioneer companies on construction and forestry work or loading and unloading supplies in depots. Ironically they became the most highly intellectualised unit of the British Army. The history of this period has been documented by the author in detail in two previous books, *Jews in North Devon during the Second World War* and *The King's Most Loyal Enemy Aliens*. Perhaps because at fifty-one he was one of the oldest recruits, Martin Freud spent his entire army career stationed in Ilfracombe. On 24 October 1940 he sent a telegram from Ilfracombe to his son in Camp 7, Hay NSW, Australia. It simply read: 'Am Pioneer 219 Coy AMPC, Ilfracombe North Devon. How are you? If released, try to continue studies overseas.' The following month on 27 November he wrote again from Ilfracombe to Walter in Australia, this time a letter:

> I think I could have you released for the AMPC, there is not the slightest possi-
> bility for an alien to join another unit. I also think that conditions are absolutely
> unfavourable for an alien of military age to go on with his studies. Life in the
> AMPC would not harm you. You might even like it if you had nice comrades.
> There are all sorts, nice lads who studied in Oxford and speak a wonderful
> English and masters from Berlin like in your Faversham School. The greater
> chance is that you hear nothing but Yiddish and Berlinerisch and forget your
> British education ... I understand that you would like to come back and fight in

the airforce – but this is – for the moment impossible. You had [sic] to do same work as I do, clean kitchens, scrub floors, move furniture and so on.[14]

During the period between their next correspondence the following year, Martin continued in the army at Ilfracombe and Walter remained behind barbed wire in Australia. On 6 June 1941 Martin wrote to Walter with news that he was being invalided out of the army:

> I had a rather hard time in the army, but I have been discharged on medical reasons. On the 14th of this month I shall be a civilian again and I do not know what sort of work I shall be able to find. But I am not afraid, there is plenty of work now and as I am an ex-serviceman have nearly the same rights as a naturalised person. My health was not too good, but I was given the usual twenty-eight days leave and I have fully recovered. I don't look much different from what I looked when we were in Davos together, hairs a little greyer of course and less fat ... I even do not know where I shall live in the next months. I go back to Holly Terrace in a few days, but since my long absence relations with Lisa are not what they were. I think that we shall separate and I do not know which party will continue to live in Holly Terrace.[15]

At the end of this same letter, Martin informed Walter that Esti and Sophie were now living in Nice and hoping to secure visas to America. He had tried to send money out to them but this was proving difficult because they had adopted false names. Sophie Freud narrates their escape in full in her book *Living in the Shadow of the Freud Family*. On leaving the army, Martin was sent to be trained as a fitter for war work. In the coming years he kept in touch with Princess Marie Bonaparte who had done so much personally to secure the family's release from Vienna in 1938. He wrote to her with a summary of his early wartime experience:

> Dear Princess,
>
> It is quite a long time since I have heard form you or you have heard from me directly, but of course I know everything about your dangerous and rather sad adventures. My own experiences during the same time were by far less dangerous but altogether a little absurd. You might remember my activities as a manufacturer of toothpaste; later I worked as a clerk to a Chartered Accounted, then came internment, after 3 months of a rather

soft life in internment camp I had 9 months as a private in the British Army (Pioneer Corps). Most of this time was spent in washing dishes and scrubbing floors for New Zealanders, A.T.S. Girls and so on. They invalided me out – I think for the reason that I am a few years over military age. Later I joined a Government training Centre and was trained as a 'fitter'. It took me about 3 and a half months to pass my 'Trade Test'; in was work, as much as I like the idea on principle, I felt mostly out of importance or responsibility. Some of the things that happened to me were rather funny and I used my different experiences for a couple of short stories, which unfortunately according to war conditions could not find a publisher. Since the beginning of this year I am a member of the 'Civil Defence', not too exciting a job for the time being but in case of Air Raids it would be just the thing I would like best of all.

The real subject of my letter is not to report about myself, the first paragraph was only an introduction. Anna told me that you were working on St Christophorus and needed some material which you could not find in South Africa. I volunteered to find it for you in the British Museum; it took some time as not all the books are available, specially the old and more valuable Scripts are not for the time being. Anyway, I have been able to find a text which I hope is that what you need.[16]

In the same month as Martin Freud's discharge from the army in June 1941 Hitler invaded Russia, thus ending his threats of an invasion of Britain. The British government reconsidered the position of internees in Australia. Thus began their gradual release from these camps. Captain Julian Layton was sent out to Australia by the British government to persuade them to return to England and enlist in the Pioneer Corps. Some decided to do so, while others remained in Australia and made new lives for themselves there. There was no question of Walter wanting to remain in Australia. Like his father, he volunteered for the Pioneer Corps. Eventually Prime Minister Winston Churchill conceded the whole internment affair was 'a deplorable mistake'. One of his government Ministers, Major Cazalet, described it as 'a bespattered page of English history.' Walter Freud was amongst the first batch of men to return to England aboard SS *Gleniffer*. It left Australia on 2 June 1941 carrying 139 internees and arrived back at Liverpool at the end of August. The majority of his fellow internees who had also signed up for the Pioneer Corps left Australia on the SS *Stirling Castle* on 12 October 1941, docking in Liverpool in November. Walter wrote of the return journey:

> The journey home took as long as the outward trip, but was infinitely more comfortable. I had a cabin to myself and there were lots of Chinese and other stewards to look after our creature comforts. In the morning they would call 'Bathy-laddy' to indicate that my bath was ready, at 11am they would call 'Iceleam lady' and continue with similar coercions for food and drink for the rest of the day. We arrived at Cristobal, which is at the Caribbean end of the Panama Canal on the 6 August 1941, and I was given a pass by the ship's captain, Mr W.G. Harrison, to go ashore. The town was just one large brothel for the Americans, who were guarding the Panama Canal. Every window of the main street, and there were few others, was festooned with nude bosoms which were attached to the women in the background. The American sailors would parade up and down that street, selecting suitable bosoms and then disappear for a while. I had been given some money, but restricted my purchases to bananas, I had been told that bananas were not to be had back home, and I wanted to surprise them. Unfortunately, the banana's ripened in my cabin and I ate my last banana and threw the last banana skin into the Mersey.

Once back in England, there was a delay of several weeks with Walter's call-up papers and, much to his frustration, he found himself back behind barbed wire on the Isle of Man. That frustration was expressed in letters between him and his father at the time, although only Martin's letters appear to have survived. On 19 September 1941 Martin sent his son a pound postal order for the Douglas Post Office on the Isle of Man and told him:

> In a way it is quite good that you have to join as it is of very great importance for every alien who wishes to stay in this country after the war, that he did something to help in the common cause … I suppose that you will be sent to Ilfracombe, a lovely place on the seaside where you will have quite a good life. I have lots of friends there and that might be helpful … All the best and enjoy to be lazy [sic], in the army you will have to be out of bed very early.

The following month, he wrote to Walter again about the delay his son was facing in internment. Already he was thinking about the defeat of Hitler which, unknown to them at that time, was still four years away:

You should try to make this delay not too tragical [sic]. Today there is only one important matter: the progress of the war. I think matters have improved a lot and Hitler's defeat will mean for all of us hopes and a future. It really does not matter so much where you pass these autumn weeks, although I agree it must be very unpleasant to be interned again. But it matters a lot that Russia and USA are now on our side and that I see the possibility for you and Sophleim [Walter's sister Sophie] to live free and happy after victory.[17]

Finally Walter's papers came through and like his father before him, he was sent to Ilfracombe for basic military training. He was issued with army number 13805972, again the first four digits denoting his status as an enemy alien in the army. There he linked up with other internees who had returned from Australia. They too had been sent to Ilfracombe for 4–6 weeks of army training which consisted mainly of square-bashing on the Victorian seafront, often watched by groups of bemused locals. Walter did not make a very good start at the training centre, as he described in his unpublished memoirs:

My start as an 'Auxiliary Military Alien Pioneer' in Ilfracombe was not propitious. We were kitted out and instructed how to make our beds. They had to be 'just so', no doubt because soldiers who could make beds according to a regulation of 1813 would be better at killing the enemy than those who could not master this art. I folded my blankets and my brand new uniform as instructed; I was then allowed out into the town. When I returned soon after, part of my new equipment had disappeared, it had been stolen. It was obvious that some racket was going on, involving the robbing of new recruits. I got the blame, but my sense of justice revolted. I had done everything by the book, exactly as I had been told, and I could not help being robbed. When my sergeant noted that I was not going to take my punishment without a protest and that I was prepared, if necessary, to go to a higher authority, he relented and let me off the fatigue to which I had been condemned. After much difficulty, I even had my stolen stuff replaced. This Headquarters in Ilfracombe was a terrible place, nearly everybody seemed to be involved in some private racket, usually connected with stolen army property and nobody cared for us, the new recruits. Except for learning how to make beds and how to salute, I was given no other training. Now I have learnt to recognise the difference between well and badly run units or organisations. Fifty years ago I was more innocent and easily deceived. Ilfracombe represented base-service of the worst kind: the Germans have a word for it, *Etappenschweine* (military contempt).

Walter's period in Ilfracombe was as frustratingly boring as that of his father. He tried to use his engineering skills to transfer out of the Pioneer Corps, but to no avail. Any hopes of a transfer were soon dashed as he found himself clearing fire damage in the town centre of Barnstaple, some twelve miles south of Ilfracombe:

Before I had learnt even these relatively easy lessons of warfare, and while I was still saluting everything in uniform, such as postmen and land-army girls, I had my first and sudden call to action. In case a grateful country should ever wish to bestow on me a posthumous decoration for my rapid and whole-hearted response, I would like to explain straightaway that this action did not involve a bayonet charge against a machine-gun nest, nor the defence of Buckingham Palace. No, but a fire had broken out in a food storage depot in nearby Barnstaple.[18] At that time, I thought that it had been caused by a German bomb, but I have recently been assured that no German bomber ever penetrated to North Devon. The fire had been put out, leaving a smelly mess of charred and watery bags of flour, sugar and other staple foods. My action consisted of helping to clear up after the firemen. Equipped with high Wellington boots, I and my colleagues shovelled and carried the messy residue of that fire onto lorries.

The incident which Walter was involved in was the fire at the Albert Hall in November 1941, on the site of the present-day Queen's Theatre in Boutport Street, Barnstaple. The glows of the fire exposed the town to enemy attack that night and it was soon 'covered' by searchlights. German bombers returning from raids on Swansea and Cardiff would have seen it easily. The fire also affected the adjacent Tonkins Egg Store such that the following day the gutters ran with stinking batter pudding. It was this mess that Walter found himself clearing up. Once it was done, he was back in Ilfracombe for the final part of his training, but before he completed it, he fell ill with pneumonia. He was transferred to an army hospital as his condition was serious. He later wrote about his experience there, a story which highlights his forthright defence of his Jewish roots in spite of not being a practising Jew:

A Catholic Army Chaplain was very active there, and whenever somebody was very ill and at the point of dying, he would do his best to try and snatch his soul. I had a very high temperature and was hardly conscious and that man sat at my bedside, showing me religious pictures of saints and impressing me with the benefits of dying a Roman Catholic. With my last effort of will I told him time and time again that I was born an Austrian Jew and wished to die as one and in peace. Luckily I recovered.[19]

After recovering from this bout of pneumonia, Walter was posted with No. 87 Company of the Pioneer Corps which was then stationed at Pembroke Dock near Milford Haven in west Wales. The men were billeted at the Defensible Barracks, a large Victorian fortification surrounded by a moat. Once again Walter was in the company of other Continental intellectuals and professionals. They were under the command of elderly British non-commissioned officers (NCOs) who had served in the First World War, and had been drafted into the Pioneer Corps because of some physical shortcoming like impaired vision or lack of education. Ironically, from time to time, Walter and his colleagues were asked to help with the administration and paperwork for their NCOs who could barely write a sentence. Walter has a fair amount to say about the NCOs in his memoirs:

Our officers were of the same calibre as the location. After they had been flung out of every other unit in the British Army for total incompetence, madness or political unreliability, they landed with us. I well remember one of our Commanding Officers, who had been with the Company in France, a Major Wilson. He felt the urge to have a private Praetorian Guard. He selected the tallest of us, bought them, with his own money, fancy uniforms and they had to be in attendance at all times. When he marched across the barrack square, his 'Guard' had to march around him like Caesar returning in triumph from Gaul. Except for this eccentricity, he was quite harmless and left us digging in peace. Another one of our COs had one arm only, and when he drove his car he made sure to acknowledge every salute. The car would then career driverless in zig-zag fashion across the square and one had to jump smartly out of the way to avoid it.

Our English NCOs were of a similar calibre as the Officers. They were all elderly regular soldiers, who had been in the Army for years and had ended up with us for some shortcoming. Nearly all of them were only semi-literate, and we foreigners would oblige by conducting their correspondence. They were probably not to blame for this; when they went to school, just before the Great War, the educational facilities open to them were inadequate. All their money would be spent on beer, of which they could consume prodigious amounts; ten pints an evening would be nothing out of the ordinary. Compare this with my capacity, which was half a pint; after one pint I got a headache and fell asleep. None of them was in any way sadistic or unpleasant and they left us in peace, which could not always be said of our own, the 'alien' NCOs, who had to show off their newly gained authority. The only serious drawback of the British NCOs was their lack of hygiene. When on Sergeant Mess duty, I had to carry out and empty Wellington boots which were filled half way up with piss; they had been used as chamber pots. They also had the tendency to use the grate of the fireplace, which all sergeants had in their rooms, to deposit their excrements. But one didn't have Sergeants Mess duty very frequently.[20]

While stationed at the Defensible Barracks No. 87 Company, which consisted of 350 men, he was engaged on construction and digging work. They dug trenches 4ft wide by 4ft deep for miles and miles along a particular area. Once these sections were completed, they moved to the next one. Walter comments: 'A machine could probably have dug them in one hundredth of our time. Except for digging, there was absolutely nothing going on in Pembroke Dock, no girls, no shops, no amusement, it was a dead place.' In January 1942, Walter received a letter at the Defensible Barracks from his father informing him that his mother Esti and sister Sophie had escaped across France and were temporarily staying in Oranport, North Africa. They were due to travel to New York via Casablanca, Moroco on the ship *Serpatina*. Numerous regular letters from Martin to Walter dating from 1942, some of which are in German and others in English, reveal that his father was travelling around the country with The National Dock Labour Corporation as an auditor. During the periods when he was back in London, Martin served as a Civil Defence Warden on the Holly Lodge Estate near his home in Highgate, north London.[21] One bizarre wartime incident that occurred in Highgate in 1942 provided the basis for a short story by Martin, entitled *Strawberries*:

Sigmund Freud with sons Martin and Oliver in the First World War © The Freud Museum, image reference IN 76

Martin Freud's Regiment in action during the First World War. Courtesy of the Freud family

The Austrian Field Artillery in action in the First World War. Courtesy of the Freud family

Martin Freud with his regiment on the frontline in the First World War. Courtesy of the Freud family

Martin Freud in uniform of the Austrian Field Artillery, decorated for bravery during the First World War. Courtesy of the Freud family

Martin Freud in the Kadimah (Jewish Duelling Fraternity). Courtesy of David Freud

Martin and Esti Freud's wedding breakfast, December 1919. From the left around the table: Oliver Freud, Ernst Freud, Anna Freud, Sigmund Freud, Martha Freud, ?, Minna Freud, Martin Freud (the bridegroom) and Esti Freud, née Drucker (the bride). Courtesy of David Freud

Martin Freud. Courtesy of the Freud family

The young Walter Freud
in Vienna. Courtesy of Ida
Fairbairn

Martin Freud with son Walter on holiday in Grado. Courtesy of Ida Fairbairn

Sigmund Freud arriving in Paris from Vienna with Princess Marie Bonaparte and William Bullitt, June 1938 © The Freud Museum, image reference IN 3831

Sigmund Freud, 1939. Courtesy of Ida Fairbarin

The Sigmund Freud and family memorial at Golders Green Crematorium. The flowers were placed here by the City of Vienna to commemorate the 150th anniversary of Sigmund Freud's birth in May 2006. Courtesy of Eric Willis

Martin Freud in Pioneer Corps uniform, Ilfracombe, 1940 © The Freud Museum, image reference IN 483

Oath of Allegiance.

I, *Anton Walter Freud*
swear by Almighty God that I will be faithful and bear true allegiance to His Majesty, King George the Sixth, His Heirs and Successors, according to law.

(Signature) *A.W. Freud*

Sworn and subscribed this 2 4 day of *January* 194 7, before me,

(Signature) *Claude A. Lewis*

~~Justice of the Peace for~~

A Commissioner for Oaths.

Name and Address (in Block Capitals) *CLAUDE ADRIAN ESCOTT LEWIS MARKET STREET LOUGHBOROUGH. LEICS*

Unless otherwise indicated hereon, if the Oath of Allegiance is not taken within one calendar month after the date of this Certificate, the Certificate shall not take effect.

W1 0911 25 bks/3/45 W1 & Sons Ltd. (69)50942—24

Walter Freud's signed Oath of Allegiance to King George VI. Courtesy of David Freud

Walter Freud, Special Operations Executive. Courtesy of David Freud

Members of '12 Force', Special Operations Executive of which Walter Freud was a part. Rear row from left to right: Frank Kelley (Franz Koenig), Etti (Ettlinger), a FANY, Peter Priestley (Egon Lindenbaum), Hugh Falton (Hermann Faltitschek). Front row: Buston (called Busti), Alan Grant (Noe Czuppa), Michael O'Hara (Fred Berliner). Courtesy of Eric Sanders

Special Operations Executive from left to right: H. Faltitschek, Vrkos (Security), H. Hladnik and Theo Neumann. Courtesy of Eric Sanders

Walter Freud working for War Crimes Investigation Unit, Karlsbad, Germany in July 1946. Courtesy of David Freud

Walter Freud and Annette (née Krarup). Courtesy of Ida Fairbairn

The house on the Vallø Castle estate where Aage Krarup lived with his family and where Annette Krarup grew up. Courtesy of Ida Fairbairn

Aage Krarup giving a speech at Vallø Castle on Liberation Day, 5 May 1945. Courtesy of Ida Fairbairn

Vallø Castle, Denmark.
Courtesy of Ida Fairbairn

Major Walter Freud with Martha Freud in
Maresfield Gardens, 1946. Courtesy of David
Freud

Martin Freud outside his tobacconist shop, near
the British Museum, early 1950s. Courtesy of
Caroline Penney

Wedding of Walter Freud and Annette Krarup in Vallø Church, Denmark, 20 August 1947 Courtesy of David Freud

Walter Freud (7th in back row), Club of International Students at Loughborough College, 1947. Courtesy of Ida Fairbairn

(Left) Annette Freud with the three children. From left to right: Ida, Caroline and David, 1955. Courtesy of Ida Fairbairn

(Below left) Walter Freud. Courtesy of Caroline Penney

(Below right) Martin Freud, 1950s. Courtesy of Caroline Penney

Annette and Walter Freud celebrate their Golden Wedding anniversary, 1997. Courtesy of Ida Fairbairn

When I went up to Highgate Village, on duty as a warden, the tiny market place was blocked by a funeral procession. You know, the big Highgate Cemetery is only round the corner. I could not see what had brought the convoy to a standstill, maybe it was only the traffic lights. The sun was shining bright and Mrs Gay, the greengrocer, put a few baskets of strawberries in her windows. Although not many people were about, a queue formed quicker than anything else I had seen forming itself in English life. Now one of the big Rolls Royces of the funeral convoy was only two yards from the head of the queue and a youngster in black sitting next to the door, opened it very cautiously and slipped out, to join the queue; some more mourners followed and in a few seconds nearly everyone f the big cars had a door open. A tall, sinister man in a top hat, who looked as if he were responsible for the funeral arrangements stepped also out into the street and shouted something, raising both arms to heaven in a desperate manner.[22]

Returning to Walter and the Pioneer Corps, during 1942 the men of 87 were issued with rifles and given training in their use, along with training in the use of explosives. On 28 April 1942 Major Geoffrey Garratt, who had been posted to the Pioneer Corps because he was an active Communist, was giving a demonstration using live explosives. It ended in disaster, as Walter narrates:

He managed to kill himself, and a good proportion of the Company, without the help of a single German. He lectured on the technique of handling and laying land-mines. These lectures were held in the NAFFI canteen of our Defensible Barracks. They were attended not only by us, but also by a party of Royal Engineers. One day during these lectures, two of these mines exploded, killing everybody present, perhaps fifty people. As I survived to tell this sad story, I did not, on that day, attend those lectures, but worked on an outside working party. For days afterwards, we had to collect parts of bodies, which had been blown all over the place, hands, chests, heads, etc.

A fellow member of Walter's Pioneer Company also wrote about this incident. Garry Rogers (born Günther Baumgart) served first in 87 Company and then in 1943 transferred to the First Royal Tank Regiment. He wrote in his memoirs *Interesting Times*:

We were now issued with Lee Enfield rifles and received training in the use of weapons. One such training session led to a disaster. The cause was never discovered, but during a training lecture on grenades, a live grenade exploded and caused a major accident in which five soldiers were killed and a number badly injured. The force of the explosion was so severe that it blew out windows and even damaged thick walls. One soldier was blown clear out of the window and into the moat.[23]

That day seventeen men died, two of whom were 'alien' Pioneers: Corporal Heinz Abraham, aged twenty-three (13801220) and Private Heinz Schwartze, aged twenty-two (13801014). The others were British-born soldiers from the Pioneer Corps, Royal Engineers or King's Own Scottish Borderers. All are buried in the Pembroke Dock Military Cemetery which is maintained by the Commonwealth War Graves Commission.[24]

During the summer of 1942 Walter was sent on a special weaponry course. One of his fellow Pioneers, Colin Anson (born Claus Leopold Octavio Ascher in Berlin), recalls:

Walter and I were in different sections of 87th company of the Pioneers Corps, and so never had any contact until we were both part of a group of volunteers who attended a course of field craft and weapons training and the like, in a tented camp in South Wales, lasting perhaps two weeks.[25]

Afterwards they returned to their Pioneer section engaged on the large scale construction of Nissen huts in preparation for the arrival of American troops in Britain. America had reluctantly joined the war after the Japanese bombing of Pearl Harbour, in the Pacific Ocean, the previous Christmas. Thousands of American troops had to be accommodated in army camps across Britain. Many of the 'alien' Pioneer companies, including 87 Company, were given the task of constructing these camps during 1942. The huts consisted of a double layer of corrugated and curved iron sheets, fixed to a ribbed skeleton. Each hut was approximately 40ft long by 20ft wide and 'we could put them up in double quick time.' It was during the summer of 1942 that a mysterious Swiss gentleman by the name of Hartmann mixed among the men of 87 and 88 Pioneer Companies to ascertain their motivations and aspirations. The government realised they could be vital for covert operations, interrogation of POWs or as agents to be dropped behind enemy lines. As a result, some ex-German refugees were approached and asked whether they would be prepared to volunteer for special duties. Just over a hundred men were selected to form the only German-speaking Commando unit in the British Forces called 3 Troop of No. 10 Inter-Allied Commando. They trained in Aberdovey in North Wales and Arisaig in the Scottish Highlands. Their story has been told in full in Peter Masters's book *Striking Back* and also in *The King's Most Loyal Enemy Aliens* (a book by the author). The Austrian members from the Pioneer Corps who passed the selection interview in London eventually trained for an Austrian branch of Special Operations Executive. That included Walter Freud. None of the men knew in those early days what unit they were to be trained for; they only knew that they had signed up for special duties. The intention was to train them to 'set Europe ablaze', as Churchill said in 1942. This would be achieved through sabotage of the Nazi war machine's communication and supply network. It was also envisaged that those who were dropped behind enemy lines would liaise with partisans and underground resistance. Walter's secret service file now declassified at The Public Record Office shows that in June 1942 he was being vetted as a 'possible trainee' for SOE.[26] The form used was SO2, headed by MI5, and he gave his address as 87th Coy Pioneer Corps, Defensible Barracks, Pembroke Dock. The comments at the bottom read: 'Grandson of renowned psycho-analyst. Nothing recorded against.' It was signed and dated 16 June 1942.

It was at least six months before Walter was sent to the STS (Special Training School). In the interim period he remained with 87 Pioneer Company. Shortly before Christmas 1942, he moved with his Company to the Ordnance Depot at Long Marston near Stratford-upon-Avon. Here their duties were largely confined to unloading supplies coming into the depot and loading the outgoing consignments. They handled everything except food, munitions and weapons. It was an icy-cold winter. The men were accommodated in tents with no hot water or heating whereas the NCOs were billeted in solid buildings. Walter wrote of that period:

Our accommodation there was most miserable, in small four-men tents. It was raining all the time and the tent floor was always under water. It was

December and icy cold. There were no facilities like hot water for washing oneself or one's eating utensils. All our Officers and NCOs disappeared; they had managed to get themselves accommodated in solid buildings and left us to our devices and severely alone. Within days we became like Russian POWs, unshaven, dirty and dishevelled. We slouched off to work after breakfasting on ice cold porridge, and did a minimum of loading and unloading. We wore all our uniform items, battle dress, fatigue dress, overcoat etc, all the time, day and night and by the looks of us we might as well have been at Stalingrad. There, at that very time, the crucial battle of the war was fought two thousand miles to the east of us. I confess it was not quite as dangerous at Long Marston as at Stalingrad, but my best friend Ernst Wedel had one of his legs squashed off when a load of steel plates fell on it.[27]

Eventually the men were moved into Nissen huts with a stove for warmth and a communal shower, considered pure luxury after their previous accommodation. Like so many 'alien' Pioneers, Walter was frustrated by his time in the Pioneer Corps. He could not envisage spending the rest of the war in a non-combatant labour corps digging for victory. It was not enough. He wanted to do something more active for the war and play his part in the defeat of Hitler. Fate had something else in store. His charisma and flare meant that he would prove to be ideal for special duties.

Special Operations Executive

In January 1943, Walter left the Pioneer Corps 'without shedding many tears. Its cap badge, showing a pick and shovel was not one I was very proud of.' On 20 January 1943 he was posted to the Special Training School (STS) at No. 1 Stodham Park near Liss in Hampshire, a requisitioned country mansion. This first phase was designed to filter out those who were unsuitable for SOE operations. At Stodham Park, Walter trained with 25–30 other ex-refugees from the Pioneer Corps, the majority of whom were ex-Austrians. They became known as '12 Force', a self-designated title. The idea behind forming this particular group was to eventually parachute them in twos and threes behind enemy lines back into southern Austria. There they could link up with anti-Nazis and provide an Allied presence in the region, with a brief to also capture the strategic aerodrome of Zeltweg in Styria, southern Austria. During his training in SOE Walter became very close to ex-Viennese refugee, Eric Sanders (originally Ignaz Schwarz). Eric had arrived in England from Vienna in October 1938, volunteered for the army after the outbreak of war and in February 1940 enlisted in 88 Company of the Pioneer Corps. His company served with the British Expeditionary Force in France in the spring of 1940 and was evacuated after Dunkirk in June 1940. From SOE days Walter and Eric became life-long friends until Walter's death in 2004. Eric recalls the first time he met Walter at Stodham Park:

On Thursday 21 January 1943, seven men and I left the 88 Company of the Royal Military Pioneer Corps in Sennybridge to be transferred to the SOE. Not that we knew that. All we knew was that we were to be trained to do a special job. After having signed the Secrecy Act in London we were taken to Liss, a small town in Hampshire. Five men from the 87 Company welcomed us, having arrived the day before. One of them was Walter Freud, an ex-Austrian like me. We became friends almost immediately. My secret diary entry half-way through the course reads: February 1943: Walter Freud is my age, very intelligent, slim, nice-looking with narrow attractive eyes, a good runner and good at most things, usually just a little bit better than I and I like him best of all. I am told that he is Sigmund Freud's grandson. Unfortunately I don't know anything about Sigmund Freud except that his name is a famous one. It does not mean anything to me and it doesn't stop me from liking Walter.[1]

That same year Walter's father was still travelling the country as an auditor for The National Dock Labour Corporation. He wrote regularly to Walter, letters always forwarded to Walter's secret training address. Martin had no idea where his son was, only aware that something had changed. That much is evident in a letter he wrote to Walter at the end of January 1943: 'I suppose you have reasons (honourable reasons of course) to keep your whereabouts, unit and occupation, a secret, and I am glad you find the new surroundings comfortable.'[2] The first report about Walter's progress as a trainee survives in his personal file. Written by CSM Webb and dated 29 January 1943 it described Walter as 'very sensitive, keen on all subjects, but inclined to ask rather unnecessary questions … Doesn't conform to rules and regulations so readily and has to be told two or three times to do a thing.' This was certainly a characteristic trait of many Continental intellectuals in the British Forces, especially those in the aliens Pioneer Corps who always questioned orders from the British officers. By 5 February, when the next progress report was written, Walter had improved in CSM Webb's eyes: 'This man appears to be undergoing a change. He is working much harder and taking even keener interest. He is not talking so freely now but is still inclined to be argumentative … He has both the ability and brains if he cares to apply them.' On 12 February, Webb wrote in his file:

He has all the qualities there i.e. brains, agility, physique, etc. but these tend to be spoiled by his lack of self-discipline and his inclination to be sulky. Resents having to do as he is told and gets argumentative ... He has been slightly reprimanded by the Commandant for talking out of turn and it will be interesting to notice his re-actions to this.

Less than a week later Webb was able to write in Walter's file:

Re this man's reprimand and his reactions to same. He has taken it very well and appears to have learned from it. He has not been so forward as usual ... Rather liable to cut corners when out of sight in order to gain a little time. This was shown at a recent PT lesson when he cut off a corner in the obstacle course which everyone else took and which he had specially been told about. Continues to work hard and use his ingenuity.[3]

On 15 February 1943 Walter signed the Official Secrets Act at Stodham Park. He still had no idea that he was being drafted into SOE. His code number on his personal file, allocated to protect his original identity, was 12 'C' 4.[4] Training at every stage was now extensive and demanding. The men learned unarmed combat, weaponry, how to make home-made explosives and open locked doors, how to drive trains and derail them, sabotage, radio technology (the use of suitcase radio sets to send and receive messages), cryptology and how to conduct one's behaviour under interrogation. Walter was exceptionally proud of what they could achieve:

We were given a British Escort Officer, Captain J. Bennett, and a wide variety of instructors. Naturally they included PT instructors to make us a hundred percent physically fit. They also taught us unarmed combat, in which a knife did not count as arms. As far as I remember, stabbing somebody in the kidney area is sure to lead to his rapid death. Looking back, I believe that all that unarmed combat was a waste of time and effort. I have not heard of a single case of a British Agent engaging in unarmed combat with, say, a German sentry and getting away with it. In addition to PT, we had very good instructions in weapon technology, when we were made familiar with every type and make of small arms, rifles and light machine guns. I am mechanically minded and enjoyed these courses. In my heydays, I could strip and reassemble blindfolded any such weapon made in Europe and America. Assault courses also featured prominently in our training. These types of elaborate obstacle race have now been made familiar on TV programmes. They included jumping over walls, swinging Tarzan-like on ropes across rivers and such like.[5]

On 20 February 1943 Walter and fellow trainees left Stodham Park for the next STS which was located at Arisaig House, Arisaig near Mallaig in the western Highlands. After the first five days at Arisaig, Lt Col Fooks was able to write in Walter's personal file on 25 February: 'He is certainly most intelligent, but is inclined to be conceited and to resent contradiction. He gets rather sulky if he has to do something he dislikes (e.g. early morning PT) but can do anything well if he tries – which he usually does.' On 4 March the report in his file was brief: 'He has improved a great deal within the last week – is less inclined to sulk, and is working most enthusiastically.' At every stage, the men's ability and suitability for SOE assignments were at the fore of their instructors' minds. On 11 March, Walter's training report reflected his steady improvement:

> Is maintaining the improvement already shown in his manner and will to work, and as a result, his undoubted ability is more evident. He is much more willing, displays more dash, and is less the spoilt child. He stripped to the skin on an icy day and plunged into the sea, swam out to retrieve a fish that was floating some distance out. He would not have done this a few weeks ago. He should be a very useful man if these improvements continue.

Training at Arisaig was more rigorous and the physical pace had increased to include negotiating tough assault courses and the use of weaponry.[6] The men had to be 100 per cent fit to be parachuted into occupied countries and what they underwent at Arisaig overlapped with elite commando training. By the time the SOE trainees were in Arisaig, Walter was paired up with Eric Sanders for exercises. Eric states:

> I recall an assault course in which Walter had to pull me across the canal in the grounds. I was assumed to be wounded and holding on to a piece of wood. The piece of wood did not trouble us but the stink of the water, the dead dog floating past and the explosives thrown in by one of our training officers did. Our run was timed and we came second but without me he would have

done better. Walter ran faster than I. On another exercise we were assumed to be arrested and were being questioned separately about our joint actions the previous day. We had ten minutes to agree on what to say. That was, of course, not enough time to cover all details. Walter's judgement of what I was likely to have answered to certain questions which we had not covered was so good that our interrogators were unable to break our cover story. Luckily they did not use Gestapo methods.

Training in Arisaig included not only physical fitness and aptitude exercises but also learning how to derail a train. Walter wrote of this:

The place was romantic alright, but equally wet. The romance was provided by the piper, to whose accompaniment we dined in the mess. The wetness was provided by the Atlantic sky, which shed its moisture at landfall over Arisaig. Every morning before breakfast, our PT Sergeant Major took us for a nice long cross-country run through the sodden landscape. This was sheer misery, exhausting, wet and cold. If anybody should ask me about my idea of hell, it would not be fire and brimstone, but a wet Scottish moor at 6am on a February morning.

Another one of our instructors at Arisaig had been Head of the Police in the International Settlement of Shanghai and he had the reputation of being a deadly shot with a revolver. He taught us a lot; by the end of the course we could hit any target with anything from a 0.22 Browning to a 0.45 Colt. At Arisaig we also learnt how to drive trains and how to derail them. The poor line from Fort William to Mallaig was plastered with plasticine 'explosive', which meant that poor us [sic] had to spend many a freezing night stalking the guardians of the line. Both sides took these training exercises very seriously. Derailing a train is not an easy exercise. If a section of straight rail is cut out by two explosions, the train will usually jump the missing piece and continue unharmed. If an attempt is made to cut out a longer section of rail, the sleepers in between will usually hold the section in place, again allowing the train an undisturbed run. The explosives have to be placed on a sharp curve and even then the train is not always derailed.[7]

Weaponry training could sometimes be dangerous as Walter recalled about fellow recruit Peter Priestley (originally Egon Lindenbaum):

He lacked co-ordination both in mind and body: hand grenade practice with him was hazardous because he would throw the grenades straight up instead of forward. But he volunteered to go on a dangerous early mission to Italy, in spite of being terrified. He shamed others who, better educated and endowed, refused this opportunity of a likely early death.[8]

In fact Priestley was dropped at the wrong height and location, landing near a German army camp. He was taken POW and fortunately survived his imprisonment in Tolmezzo prison and, later, Udine.

On 21 March 1943 the SOE group moved from Arisaig to Wilmslow near Ringwood, Manchester for parachute training. The local country estate of Tatton Park was used as their dropping zone. It was during the training here that one of the men, Hermann Faltitschek (aka Falti), was injured during his first parachute jump and broke his spine in three places. He managed to stumble back to billets where he eventually collapsed and was taken to hospital where he received treatment. He chose not to be invalided out of SOE but went with the others to Italy in 1944, assigned different duties because he could no longer parachute. It was while Walter was doing a practice jump at Ringway that he blacked out in mid-air and failed to roll upon landing. He hit his head on the ground and suffered a head injury, necessitating treatment as an outpatient at a nearby hospital. On 25 March the accident was reported briefly in his personal war file: 'Is very enthusiastic about his work, but has had rather a heavy fall and seems rather shaken by it.' His commanding officer added: 'With regard to security, he is inclined to be slack and needs to be continuously reminded.' Eric Sanders's diary entry for March 1943 also mentions Walter's fall:

We had one more jump on Friday that week, in quick pairs, at midday. I was No. 2. This time there was quite a strong wind and I tried to turn myself in order to face the correct way when landing but was not at all sure and landed half-way through the attempt. Walter Freud apparently blacked out in the air and hit the ground with his head. When I reached the hut where we returned our chutes he came out but didn't remember anything and seeing him like that depressed me. Back at our billet in Altrincham, he went straight to sleep and I sat down beside his bed all the afternoon. Actually he had been tense and very nervous the last few days, bordering on the hysterical. I sensed it had nothing to do with the jumps. He has had a couple of periods of introversion and when he does I leave him to himself.

Further parachute training was carried out in Italy the following year. Eric Sanders recalls one particular training exercise with Walter while they were at Wilmslow:

> One of our night schemes took place some twenty miles from our base and our officers decided the night air would be healthy for us. We had to make our own way back. Although it was not the shortest route, Walter had worked out that the safest way was to follow the track of a railway line. We were both extremely tired and once or twice I cursed his idea in my mind. But, typically, he turned out to be right. We arrived at least an hour before everybody else. On that leisurely stroll he told me that his grandfather psycho-analysed every one in the family. I did not really know what that realistically entailed but wondered whether these moments of introversion had something to do with it.

From Wilmslow the men were sent to Brockhall near Flore in Northamptonshire where they underwent further extensive training from 3 April until 1 June 1943:

> When we were stationed at Weedon in Northamptonshire along the Grand Union Canal, Captain Bennett devised another handicap race. We had to swim across the canal, dragging nominal non-swimmer with us. When we were in the middle of the canal, Captain Bennett exploded underwater charges below us. These paralysed us and both swimmer and non-swimmer gently sank to the bottom. Luckily we were pulled out before irrevocable damage was done, or a lot of good training money would have been wasted.[9]

One of Walter's comrades Stephen Dale (Heinz Günter Spanglet) later wrote of this period of training:

> It gradually became clearer what the purpose of our training might be all about. We were by this time about 30 people in total and training got more specialised and more strenuous. Our stamina improved and on one occasion, while still at Brockhall, within the space of about 34 hours or so, we covered 60 miles on foot in battle order, and in between had a small exercise and

two or three hours' sleep. When we got back to Brockhall most of us felt fit enough to go out to a dance in the nearest village.[10]

Walter continued to show improvement in this phase of training. The instructor at Brockhall wrote the next report in his personal file, dated 16 April 1943. Again it reflects the requirement to be physically fit but also intellectually up to the task of special operations: 'He is extremely intelligent, and has all the physical qualities necessary for the work. He is, however, inclined to resent discipline but has also improved in this respect, and I think will be useful.'

After Brockhall the men were posted to Anderson Manor near Winterbourne Kingston in Dorset for a period of almost eleven months until April 1944. Anderson Manor had been used in 1942 for the secret training of the Small Scale Raiding Force (SSRF), an early raiding unit that sent small teams on coastal raids of North Africa and France. It was at Anderson Manor that SOE trainees were sent on regular route-marches and taken by lorry to unfamiliar deserted countryside to find their way back to base. There was still no mention to them of the term SOE, although the nature of their intended operations was becoming apparent from the training. This included negotiating a small assault course, every kind of weaponry training from pistol to bazooka, radio communication and basketball; 'plus,' comments Eric Sanders, 'a lot of fraternisation in the village, the details of which fall under the national secrets act!' During the summer of 1943 Walter Freud received a letter from his father, at that time working for The National Dock Labour Corporation in Goole, Yorkshire. He told Walter:

> Due to bad management from my side, my two girlfriends met in the flat on Monday afternoon and Molly (the new one) walked out in a terrible temper. Good that you returned her book; she would have started legal proceedings otherwise. I think you disliked her anyway. The whole scene was pretty good light comedy. I entered with Molly and found Hilda undressed for sunbathing and most cheerful.[11]

In September 1943 the men were sent from Anderson Manor to Portland Bill near Weymouth for a short assignment. Their brief was to scale the castle walls there, as enemy special forces who had secretly landed at

Portland Bill (a British naval and army Headquarters) and capture it for
the enemy. They had three days before the invasion deadline in which
to put five major defence posts out of action. The man in charge of
the exercise was ex-Berliner Yogi Mayer, a fellow member of SOE. The
whole of the island's defence forces, navy, army and home guard were
on 'action stations' for these three days, but they did not know who was
going to invade nor what they looked like. Eric comments humorously:
'Actually I looked more attractive than usual, having had my face black-
ened for the operation. During the early morning hours of the last night
each of the different groups went into action simultaneously.' Walter
proved his extraordinary capabilities and characteristic flare during that
night-time operation:

> Our Commanding Officer, Major Metherell, was a tough ex-Black and Tan
> man, whom we called the Gauleiter. The exercises he conducted were by far
> the most realistic. Had these exercises been for real, none of us would have
> returned home alive. On one of them, we had to storm the Command Post
> of Portland Bill, which is now a prison. It was protected by a near vertical wall
> of 20ft and more; the wall is still there for anybody to inspect it. I and some
> of my colleagues managed to scale it and infiltrate into the camp. For visiting
> cards we put plasticine 'explosives' into most of the anti-aircraft guns. The
> following morning, the Commander of the Portland Command Post phoned
> Major Metherell and told him that his, Metherell's men had been unable to
> penetrate his Command, and that there had been no sign of us. Metherell
> replied 'Oh what a bad show, but could the Commander perhaps have a look
> into the barrels of his anti-aircraft guns'. It took some time for them to scrape
> off all that plasticine which we had stuffed everywhere, it was a real 'Guns of
> Navarone' job.[12]

Walter was the only member of the team who had managed to penetrate
the castle without being seen. That unforgettable occasion remains forever etched in Eric Sanders's memory. In his wartime diary he recorded
just how difficult it was to get inside:

> September 1943: This was when fake reality turned into theatre. Jimmy
> Bennett gave me permission to roam about the island in case I could do
> something useful – I hoped. It was a moonlit landscape, everything in sharp

outlines with strong shadows. I walked up the hill to the Verne and wandered completely around it, wondering whether I could manage to get in. The walls were made of three layers of huge Portland stone blocks, the top edge of one I could just reach with my arms fully extended. The grooves between them were too small to get enough of a grip to pull myself up. What is more they were leaning outwards from the bottom to the top. I walked close to the walls on the inner edge of the grassy moat which held no water. When I came near the main gate there was a sentry standing. I threw stones into the opposite direction vaguely hoping he might go to see where the noise came from but, of course, he did not move. Afterwards it turned out that Walter Freud had indeed managed to climb over and get in but was captured inside. How he managed to climb in I don't know. He was obviously braver than I and often displayed a dash of recklessness and disregard for his own safety.

Years later, reflecting on the above comments about Walter's reckless-ness, Eric said: 'This was, indeed, a correct description of Walter. He was driven by a similar motivation to mine, to do something concrete about Hitler's and the Nazis' downfall. He spoke scathingly about a handful of our lot who backed out when it came to being flown to Italy for going into action.' During October 1943, the men were granted a period of leave and Eric went to visit Walter at his home at 1 Holly Terrace in Highgate. It was not the first time Eric had been there. Of a previous occasion there he wrote: 'I marvelled at the grape vine growing against the wall of their house. I also met his father, Martin, who did not actually display any interest in me.' The second visit in October 1943 is chroni-cled extensively in Eric's diary:

I met Walter Freud on Friday [Freud-day?] afternoon and we went to pic-tures, seeing 'Colonel Blimp'. He asked me to come in uniform to a party at his place towards the end of the fortnight and 'impress' one of the group of friends who'd be there who always bragged about having kept out of the army. I found out that Walter had boosted me up in their eyes and they were curious to find out what I was like. He was right about that rather unpleasant young fellow who made a derogatory remark about my showing off with the parachute on my uniform. I told him that I was supposed to wear it and that it only indicated the five parachute jumps we had done just as the uniform indicated that I was in the Army. I added that it was, of course, up to him whether to do something in the war against Hitler, given that he was a Jew, but as he had decided not to do so it might be wiser for him not to open his mouth about it so much. I don't know whether he interpreted that as a threat which it was not meant to be, but he not only shut up after that but avoided coming near me. Apparently Walter had also described me as having a lot of success with girls – why, I don't know. A pity it's greatly exaggerated. To tell the truth I was not overly enthused by his visitors. They were a little naïve and very much upper class.

In November 1943 the men were back at Anderson Manor where they were required to anglicise their names in case of capture during overseas operations. If their original German or Austrian identity was discovered by the Nazis, they would have been tortured and shot as traitors rather than being treated as conventional POWs. As a further security measure they were officially attached to the Royal Fusiliers with no mention in their papers of SOE. Walter Freud and his colleagues were now part of the Royal Fusiliers but unlike them, Walter refused to change his name. The reason he gave was that he left Austria as a Freud and wanted the Nazis to know that a Freud was returning. 'At least,' he wrote, 'I would perish under my own name.' Eric Sanders recorded the occasion in his diary:

November 1943: I took the plunge and Erich Ignaz Schwarz became Eric Ian Sanders. Some others picked interesting names. Noë Czuppa became Alan Grant, Helmut Fürst (Lofty) chose the name of the estate where we were: Anderson, Georg Breuer became George Bryant, Spanglet (Ziba) transformed into Stephen Dale, Hermann Faltitschek (Falti) became Hugh Falton, Franz König became Frank Kelley and Egon Lindenbaum chose Peter Priestley. Walter Freud refused to change his name, explaining to the black-suited man from the War Office, 'I want the Germans to know that a Freud is coming back'. Oddly enough it didn't sound bumptious at all.

Eric recently added commentary on this episode and said: 'My last remark was confirmed by others' comments. "He is fighting his personal war," one of them, I think it was Alan Grant, said to me. Walter proved his personal courage when he went into action from Italy and, separated from his partner during the drop in Austria, was on his own.'[13] Walter's unpublished memoirs reveal that he did change his name temporarily for a training exercise:

Our laundry was sent for washing to the village, and we were told to mark
our laundry bundles with British names. I thought I could not do better than
call myself Corporal Metherell. The inevitable happened. I got back Major
Metherell's laundry and he got mine. The next day, in addition to a severe
ticking off, Special Force Orders contained the following item: Nobody in
Special Force is permitted to use the name of Metherell.

The men remained at Anderson Manor until April 1944. While at
Anderson Manor Walter was absent without leave on one occasion from 5 March, staying at his father's home at 1 Holly Lodge in
London. His father was away from London at this time working for
The National Dock Labour Corporation. Walter's personal SOE file
notes that he was reported to have measles. It appears to have been
severe enough for a period in hospital. A letter written by his father
on 7 March refers to Walter being in hospital and offers the hope that
he will soon be discharged. From hospital Walter returned straight to
SOE training. His father wrote to him on 21 March: 'As a matter of
fact I have not heard from you since the ambulance took you away
and left me a blue printed form instead. I know only from rather
incomplete reports that you rejoined your unit again after only one
day's stay at home, looking rather thin.' The following month, on 12
April 1944, the men moved from Anderson Manor to Hetherop Castle
near Fairford in Gloucestershire for the final phase of their training
in England. There Walter remained until his posting to Italy in July
1944. Correspondence from his father was now being sent to: 'Fusilier
A.W. Freud, 13805972, PO Box 992, Wimpole Street, London W1.'[14]
Ten days later his father told him: 'Not much has happened during the
week since you left. More bombs of course but nothing too near the
flat or Maresfield Gardens.'[15]

During the period at Hetherop Castle, Walter volunteered as a radio
operator. His friend Eric Sanders was also selected to be wireless operator, this time for Theo Neumann's team. From 30 April until 14 May
1944 both men were sent to Dunbar, Scotland to receive instruction in
Morse code. Walter wrote of that period in Dunbar:

We learnt sending and receiving messages by Morse code, de da de da de.
Each word consisted of a group of five letters and the aim was to send at least

twenty letters per minute. Sitting by a table on a comfortable chair, in a warm room, I had little trouble in reaching this target. But it was a different matter during field exercises. Then, one was lying in a wet field, in half or pitch darkness, and one had first to climb a tree to fix the aerial. One's pencil would break, the Morse key would sink into the ground, the battery would be on its last legs and an unfriendly goat would eat one's message pad. Twenty words a minute! – more like twenty words an hour.

Dunbar had one great advantage as a location: there were a number of army radio stations, and these employed FANYs as operators. I think FANY stood for 'First Aid Nursing Yeomanry' and they were a sort of middle-class ATS; they had to buy their own uniforms. My relationship with Jean had, after six happy years, cooled due to no fault of mine, and rather naturally I fell heavily for one of them. The lady in question however, preferred to play the field, and the field was very wide.[16]

During their seven days in Dunbar, Walter and Eric had twice-daily radio contact with their base in London. Their tasks involved receiving coded messages, decoding them, encoding replies and sending them. There was no officer in charge. They were on their own and enjoyed socialising in their spare time. Eric wrote in the secret diary:

May 1944: We took the Edinburgh train on Sunday, 30th April and are stationed in a stately home just outside a little town called Dunbar. It's smashing. The radio sets are so powerful that we can put a large nail into the aerial socket and still receive every letter loud and clear.

On the second day here, Walter Freud, Falti and I went into a little tea shop run by a little stout man who stood there, his eyes following us, as we entered and sat down. We ordered high tea. When I asked him for his nationality, guessing that he was French he said that was an insult and, in a kind of dry humour, threatened to throw me out if I didn't guess right. Then he said, 'I'm a Jew.' I told him that we were too, and he became transformed. He comes from Kovno. Falti tried to speak Russian to him but he couldn't understand as his language is Litvak. He was very animated and especially excited when telling us about the prayers and services back home in Russia. The whole situation was so unexpected that I fell under its spell. So did Walter who complained afterwards that he was not sufficiently Jewish, himself. That is strange as from what he has told me he never had any non-Jewish friends back in Vienna, never had been in the home of any non-Jewish family and was surprised that it had not been the same with me.

The main wing of the mansion houses a group of FANYs. FANY stands for First Aid Nursing Yeomanry behind which name, I have been told, is hidden a regiment of selected women also doing special services, of the kind the SOE organises (although some of them seem to be used as drivers of high-ranking officers). In the first few days they passed us without acknowledging our existence. We wondered whether it was snobbery or security.

Whichever, it has changed since then. I met one of them, Chris, who is studying Economics. One French girl, Angelle, finds Walter Freud delightful but spends a lot of time with O'Hara. She is one of those noisy people who aren't really noisy. Then there is Jill Lightfoot whom I find delightful. Her bright-eyed sunny face and her trills of laughter give her an innocent child-like quality. Walter has started going around with her. I enjoy just watching her, she is so good to look at. One day when she came walking happily towards Walter and me she was raising her arms doing an uninhibited pirouette which caused her dress to billow out high above her lovely legs. That moment, one arm stretched out towards the sky seemed to reveal the outline of her beautiful body like a Greek statue only very much alive. It gave me a real thrill without any sexual concomitant, just pure joy at the picture before me. She was very unhappy about our leaving but I realise she meant Walter. She seems to have developed serious feelings for him.

Eric annotated the above diary entries with the comment:

Walter told me later that she had wanted to marry him. It fitted to my observations. At about that time he gave me a book by his grandfather as a present. Inside the cover he wrote, 'To Eric, with whom I would like to have gone into action.' My reason for mentioning this is that during our first year in SOE I, too, had wondered whether the fact that our training officers allowed us to do so many exercises together meant that we might go together when it became earnest. I am not even sure whether they did not consider it. As it happened, by the time we embarked on the second year, they had decided otherwise. In any case I do not believe that they would have allowed two good wireless operators to be in the same team.[17]

Whilst Walter was at Dunbar he met a woman also at the STS there by the name of Christine White. They struck up a friendship and when Walter was back at Hetherop Castle he requested permission from his Commanding Officer to visit her on his next period of leave. The SOE instructors kept a close eye on all their trainees' fraternisation and Walter was no exception. His movements regarding Christine White were recorded in his personal file, entry dated 30 June 1944:

> During his leave is visiting, or meeting, Christine White, posted to STS 54 w.e.f. 24.6.44 from Dunbar. He had or originally intended to visit her in Dunbar had she still been there. Immediately Vol. White knew of her transfer she sent a telegram to 12 C.4 informing him that she was arriving there on Saturday. At first 12 C.4 wanted permission to go there on the next day (Sunday). When asked how he would find her he said that he would go up to the School, and ask for her. Permission was refused. Capt Clitheroe was advised of this on 24.6.44 so that action could be taken if necessary.

In June 1944 the first of Walter's SOE colleagues left Hetherop Castle for Italy. They consisted of Otto Karminski, Alan Grant (Noe Czupper), Teddy Lees (Erhard Saar), Stephen Dale (Heinz Günter Spanglet), George Bryant (Dr Georg Breuer), Fred Warner (Manfred Werner), Frank King and Jack Rhodes. The next to be dispatched included Walter in July 1944:

> Before I left, I was kitted out on the 8th July 1944 at 10am, according to the still existing letter. This took place in what appeared to be a private apartment in an exclusive part of London, Canning Place, near the Albert Hall. The lady who conducted it called herself Mrs. F.M. Moore and she brought along her ten-year-old daughter. I thought this was a serious breach of security, as one should not involve children in such affairs. She, the mother, was an obvious amateur. She acted and sounded like a rich, well bred and connected society woman 'who wanted to do her bit for the war'. I got a pair of very superior handmade boots, which I used to wear for years after the war, also for skiing. My trousers were not dissimilar to standard uniform trousers, but made of a better and lighter material. Above that, I wore the normal battledress blouse, with signs of rank. On top of that blouse, I was issued with a sand coloured neutral gas cape. When wearing it, one would look from a distance like a

tourist, or a soldier, or a workman, or a farmer; almost anybody could have worn it without arousing suspicion. It was also waterproof and as such a very useful item of apparel and camouflage … My further equipment consisted of a luminous watch, a compass and my radio codes. These codes were of the 'one time pads' type and unbreakable. They consisted of random letters in groups of five. One wrote down one's message underneath these letters and the combination of the random letter and a letter of the message gave a third letter. This third letter was determined from a table, and this was the one used for transmission. As long as the 'one time pads' were not stolen or copied, this type of code was quite safe.[18]

The same day that Walter was kitted out in Canning Place, his Commanding Officer filled out an application form for his promotion to the rank of second lieutenant, although it would be several months before the recommendation was approved. The reason given for supporting the application was 'a highly trained agent to be used for responsible work in the Field.' Proposed employment was given as 'operational duties in the Field.'[19] Before going overseas, Walter was granted a week's leave which he spent with his father in the flat at Holly Terrace. The flat afforded a panoramic view of London with the German bombing of the city. Walter described two occasions in his memoirs:

> At the time the V-1s, the pilotless flying bombs, were coming over to attack the capital. I recall being in the Marble Arch Branch of Barclays Bank, when one of those doodlebugs came over. One knew that when their engine cut out, one had about half a minute before the thing would come down and explode violently. When the engine of this particular one stopped, everybody, staff and customers, dived underneath the solid oak counter of the Bank to await the bang. It missed the bank, so there was no scattering of pound notes or bodies. From my Father's flat, one had a good view at night of the attack. One could see the V-1s approaching from the south-east, gliding down and suddenly crashing with the brilliant flash of an explosion.[20]

On 16 July 1944, after eighteen months of intensive training, Walter finally left for action overseas.[21] He was posted to Italy in readiness for his drop into Austria, now with Special Forces number 328065. Eric Sanders recalls his friend's sudden departure: 'Walter one day had disappeared from Hetherop Castle, our last English stately home. At the beginning of August Theo Neumann and I spent six weeks in London preparing to be flown to Italy. During that time I received two aerograms from Italy; the second aerogram was from Walter.' It read:

> Dear Eric, Here is an amazing number of old acquaintances and friends assembled … we're having quite a good time in a villa … morals are very high … the food is very good, an excellent cook … we're not in a town where morals are lax, it's either marrying or nothing … Regards to everyone, your old friend Walter. GIVE MY REGARDS TO THEO AND KEEP WELL!

Messages were added all over the place in the letter:

> 'There is no piano here, therefore no use coming, O. (Otto Karminski); Give my regards to Barry, Ziba (with whom Barry had the duel); Alles Gute noch, von Deinem Steirer Seppl (All the best from your Styrian Seppl); Time you answered my epistle, and greetings all the same, Old Chopper (Alan).' Seppl Rasborscheg amazingly had written in German. This was the last communication I received from Walter Freud during the war.

Walter and his colleagues had received some of the most rigorous training that the British Army had to offer. They were now fit enough to go into action. He reflected on his achievements thus far:

> When I left for Italy, I was physically perfectly fit. I could handle explosives and every type of firearm. I could drive trains, open locks, make my own explosives, transmit and receive wireless messages. I had learned how to drive cars and motorcycles, and how to arrive gracefully at the end of a parachute. Whatever the shortcomings of the Special Forces were, and Italy they were quite a few, there was none in the training in the UK. All my instructors had been, without exception, sympathetic and friendly and that included even the PT Sergeant Major at Arisaig. With a number of our instructors, particularly the Captain Bennett, I have kept in touch for fifty years since the end of the war.[22]

In the coming weeks and months Martin Freud wrote regularly to his son, although he had no idea that Walter was in the Special Forces. On 23 July

1944 he wrote to him from 1 Holly Terrace, making the first reference to the turn of the war. This is post D–Day: 'Developments everywhere are now very quick and decisive. Let us hope for more good news.' Martin's health was not brilliant; kidney trouble similar to that which had dogged him in Vienna returned. He told Walter in a letter dated 20 August 1944 that he had consulted a specialist and been put on a special diet of extra eggs and milk. The letter was addressed to Walter: c/o Head Censor, No. 6 Base Censor Group, C.M.F. (Central Mediterranean Force). By this Martin may well have guessed that Walter was overseas, but with no idea of his precise operations or unit. By October 1944, Walter's promotion to second lieutenant had finally come through. His father sent his congratulations on 7 October: 'You can imagine how very pleased and proud I was when I received the good news of your promotion.'[23] At the end of the year in December 1944, Martin himself received promotion to Senior Auditor for the The National Dock Labour Corporation with an annual pay rise of £50. He was now able to send Walter money to supplement his army pay.

Behind Enemy Lines

July 1944: at the age of twenty-three Walter was fully prepared for whatever lay ahead. His exact assignment behind enemy lines had not yet been allocated; he still had final practice parachute jumps to complete with his colleagues in Italy and he travelled on a troopship through the Gibraltar Straits to join his fellow SOE colleagues who had left the previous month. His reflections of the journey in *Before the Anticlimax* are scathing of the class divide aboard ship:

> Nothing is quite so likely to convert one to extreme communism than a journey on a troop ship. Nowhere else is class distinction more pronounced and more strictly enforced than on a troop ship. The whole ship was festooned with notices like 'Out of Bounds for Other Ranks' and 'Only for Officers of the Rank of Major and Above', 'Out of Bounds for Women', 'Out of Bounds for Men'. Any chance meetings between members of different social groups, or between opposite sexes, had to be avoided at all costs. It was war-time, we served a common purpose and we were literally 'in the same boat', but the concept of a sergeant having a glass of beer at the same bar as a lieutenant, was quite unthinkable. If we had been torpedoed and sunk, I am sure that even the life boats would have carried 'Out of Bounds' notices. Only the Captain of the ship had complete freedom and even he, if it was a he, was probably not allowed into the Ladies' loo.[1]

Once in Italy, he was stationed with his colleagues at an olive processing factory at Fasano near Monopoli on Italy's Adriatic Coast. A few weeks later the men were joined by the rest of the ex-Austrian SOE trainees, including Walter's friend Eric Sanders. On arrival the impact of the war for ordinary Italians was clearly visible to Walter:

> There can have been few ordinary Italians whose life was remotely as pleasant as ours. The war had brought them nothing but hunger, destruction and misery – the three riders of the Apocalypse were indeed riding across this normally pleasant and fertile land. The Germans had taken a full measure of revenge for the desertion of their Italian ally. As the Germans slowly retired north, they wrought havoc with Italian installations.[2]

It would be at least six months before the men went into action. In the interim period their intensive training continued with parachute jumps near Bari and mountaineering expeditions in the Abruzzi Mountains, east of Rome. Walter wrote of this time in Italy:

> At that time, we developed a method of jumping together with our heavy equipment, without hurting us on landing; a sprained ankle could then be equivalent to a death sentence. The method consisted of wearing the chute on the back, and in front, on our chest, we carried the heavy equipment in the rucksack on a twenty five foot long rope, so that it dangled beneath us. Thus, we were unencumbered on landing. It worked better in training than 'on the night'! During the operational jump, one of us, H. Schweiger, instead of lowering his baggage gently, let go. The twenty five foot drop was too much for the rope, it broke and Schweiger irretrievably lost all his equipment.
>
> The training of parachute jumping in Southern Italy had one major drawback. After each jump, the chutes would be bundled up, put on a lorry and returned to the depot for repacking. We found that chutes went missing and the Authorities naturally suspected us of having converted them to underwear for the girlfriends. But we were innocent! When the lorries were on their way back from the dropping zone with our chutes, the Italians would stand on their balconies, under which these open lorries would travel. With the help of fishing lines and hooks, the Italians would catch hold of these chutes and pull them off and up. As there were almost no other materials for dress making available, parachute nylon was much in demand.

By the end of 1944 Walter was working in Italy alongside German POWs who had been given manual tasks by the Allied Forces. The psychological pressure of being on alert for action and the ensuing delay began to take its toll. Walter found it particularly difficult and wrote:

Towards the end of 1944, my mental state started to deteriorate. One can remain keyed up only for a limited period and my period was apparently up. I wanted to get on with it, to do something useful, instead of more and more useless training. I was also not in tune with some of my new colleagues. These were not, like me and our original lot, Jewish refugees from Hitler's persecution, but German POWs of Austrian descent, who, after having been made POWs, had volunteered to fight for their captors. Who could tell if they were not Fifth Columnists, trying to infiltrate the organisation of the Special Force? My fears were not groundless; after the war it became known that the Dutch Country Section was completely undermined by the Gestapo and many brave lives were lost because of the carelessness of the London organisation in Baker Street. The absence of security checks in the messages from the agents in Holland were either not noticed or ignored by Baker Street, the British Headquarters, and the Gestapo more or less ran Special Forces Holland. British Intelligence prided itself that they ran most of the German spy rings in this country; unfortunately Gestapo did do the same with our lot in Holland.

Eventually the time came for the men to be assigned their mission behind enemy lines. Major Metherell discussed with Walter possible options, including being dropped into a region near the Semmering Pass. The railway pass over the Semmering was considered one of the targets because of its strategic importance as a main supply line of the German forces in Italy. Built in the 1850s by the Rothschilds, the railway ran from Vienna south-westerly towards the Adriatic. The Semmering Pass was located towards the eastern end of the Alps, about fifty miles south-west of Vienna, served by some elaborate viaducts and tunnels:

The general idea was that I should be dropped together with a canister of explosives. This should then be used to blow up one of these viaducts. If successful, it would have taken a long time to repair the line. We made a sand table of the area (a three dimensional model) and the operation was discussed in great detail. We even had some aerial photos taken. However, at the end it was judged not feasible. The explosives could not have been dropped with sufficient accuracy; they would most likely have got stuck in some ravine. Anyway, successfully or not, it would have been a suicide mission as there would have been no escape from the area afterwards.[3]

The missions did not run according to plan. It was a risky venture. The men, including Walter, were dropped from the wrong height or location, resulting in landing miles from their intended drop zone. They had to survive for days or weeks without their companions. In some cases their equipment was dropped after them but landed in the wrong place. Without equipment the men could not radio their whereabouts to HQ and they found themselves alone in enemy territory, reliant on their training and quick-thinking for survival. With one exception all survived the war and their mission in enemy territory. Of those who were eventually parachuted behind the lines, two of Walter's colleagues were known to have been taken prisoner: Stephen Dale (Heinz Günter Spanglet) and Peter Priestley (Egon Lindenbaum). Butch Baker-Byrne (Robert Becker) was dropped twice into Germany and Michael O'Hara (Friederich Berliner) was the only one to have been killed. He was captured, tortured and shot. He had also acted as dispatcher for Italian partisans and given the orders to jump. Austrian-born Charles (Karl) Kaiser was group leader of Operation Hamster and on 20 April 1945 was dropped behind enemy lines with Harry Williams (Harry Wunder).[4] Their destination was Rossbacher Alpe in Styria which was formerly a province of Austria; their brief was to attack communications of Bruck-Leoben and Bruck-Graz. Kaiser came to Gleinalpe where he succeeded in contacting a local resistance group and later a deputation of Hungarian Air Force officers coming from Zeltweg airfield. From 8 May, Kaiser was operating in Knittelfeld, a Styrian town, and two days later at Zeltweg aerodrome. Together with twenty men he marched into Knittelfeld where he was supported by local resistance of around 200 men. Public buildings were seized and the Germans agreed to withdraw. On 9 May he met with the Russians in Leoben, the second largest town in Styria, and organised Russian protection against SS troops operating in the area. He also tried to arrange the movement of Russian forced labourers from Knittelfeld to Leoben in exchange for

British POWs there. As a result of going into action, both Kaiser and Williams were commissioned as second lieutenants.

Finally in April 1945, Walter's moment had come. Two parties were to be dropped simultaneously into Austria in a mission codenamed Operation Clowder. Walter was to be the radio operator of the smaller party. As he prepared for the mission, reality finally dawned:

> I wondered what sort of reception I would get in Austria. Would the population receive us with open arms, as liberators, or would they lynch us at the first opportunity? Would they consider us as Austrian patriots, trying to save them from the catastrophic results of Hitler's war, or would they treat us as multiple traitors, as Jews and as Austrians who had gone over to the enemy? I had no idea and neither had anyone else.[5]

Practical preparations began for the impending operation. Walter was issued with quite a large amount of money: German marks, some other hard currency like Swiss francs or US dollars and gold coins and twenty-five francs louis d'ors. He was also fully equipped for the task:

> Our luggage was divided into three parts like ancient Gaul. The heavy stuff, like the radio transmitter-receiver, the explosives, the bulk of the ammunition and the food, was in a separate container. This container would be dropped by parachute by the crew of the aircraft, for us to retrieve on the ground. The more personal belongings, such as sleeping bag etc. would be in our rucksack, which would be dropped with us by the method already explained. Finally, I carried the most important items in my pocket, including the radio codes, maps, compass, hand guns and money. I packed in such a way that even if I lost everything but the clothes I stood up in, I would still be in a position to survive for some time. Our weapons had to be tried and calibrated; each of us got quite an arsenal. There was a 0.30 American carbine, a wonderfully light, reliable and accurate rifle, the best of its kind. Then there was a 0.38 automatic Pistol, easy to use, not heavy, and yet quite effective. Lastly, I had a 0.22 Belgium automatic Browning; it looked like a toy, it was tiny and could be readily hidden in one's clothes.[6]

The intended dropping zone was aerially photographed beforehand and the men briefed about their operation. The drop was to be a mountain meadow high above the Mur valley in southern Austria; the nearest town Judenberg (which rather appropriately translates as Jewsborough). It was a highly risky mission because it was to be a blind drop, i.e. there would be nobody there to receive them. Walter's companion and boss for the drop into Austria was Hans Schweiger, an Austrian ex-lawyer and older man. Although Hans was not agile, he was reliable and careful. The other group for the drop consisted solely of German-speaking refugees who had anglicised their names. Their leader was George Bryant, another Viennese lawyer and grandson of Dr Joseph Breuer who had co-operated with Walter's grandfather Sigmund Freud on the book *Studien Ueber Hysterie* (1895). The wireless operator for this group was a German refugee, Frank Kelley (Otto König). The two other members, both originally from Hamburg, were Fred Warner and Eric Rhodes. The brief for both groups was threefold: first, to make contact with the local population and establish whether they would co-operate with the Allies; second, to carry out acts of sabotage on railways and communications; and third, to establish a British presence in the area because the Russians were advancing towards Austria. If possible, they were to take the strategic air base of Zeltweg in southern Austria.

The airport of departure was between Sienna and Livorno. Sienna had already been liberated by Allied Forces. On the night of 24/25 April 1945 the men boarded the plane for the two-hour flight to the dropping zone. The distance was some 320 miles. It meant that the men were about to parachute into enemy territory in the middle of the night in pitch darkness with no moonlight and no one on the ground to meet them. It was highly risky as Walter was shortly to find out. He described the drop in detail in his unpublished memoirs. It gives an insight into not only the mission itself but his feelings in the tense moments before he jumped out of the back of the plane:[7]

There were a number of other passengers in that plane, in addition to our two parties of six. I recall an American Secret Agent with whom I had a long conversation about the use of salt in food. He explained to me that the right amount of salt was necessary to bring out the full flavour. It helped to pass the time! The pilot was not British, but either an American or a Pole. Schweiger had discussions with him before take-off: the pilot confirmed that he knew where to drop us, which, as it turned out, was a bloody lie. We had arrived at the airport at dusk, been given our chutes and made sure of our luggage. The whole scene was very dark and sombre like an under-exposed black and white film, and very nervous making. After much hustling about, we eventually climbed into the aircraft. We had the normal complement of gunners and as soon as we were airborne, they tried out their guns, which was very noisy and not calming on the nerves. We had with us a dispatcher, who would see to it that our parachutes were properly fitted and that we would jump at the right moment. I imagine that he was also responsible for dropping the container with the heavy luggage after us. It was almost pitch dark in the plane and pitch dark outside. Flying over enemy territory was an unpleasant experience. One cannot admire too much the bomber crews who did this voluntarily night after night for years.

The green light appeared inside the plane. I could feel the dispatcher touching my shoulder. I quickly stepped out through the open door into the darkness. We were lucky that we could jump at our first attempt. Once my parachute had opened, which it did within a few seconds, I seemed to be hanging in the air for hours. I gently lowered my heavy rucksack on its 25ft line, so that it dangled below me. Unfortunately, its pendular movement was very strong, much more pronounced than during training, and it pulled the bottom strap of the chute away from underneath my behind. As a result, I was uncomfortably supported by my leg straps on my testicles. At long last, I guess after 10 minutes, I landed gently. Although it was almost completely dark, there was a bit of moon and it was obvious to me that I was not at my mountain meadow but in a wide open valley. I could not hear our plane. I couldn't see it, but even if I could, I would not have flashed the 'OK' signal. I had no idea where I was, but it was obvious to me that I was somewhere where I should not be. I believe that I was dropped not from a thousand feet above ground but more likely from seven or eight thousand feet. The reason was not far to seek. The highest mountains in that area are about 8,000 ft above sea level and a pilot would be very foolhardy to fly below that level on a dark night. The Mur valley is only about 1,200 ft above sea level, so I was probably dropped from 7 or 8 times the prescribed height, taking eight minutes at least. During this time I would have drifted for miles.

The second group consisting of Frank Kelley, Fred Warner and Eric Rhodes were dropped after Walter, but like Walter's experience, they were flown to the wrong location and parachuted out of the plane at the wrong height. Fred Warner narrates a similar tale to Walter in his unpublished memoirs entitled *A Personal Account of SOE Period*. Fred found himself alone in enemy territory without his colleagues, eventually making his way to Zeltweg aerodrome, arriving after Walter.

After landing, Walter untied himself from the uncomfortable parachute harness and scouted around for the others. He had no idea whether or not they had been dropped. There was no one in sight, and he had not flashed the 'OK' signal with his torch. Now he had to be extremely careful not to alert the neighbourhood of his presence in the area. The only sound was the distant barking of dogs. Many thoughts must have flashed through his mind at the time and a great deal of uncertainly. His priority was survival. In the pitch dark he did not attempt to find the container with his luggage that should have been dropped after him:

When we were planning the operation, we had arranged a rendezvous for meeting after the drop. It was to be at the south-west corner of the mountain meadow, our selected dropping area, across a little stream. I had had a jocular argument with Schweiger about that location. I told him: 'Look, if we have to cross that stream, we shall get wet feet.' I was no great friend of wet feet in winter. But Schweiger was adamant that this was the best location for our meeting place, for reasons which I have forgotten. So now I looked around for that stream. I could hear some water running in the distance. I quickly hid my parachute in some undergrowth and went off to find that stream; it was not far away. In I went, in accordance with Schweiger's orders. I went in deeper and deeper into the ice-cold water; it was running so fast that it almost knocked me over. When it had reached my belt, I realised at long last that this couldn't be Schweiger's little mountain stream and returned to the bank. Now it was not just my boots that were wet and cold, but all my body up to my belt. It was reasonable to assume that I could do no more that night and hence I went a little way into the wooded slopes of the mountain, unrolled my sleeping bag and crawled inside. I did not dare to take off my wet boots in case I had to make a quick getaway.

Next morning, still cold and wet, I tried to orientate myself. This was not easy; I could be anywhere and there were few distinguishing features in the landscape which could help one to take a bearing. After a time, I understood that the little stream I had been trying to cross had been the Mur river, the biggest one in southern Austria. It is known for its strong currents and I was lucky not to have drowned in it with all the weight I was carrying. I had apparently been dropped not very far from a little village called Oberzeiring, miles from the intended dropping zone. So I set off to walk there, in order to meet the others, if indeed they had been dropped. I didn't know what else to do. I took a compass bearing and started. There were no roads or paths and I made very slow progress up the wooded mountain slopes. There was still quite a bit of snow about. In order to get to our original rendezvous, I had to cross a mountain range. Whenever I thought I was close to the top of that range, there was frustratingly another mountain in front of me. Nearly all the food had been in the big container which was lost and after a few days I was getting hungry. Luckily, I then came across an isolated farm house, my first contact with humanity in Austria. I made sure that it had no telephone wires. I went in and asked whether they had any food for sale. Yes, they said they could sell me, or even give me, a large loaf and some Speck, very fat bacon. In that farmhouse, as in all others which I visited, there was only a young mother with a baby and perhaps one or two toddlers, and the old grandfather. Everybody else had been geared into the German war machine. The men from sixteen to sixty were in the Army, the over-sixties were in the Home Guard, the women worked in the munition factories and the adolescents were doing anti-aircraft duty. My identity was never questioned, nor did I give any explanation. If the inhabitants should be questioned by the police, they could honestly say that they had no idea who I was. I moved on. On my way, I visited a few other farmhouses, always making sure that they were well isolated.

After some further meandering, all steeply uphill, Walter came across a deserted *alm-huette*, a mountain hut where the cows are driven during the summer months. It was here that he decided he could rest for a couple of days. It was not easy to break into the hut. In training he had been shown how to force entry using a bicycle spoke, but with no bicycle to hand he still succeeded in getting in. When it was dark he risked making a fire to cook something. He wrote, 'afterwards, I was violently sick.' Whether this was the result of mild food poisoning or the build-up of fear and nerves is not clear. It was now clear that he would not be linking up with his colleagues even if they had been dropped. He was alone, fending for himself in a hostile terrain with little equipment. He must have wondered how he would ever get out again and back to

England, but for now survival was paramount. There was one marked incident while he was in the hut:

While I was at that Alm-huette, I heard a shot fired; I thought that it might have been fired by my party, but I was too careful to fire back. After the war, when I compared notes with my former colleagues, I found out that a shot was fired by Fred Warner, who was surprised by a German searching party. After one or two nights in that hut, I got my strength back and continued on my trek ... I continued to slowly make my way towards the original dropping zone. After some time, I began to realise that Schweiger, even if he had been dropped, which I did not know, would not be waiting for me any longer. It was obviously pointless for me to continue in that direction and I had to think of something else. I had with me a small radio receiver. With that radio receiver I could hear how the war was proceeding. My bigger receiver-transmitter was lost with the heavy luggage. One day, I heard that the British were at long last breaking through Italy and I thought that the time had now come for me to go to 'my' aerodrome at Zeltweg, to claim it for His Britannic Majesty. I turned around to make my way towards the town of Scheifling, which was the nearest town situated on the main road along the Mur valley. Zeltweg was along that same road, some miles further to the east. By that time I had had enough of mountains, so I kept to the small roads which led down to the valley. I met few civilians. In my gas cape, I looked not dissimilar to the local woodcutters. I also came across some women evacuees from the bombed towns, who were apparently taking their morning constitutional. I gave them a cheerful 'Heil Hitler' and walked on.

Then my life was saved by a grandmother. As I went down the road, I was joined by an elderly local woman. She started to talk to me at once. We came to a little footpath branching off our road and leading across some fields. She asked me for my direction. I said 'Scheifling' and she said that she was going there too and that this little footpath would be a shortcut. So we left the road and proceeded along that path. Not long afterwards we came to the main road along the Mur valley. I looked backwards along it and there, where my original road met the main road, I saw a detachment of SS troops controlling the road junction. Had I not met that old woman who had shown me the shortcut, I would have run straight into them and been shot before I could have said 'OK'. As it was, I was now a hundred yards further on, and even if they had seen me from the distance, they did not bother to take any further action, as I had not crossed their checkpoint. I asked the old woman to take me to the Mayor's office in Scheifling, which she did. I thanked her and hoped that all would be well with her grandson.

What followed with the mayor of Scheifling brings to the fore Walter's charisma and enterprising confidence. Walter was determined to try and secure the nearby airfield at Zeltweg for the British Forces. The airfield was of strategic importance in southern Austria. Fortunately for Walter, the mayor was in his office that day. Walter spun a tale about having top military orders and being part of a larger Allied force heading towards the town. It was of course all fabricated:

I told him that I was the vanguard of the British Army and that I had to get to the aerodrome of Zeltweg in order to earmark it for British, rather than Russian, occupation. Zeltweg is some fifteen miles east of Scheifling and the Russians were rapidly approaching that area. He saw my point at once. He told me that he would certainly take me, but unfortunately none of the cars in his little town had any more petrol, not even for 15 miles. He mentally went over the cars available to him, and then his face lit up. The fire engine still had petrol in it! That was good news. The fire engine would do splendidly. The Mayor drove and I sat next to him in the front. It was quite a modern engine, with a folding ladder on top and included all the other paraphernalia, including a siren. There was very little traffic about, but whenever he saw anything likely to cause a hold-up or looked like a check-point, he put on the siren and everybody waved us through. Arriving at Zeltweg, we asked our way to the office of the Commander. The place was full of soldiers in various uniforms: I noticed in particular many Hungarians in their elaborate head gear. Nobody asked for our passes or any documentation; a fire engine has free access to everywhere.

We stopped outside the Commander's office. I went upstairs into the ante-chamber where his secretary sat. I introduced myself in German: 'I am Lieutenant Freud of the 8th British Army, can I see the Commander please?' She paled, went into her boss's room and invited me in. I entered, saluted nonchalantly and repeated: 'I am Lieutenant Freud of the 8th British Army; I have come to take over your aerodrome.' The Commander, I believe he came from Hamburg, slumped down on his desk and started to cry, 'all our efforts, all our sacrifices, all in vain.' I, being a softy, felt quite sorry for him. It cannot have been fun for him to see a young enemy officer asking him for his aerodrome. I explained to him that I had been especially sent by General Montgomery to ensure that the aerodrome would come under British rule at the end of the war. These were of course all lies. I did not belong to the 8th British Army, nor had I ever spoken to, or even seen, General Montgomery. The Commander asked me whether I had a document with me, authorising my demand. I said that I had not, my word as a British officer should suffice. I could see that the man was in a terrible quandary. If he handed over the aerodrome, the still active SS might take a dim view of his defeatist attitude and execute him. On the other hand, the Russians were near, or even past, the Hungarian/Austrian border, less than 60 miles away and could be arriving any day. The Germans had one great fear and it was the fear of the Russians. They knew what they had done in Russia and to the Russians and were terrified of retribution. To be included in the British Zone of occupation would ensure them a safe haven.

Although the commander was in a predicament about what to do, he asked Walter for the necessary authorisation about his status and military orders. Walter, of course, did not have any of this. It was agreed that Walter should radio a message to his home station from the radio room in the aerodrome. That Walter did and the original message sent in German survives in his SOE file. Only the first line was sent in English. The whole transmission read:

Have to send messages in German Plain language – stop.
Translation of the German message:
I am at the aerodrome Zeltweg – stop
The Commander is unaware that there is a ceasefire – stop
I request exact East borders of the ceasefire area – stop
Inform me tomorrow over DHNGEHY-yellow (his code station) – stop
Very urgent – stop
I am at present guest of the compound Commandant – stop
I will use their radio station at the aerodrome – stop.[8]
Freud – stop

Walter was out of luck that day with the transmission. No one at the other end acknowledged it at the time of its sending, possibly because they would have been looking for a weaker signal from his own radio set and not the high-powered transmission from Zeltweg. Walter returned from the radio room to inform the commander that he had failed to get through. The Commander told him that the following day he would convene a meeting with the local gautleiter and Nazi bosses to decide the issue of the surrender of the airfield to Walter. That night Walter spent the evening at the hospitality of the commander and dined in the officers' mess. The whole scene before him was somewhat surreal and bizarre:

> I was astonished how formal the proceedings there were; almost like peacetime. Officer after officer jumped up, after having been given formal permission to do so, to wish the Commander good luck: Proestchen, Herr Major. Such toasts were accompanied by loud heel clicking and standing rigidly to atten tion. There was no sign of a lowering of morale; the nearest Russian might have been in Vladivostok, not fifty miles away in Eastern Austria. The food and drinks were very good.

That night Walter was allocated a room in the airfield complex, his only company a large picture of Hitler looking down on him from one of the walls. How ironic. Having witnessed Hitler's triumphant annexing of Austria in 1938, just seven years later as an officer in British uniform, but still not yet a British citizen, he was about to experience Hitler's total defeat in both Austria and Germany. The following day several meetings took place with Walter present. None of the Nazi officials wanted to be responsible for making the final decision about the airfield. There were around 20–25 of them at the meeting. It was finally decided that Walter could have the airfield if agreed by General Rendulic, the commander of the Southern Front, who was based in Linz. Then Walter had to listen to an extraordinary chain of admissions from the local Nazis:

> During that meeting, a surprising thing happened. One by one, the senior Nazi bosses approached me with: 'May I have a word with you in private Lieutenant Freud?' I said: 'Certainly'. And we would leave the big table to go to a window recess. He would start: 'Lieutenant Freud, I love the Jews. I have a Jewish second cousin four times removed, whom I protected during the whole war. I trust that this will be taken into consideration after the war'. I said, 'Yes Gauleiter' or 'Yes, Higher SS and Police Chief' as appropriate. All

this will be taken into consideration and you will be given the opportunity to state your case'. They knew that the War Crime Trials were coming and their bad conscience needed reassurance. It was not just one or two guests who wanted to 'Speak to me privately', but about half the people present. If I have to sleeve the high point of my life so far it was the moment when the Gauleiters of Southern Austria assured me of their love for the Jews. Those evil henchmen, who for twelve years had done everything in their power to humiliate, harass and eventually kill their Jewish co-patriots, were then coming crawling to me and sold their Nazi convictions and anti-semitic beliefs for a few semi reassuring words. Only two or three years earlier, these very same people fancied themselves as belonging to the upper hierarchy of the Herrenrasse, the Master-Race, and the future rulers of the world. Only they were to enjoy the fruits of the earth; all else were to be their slaves, and if deemed unfit for slavery, exterminated. I looked at them in their fancy uniforms, with braids and decorations and side-arms, trying to smile kindly at me and doing their best to imitate an impression of civilisation. They didn't even have the guts to have me shot.[9]

The next day Walter was driven by a German major to Linz on a journey which took most of the day. It was a hair-raising drive when, just out-side Linz, they were bombed by Russian aircraft: 'They swooped down low over the road and machine-gunned everything. Their aim may have been good but fortunately they did not hit me, or – as far as I could see – anybody else. But they created a lot of commotion, with everybody jumping out of their cars into the nearest ditch. It was the first time that I was being bombed, so I just sat tight, waiting for it to stop.' Walter finally arrived at the headquarters in Linz where his visit was expected. He was treated with due respect and polity. He never saw General Rendulic in person, only a handful of his officers. Walter related a story about the encounter with one of the general's officers:

One of them was very curious where I had learnt my good German. I told him that my father had had to work in Germany before the war and that therefore I had been to school there. When he showed further curiosity, I told him that my pre-war life was quite irrelevant to the present situation and that all I was interested in was the aerodrome at Zeltweg. He then desisted. By the way, the name of Sigmund Freud was never mentioned. This should not be surprising. As a Jew, he had not appeared in any German publication for the last twelve years and as most of the German officers I talked to were in their thirties, they would not have come across the name in their adult life.

In spite of not actually meeting face-to-face with Walter, the general authorised the surrender of the airbase. Walter's mission successfully achieved, he began the return journey to Zeltweg with the Major assigned as his driver. They never made it back to the airfield. The return trip did not go as smoothly as the outward one. These were still dangerous times with much uncertainty, and the car was stopped at a road block and the Major arrested by a group of Austrian units who had mutinied. Walter wrote that it was 'very dramatic, with lots of officers waving their revolvers about and getting very het up; one could easily have got hurt in the melee.' What Walter did not record in his memoirs was that these Austrians were very taken with him and what he must have said to them. He was given a typed notification from the leader of the Austrian Freedom Brigade Gruppe Ostermann which read, translated from the German:

> We have tonight from 5–6 May 1945 begun the freedom fight for Austria. Thanks to the gracious exchange/communication with the British Officer Anthony W. Freud, I beg that he should be regarded as an honorary member of this group.[10]

Having spent a night with the local resistance fighters, Walter was allocated an Austrian officer to replace the German major who had been arrested. He was driven in a westerly direction until he came to the American front line with German troops on one side and Americans on the other. He wrote:

> There were some last minute difficulties. The front line troops did not wish to let anybody pass, in case he was a deserter. My Austrian accompanying officer managed to calm another revolver waving Captain, who wanted to shoot me; it was surprising how quickly the German Officers drew their guns, as if they were handkerchiefs and they had a cold. Most probably, it was caused by the frustrations of the lost war. After this last hurdle was cleared, I made my way very carefully across a badly damaged bridge, hoping that neither side would

use me for target practice. On the other side, I soon found an American sentry, whom I asked to take me to his Headquarters. By then, I had discarded my gas cape and openly wore British Army battledress.

Once behind the American lines, Walter was interviewed by an officer from the intelligence section of that American unit. At least the officer knew the surname Freud, unlike his German/Austrian equivalent at Zeltweg: 'The name "Freud" came in good stead. He was not like his counterparts on the other side of the bridge, poor ignorant bastards, but fully conversant with current ideas and he knew his slips. He couldn't do enough for me. I was received like a long-lost son.' Walter requested permission to stay a while with the Americans, which he said was to learn how they operated. He moved with them as they advanced, taking back areas for the Allied Occupying forces. He commented:

They had learnt the art of war and Blitzkrieg to perfection. When, on their advance, they came across a town, it was encouraged by loudhailer to surrender. If the town did this and indicated it by hanging out white flags from every house, then all was well. If they didn't, the office in charge of the attack would phone the U.S. Army Air Force, rather like phoning a friend to drop in for a drink. 'Bud, can you take out town X for me?' 'Sure, will do' would be the answer. Within the hour, fifty or a hundred bombers would fly in and over the town and afterwards there would hardly be one stone left on another.

I went with the Americans through a just-captured medium-sized town. The first vehicle to enter was an armoured bulldozer, to push away the rubble to ease the way for the following tanks. The accumulated rubble in German towns had to be experienced to be believed. At that time I, and everybody else who saw it, thought that the Germans would not recover for two or more generations. One imagined that it would take them twenty years just to remove the mountains of rubble.

It was a brief but instructive interlude with the Americans. They chartered a plane to Paris for Walter on what was the first leg of his journey back to England, now his home. His reception was somewhat frosty:

In Paris, the cold showers awaited me. I was taken to the British Embassy, given a room there, but nobody would speak to me, I was not even invited to eat in their Mess or Canteen. Instead I was brought a slice of bully beef on a biscuit – in Paris of all places. I knew I looked the worse for wear, but I was still a recognisable British Officer and should have been treated as such. I was too exhausted to make a fuss. I still had most of my weaponry on me and the idea of shooting up the Embassy looked quite attractive at the time, but I desisted.

According to his SOE file, Walter finally arrived back in England on 10 May 1945, a couple of days after VE Day. He was still the rank of second lieutenant and once again received an unglamorous welcome. His return coincided with the day his father received a telegram from the War Office, informing him that Walter was missing in action. It must have been a terrible time for Martin Freud to learn that the whereabouts of his son was unknown, feared dead. The following day (11 May) instructions were issued by the commanding officer to settle Walter's pay and allowances from his time in Italy and furnish him with the appropriate rations cards and clothing coupons. Walter immediately settled down to compile a report of his time behind enemy lines, a copy of which survives in his personal SOE file. Attached to the report is a memo dated 16 May 1945 which states: 'Attached is a report made by Lieut. A. W. Freud who has just returned to this country from the Austrian theatre of war. This report is intended for the use of anyone in Security Section who is interested. Would you be good enough to circulate.' His report pretty much follows what he wrote later in his memoirs:

Immediately on landing, Freud made for the mountains in a N.N.E. direction of Bocksruck. Next day he made contact with local farmers, who provided him with food. They warned him that the Police knew that parachutists had dropped in the area, and two companies of Volkssturn were scouring the district, and so Freud decided to move away from the place. The weather became very bad, and there was nearly two feet of snow, making it difficult to walk and leaving tell-tale tracks. Freud found a loft on a farm were he made his H.Q. He was forced to rely on farmers for food. The farms were mainly inhabited by grandfathers, women and children. The old men were very reliable, never Nazi, and kept him informed of Police movements and the best roads to take. The women gave him food but gave the impression of being unfriendly and unreliable. In the main, however, the peasantry were friendly ... He was given permission to use the aerodrome's wireless providing he sent his message in German. The message attached was then arranged for despatch. (Freud actually did not manage to make contact with our people, as the set was very bad, he was right down in the valley and there was no crystal control.)

Next day, Freud was informed that no orders had been received to hand over the aerodrome but he could go to the H.Q. of the Army Group just outside Linz. He was provided with a car and driver and went to Linz, where he was interviewed by a number of high-ranking officers, all of whom were anxious to ascertain the line of demarcation between the Russians and the English in Austria. Fear of a Russian occupation was very great. Freud pointed out that unless he were allowed to take over the aerodrome on behalf of the British, the Russians would march in. This impressed all concerned. At four o'clock next morning, Freud left Linz by car for the aerodrome. The aerodrome had been moved from Linz to Waidhofen an der Ybbs. The road was crowded with convoys and they soon came up against a road-block. The Major escorting Freud, a typical Nazi type, very brutal, proceeded to charge through until he was finally stopped by a German soldier with a tommy-gun, who ordered him to put up his hands. This soldier refused to let them pass as they were under suspicion. Freud told his story once more to the Sergeant in charge of the soldiers, and said he had to get to Graz. The Sergeant escorted him to H.Q. The Commander there, named Ostermann, informed Freud that he had started an Austrian Movement of between 500–1,000 men, and that they had succeeded in cutting all roads between Linz and Graz. The insurgents were actually surrounded by Germans, but they hoped that the Americans would soon come to the rescue. Freud offered to go to the Americans on their behalf. The offer was gladly accepted, and he was given the attached credential.

Major Oesterreicher of the General Staff (who had escorted Freud this far) had on his person the necessary papers for passing through the German lines into the American lines. This major accompanied Freud and the Free Austrian Commander provided a Lieutenant for further company. Unfortunately, as soon as the first German road patrol was encountered, the Major insisted that the Lieutenant be taken into custody, and although Freud remonstrated it was useless. The Major then stated that they would return to his own H.Q. at Waidhofen a.d. Ybbs, and although Freud threatened that this behaviour would lead to trouble when the Americans eventually arrived, they did return to German H.Q.

At the H.Q. Freud stated that, in view of the surrender, he could not be detained, and he was therefore provided with another car and taken to Steyr. The Americans were already there and Freud was taken to the H.Q. of the 71st Division, and then on to Group H.Q., etc. etc. He was provided with a special plane from Nuremburg to Paris and from there returned to England. Freud merely told the Americans that he was a British Special Services Officer who had just come back from a mission in the German lines. Freud said that Steyr has not suffered much from the bombing, but that Nuremburg, Mannheim and Ludwigshafen are flat to the ground.

With the above report handed in and in spite of a disappointing reception from military officials, Walter's wartime service was acknowledged with a recommendation for promotion to rank of lieutenant. This was eventually approved and implemented in the autumn of 1945. The job of SOE agents in Europe was done but for Walter his service in British Army uniform was far from over. He was asked whether he would volunteer to serve immediately in the Far East where the war had not yet ended. He declined in favour of doing something for the occupying Allied forces in Germany because of his fluency in German. A brief report dated 19 May 1945 in Walter's secret service file records:

> The a/n agent returned to UK from operations. There is no further employment for him in the Directorate. He applies through O.C. No.1 Special Force C.M.F. (Central Mediterranean Force) for employment with the Control Commission, Austria. He wishes to continue in the Army, preferably as an interpreter. Provided security have no objection, his commission may be transferred to Open List.

On 23 May it was recorded in his file that no objections were raised to transferring his commission to the Open List. Then there followed a period of approximately three months when Walter was waiting for his posting abroad. On 3 August 1945 he wrote to his sister Sophie in France:

> I am still on leave, nearly 3 months now. However I cannot go away from London because I might be recalled any day and have to be available. It is getting a bit boring to have nothing to do for such a long time, last week I took a job with Uncle Ernst, surveying bomb-damaged houses. I still have not got

a clue when and to what they are going to recall me, anything from managing prisoners of war to The Allied Control Commission. My post war plans are all but definite. I hope to go back to College after my release from the army. I am even toying with the idea of an army career … The whole family is getting on fine, it was grandmother's [Martha Freud's] birthday on the 26th. Father speaks of nothing but food, food, and food all day long. He usually thinks he has Magenkrebs when he has overeaten. He has shaved off his beard which had suited him very well. Have you heard anything from grandmother Drucker?[11]

At this point, the family did not know that Ida Drucker had perished in the Holocaust. On 11 August 1945 Walter was posted back overseas; this time to Germany in the pool of interpreters. Meanwhile back in Britain, his exploits with SOE were the talk of the bars and coffee houses among men of the Special Forces. Harry Brooke (originally Heinz Bruck) who served with the Parachute Regiment said:

When I was on leave in London just after the war, I used to go to the United Nations Service Club in St James Square. I used to meet all those who had come back from front line fighting and operations with the Commandos, Special Services, Paras and SOE. Amongst them and our refugee circles, Walter Freud was legendary. His courage, audacity and disregard for personal safety in the service of this country earned him huge admiration, even though some of us had never met him. We heard of his exploits and his name became highly respected for his courage. He did not fear the consequences of his actions behind enemy lines and for that we had great admiration for him. Many of us felt that we would not have had the bravery to do what he had done.[12]

War Crimes Investigation Unit

After the acceptance of the formal unconditional surrender of Germany on 8 May 1945, the area north of Hamburg became full of fleeing German armies making for Flensburg. The resettlement of displaced persons and forced labourers presented a huge task for the occupying Allied Forces. Denazification and the reconstruction of post-war Germany and Austria began. That included the hunt for Nazi war criminals and preparing evidence for the war crimes tribunals. In August 1945 Captain Walter Freud was posted to the War Crimes Investigation Unit at Bad Oeynhausen, the headquarters of the British Army of the Rhine (BAOR) where he served for a year. Most of his colleagues from SOE were assigned pivotal roles in the denazification work, some remaining in Britain to work with German POWs in camps, others posted to Germany and Austria for translation work, interpretive duties and tracking down Nazi war criminals. Still enemy aliens in British Army uniform, they had not yet been granted British nationality. Walter's closest friend in SOE, Eric Sanders, became an interpreter at a camp for German POWs at Norton Fitzwarren, near Taunton in the south-west of England. After a period there, Eric Sanders was sent back to Vienna to work with Major Lasky (also a former refugee) in the legal division of the British–Austrian Legation Unit. There he was part of a team engaged in translating into English the new laws which were to be passed and approved for the newly democratic Austria by the four occupying powers (British, French, American and Soviet).

Enemy aliens who returned to Germany at the end of the war in British Army uniform came face to face with the sheer horror of the death camps and the certain knowledge of the murder of their families. Nothing prepared them or the liberating armies for the stinking piles of emaciated bodies, nor the horrific suffering of the survivors and stench of death. For those who witnessed it, the memory remained with them throughout their lives, haunting them for decades to come. This horror could not be seen or shared with any but their own army colleagues, representing the greatest trauma and bereavement of all. Hopes of finding surviving members of their families faded, and despair became a huge burden. Most, including Walter Freud, visited Bergen-Belsen concentration camp. Many of them did so in the days immediately after its liberation by British troops on 15 April 1945. The exact date when Walter Freud visited Belsen is not certain, but it was sometime after his posting to Germany in August 1945. As far as one can tell, he never wrote about it. That he visited Belsen is certain from photographs which he took of the grassed mounds where over a thousand bodies lay buried by BAOR bulldozers, and the memorial plaques marking the site. He spoke about it rarely and only, it seems, to his daughter Caroline.

Walter was assigned to No. 2 War Crimes Team which consisted of Lieutenant Colonel Norman Ashton Hill, Major Ronald Bentham Green and Captains Alan Nightingale, Richard O'Neill-Major, John Bramwell, Peter Nixon, Harry Cartmell, Brian Bone and Frederick Lee. Walter was involved in a number of cases, which included compiling evidence and searching for known Nazi war criminals. One case in which he was involved was that of the German industrialist Krupp who was thought to have helped the Nazis at the highest level and supplied munitions. Walter himself found no evidence to convict Krupp and concluded that most of the documentation had already been destroyed. However a number of other investigations were carried out on the wartime activities of the firm, including its use of foreign civilians and POWs for forced labour. Krupp had also built a large fuse factory at Auschwitz where Jews were worked to exhaustion and then sent to their deaths in the gas chambers. Gustav Krupp, the head of the firm, was listed as a major war criminal at Nuremburg, but he was too ill to stand trial after he suffered a stroke.[1] He was never tried for war crimes. Attention turned to his son Alfried Krupp who, on 31 July 1948, faced charges at a Nuremburg military tribunal. Alfried Krupp stood in a courtroom before Judge Anderson and Judge Daly to hear the guilty verdict:

> That this growth and expansion on the part of the Krupp firm was due in large measure to the favoured position it held with Hitler there can be no doubt. The close relationship between Krupp on the one hand and the Reich government, particularly the Army and Navy Command, on the other hand, amounted to a veritable alliance. The wartime activities of the Krupp concern were based in part upon spoliation of other countries and on exploitation and maltreatment of large masses of forced foreign labour.[2]

Judge Daly then proceeded to read out his sentence: 'On the counts of the indictment on which you have been convicted, the tribunal sentences you to imprisonment for twelve years and orders forfeiture of all your property, both real and personal.'

Walter Freud's biggest investigation was regarding the wartime activities of the Hamburg-based company Tesch & Stabenow which supplied Zyklon B to the Auschwitz and Neuengamme concentration camps. It was originally a firm of fumigators for ships bringing grain to Europe from America. After each trip, the ships had to be fumigated for rats and mice. For that procedure, Zyklon B was supplied by Tesch & Stabenow. During the Second World War the Nazis singled out the company to provide Zyklon B for Hitler's 'Final Solution'. At the height of the programme of the extermination of Jews, the firm supplied two tons a month for the concentration camps. Having fluent knowledge of German, Walter carried out a number of interrogations of the staff at Tesch & Stabenow as part of the compilation of evidence for the war crimes trials. He wrote about those investigations:

> And the man in charge said: 'Yes, of course. I supplied so much Zyklon B to the concentration camps. And I had no idea it was used for humans.' He couldn't deny it because we found all the receipts, but [he said] they were for the clothes of the prisoners, they were full of mice. He was a dreadful person, not only from my point of view, but also his own employees, and they all came and they said the following: 'There was a meeting between Dr Tesch and the SS, where he was told what it was for. His technicians advised the SS on how to do it because it is a dangerous powder, and you had to have

the technique of introducing it into the chambers and so on.' It had to be studied. It was Dr Tesch's staff who advised the SS on how to do it. So there was no excuse and he was hanged. He was one of the very first German technicians who were actually hanged and not excused or let free after a few years. He was an absolute die-hard Nazi, an honorary SS man, and his books were only Nazi books. It's interesting for instance that when Hamburg was so badly bombed, Himmler wrote a letter to the Mayor of Hamburg saying: 'please help Tesch to get up on his feet again.' Only Stabenow was given that privileged treatment.[3]

This was clearly one of the most significant cases which Walter ever worked on. The investigation affected him deeply. He wrote extensively again about the case in his unpublished work *An Austrian Grandfather*. During his investigations he interrogated the medical orderly who was responsible for pouring the powder into prison cells in an experiment. Walter's comments are worth quoting here in full:

The fumigant used was Prussic Acid absorbed on a chalk-like substance and the resultant powder had the trade-name 'Zyklon B', made by I.G.Farben. In the absorbed state it was relatively harmless when cold and could be handled with a minimum of precautions When heated to about 40°C (104°F) the Prussic acid would be liberated from the chalk, become active and would quickly kill any mammal breathing it in. In January 1942, at the time of the first reverses of the German army outside Moscow, there took place in the Berlin suburb of Wannsee a high-level conference to discuss the 'Final Solution' (of the Jewish Problem). This meeting decided to try gassing as an effective and cheap way of exterminating the Jews. In order to obtain the 'scientific' data, a pilot experiment was subsequently conducted at the concentration camp of Neuengamme outside Hamburg, conveniently located for the firm of Tesch and Stabenow, using Russian prisoners of war as guinea pigs. A number of prison cells inside the camp were fitted with electric heaters, the Russian POWs were locked inside, and varying amounts of Zyklon B powder were introduced through the ceilings of the individual cells. The heaters were then switched on and as soon as the temperature in the cells had reached a certain level, the Prussic acid gas was liberated and took effect. This experiment established the optimum amounts of Zyklon B, the time factor and other operating data required for later and large-scale use in the extermination camps.

I am certain of the above facts, because after the war I interrogated the SS medical orderly who was at the sharp end of that experiment; i.e. he was the chap who had to climb onto the roof of the cells in order to drop the powder into them. He was of simple farming background, but not stupid. When he signed his deposition, given quite voluntarily, he said to me: 'I am now signing my own death warrant'. While I am not quite sure of his eventual fate, I believe he was right. I am however quite sure of the fate of three senior employees of the firm of Tesch and Stabenow. Mr Tesch, his accountant and the technical representative were brought to trial in Hamburg in 1946. Their defence was that 'yes', they supplied Zyklon B to the SS, but as far as they knew at the time it was used only to fumigate the clothes of their Russian prisoners of war of which there were many. However, we found witnesses who confirmed that Tesch had been informed by the SS to what use his powder was going to be put and that he had voluntarily agreed to supply it for the purpose of killing. (I am not sure that vermin like lice will be killed by Prussic acid; this disinfection is usually carried out with steam).[4]

In the spring of 1947 Bruno Tesch and his accountant Karl Weinbacher were tried before a British Army war crimes tribunal lasting seven days.[5] One of the witnesses who gave evidence was Perry Broad who had been employed as a typist in the office at Auschwitz concentration camp from 1942 until early 1945. Little did Broad know then that he too would be tried as a war criminal nearly twenty years later in 1964 at the Auschwitz trial in Frankfurt. Both Tesch and Weinbacher were found guilty of war crimes and condemned to death. On 26 April 1947 Field Marshal Montgomery signed their death warrants and the men were hanged in Hameln prison. The technical representative, against whom prior knowledge could not be proved, was acquitted. For Walter Freud this particular investigation had a direct family link which he reflected upon after the war:

How does the above story of the supplier of poison-gas to the concentration camps relate to Grandfather? He had four sisters in Vienna, all over seventy years of age and either spinsters or widows. These four old ladies were left behind in Vienna with sufficient funds for the remainder of their lives. But these lives were brutally cut short by their transportation to various extermination camps, and by the application of the same Zyklon B gas whose suppliers I, their grandnephew, helped to prosecute. I am sure Grandfather would have approved.[6]

After the war the exact fate of Sigmund Freud's sisters became known. Two of them, eighty-two-year-old Marie and eighty-year-old Pauline, were murdered in Treblinka concentration camp in 1942. The other sister, eighty-four-year-old Rosa perished in the gas chambers of Auschwitz, and the youngest sister Adolfine died of starvation in Theresienstadt. On 27 February 1946, Sigmund Freud's sister was mentioned specifically by the witness at the Nuremburg Trials on Treblinka, considering evidence against Nazi war criminal Kurt Franz. The exact name of Freud's sister was not given, but a witness must have been referring to either Marie or Paula. The witness giving evidence was Samuel Rajzman, a survivor of the Warsaw ghetto. He had been taken to Treblinka in August 1942 where he was put into a labour unit; his life spared because of his linguistic skills. He witnessed atrocities and death there on a vast scale, estimating that between ten to twelve thousand people were killed every day, including his own wife and child. At the Nuremburg Trial he said of Sigmund Freud's sister:

> A train arrived from Vienna. I was standing on the platform when the passengers left the cars. An elderly woman came up to Kurt Franz [supervising the arrival of victims], took out a document, and said that she was the sister of Sigmund Freud. She begged him to give her light work in an office. Franz read this document through very seriously and said that there must be a mistake here; he led her up to the train schedule and said that in two hours a train would leave again for Vienna. She should leave all her documents and valuables and then go to the bathhouse; after the bath she would have her documents and a ticket to Vienna. Of course, the woman went into the bathhouse and never returned.[7]

Walter Freud lost members from both sides of his family in the Holocaust. Not only his grandfather's four sisters, but also his maternal grandmother Ida Drucker who was deported in 1942 and perished in Auschwitz:

> My maternal grandmother, then over seventy years old, was transported from Biarritz, near the Spanish-French border, to Auschwitz in Poland, a distance

of about 1,500 miles (2,300 km). The locomotive and trucks required for this, her last journey, might have been used to better purpose for the German war effort – say for example to carry the small extra reinforcement needed to capture the Caucasian oilfields which were almost within Hitler's grasp.[8]

During 1946 Walter was also assigned to the investigations of war crimes at the Neuengamme camp outside Hamburg. He was stationed in Hamburg at the time and only travelled to the camp itself a couple of times. When British troops had arrived at Neuengamme camp on 2 May 1945 they had found it virtually empty. The inmates had been evacuated towards the end of April, nine thousand of whom were believed to have been boarded onto three ships. Two of the ships, the *Cap Arcona* and *Thielbek*, were bombed in the bay of Lübeck in a British attack which had not expected the ships to be carrying survivors from a concentration camp. After 2 May 1945, the British turned it into an internment camp. Neuengamme was not intended as a full-scale death camp by the Nazis, but thousands certainly died there. It had a crematorium and punishment cells. Of 106,000 prisoners, amongst whom were Dutch and French resistance fighters, homosexuals, Jehovah's Witnesses, 500 gypsies and 13,000 Jews, only half survived. In 1943, the Nazis rounded up 2,000 of the Danish police force, all of whom were taken to Neuengamme. Medical experiments were carried out on children, and other inmates worked in harsh conditions in nearby factories. The SS guards of Neuengamme had fled, but once caught, were imprisoned in Hamburg. The camp commandant, Max Pauli, and ten others were eventually sentenced in a British court in March 1946.

Walter was assigned to other cases in the war crimes investigations, one of which was suspected Nazi war criminal Christian Gustaf Jepsen. In January 1946 Walter travelled to Denmark as part of the search to track down Jepsen. By now Walter's father knew where he had been posted and wrote to him on 27 February in Hamburg: 'I wonder how you will like Kopenhagen [sic]. I am sure it will be wonderful. My next destination is Grimsby and afterwards Newcastle.' From a letter dated 24 March 1946 it is also clear that Martin was aware that his son was working on war crimes investigations. In that letter, he passed his son sensitive information. Writing from 70 Queen's Road, Newcastle-on-Tyne where he was lodging with the Goldschmidt family, he told Walter: 'The people with whom I stay here are Jews from Hannover [sic]. They have suffered badly from the Nazis and gave me a list of their worst persecutors. It is left to your discretion to use it or throw it away.' It is not known whether or not Walter handed over his father's information to the British military authorities in Germany.

Gustav Jepsen was arrested in April 1946. The report following his arrest was dated 26 April 1946, a copy of which survives among Walter Freud's family papers. The British wanted Jepsen extradited for trial under a British court. Translated from Danish, the report reads:[9]

Group Captain A.G. Somerhaugh, Judge Attorney-General Branch, War Crimes Section, H.Q., B.A.O.R. and Captain A.W. Freud, War Crimes Investigation Unit, H.Q., B.A.O.R., presented themselves on 23rd of this month in Assistant Secretary Schoen's office to discuss the case concerning the surrender of Christian Gustaf Jepsen.

They confirmed the earlier received information that Jepsen is charged with cruelty and murder of concentration camp prisoners in Germany and they cited that Jepsen had admitted to six murders, whereas he undoubtedly is guilty of a much larger amount. With reference to the others accused in this case, all being German nationals, it was from the British viewpoint important Jepsen was handed over for judgement under the British military court, which was to hear the case. If it was not possible to hand him to the court to be prosecuted it is to be expected that the others accused will put the responsibility on him, and that Jepsen on the other hand, if his case later comes to judgement in front of a Danish court, will try to push the responsibility on to his German co-accused. The Assistant Secretary Schoen explained the view of the Ministry of Justice and stressed that it would be seen as quiet extraordinary to surrender a Danish citizen for legal proceedings outside Denmark. The charge against Jepsen was of such a nature that he would undoubtedly be sentenced to death in this country, and there would therefore be no doubt the Danish would make sure that justice was carried out. The Assistant Secretary questioned whether that the case could not be brought to justice if Jepsen only attended as a witness because he would be under no obligation to give his account on matters that could incriminate him.

Group Captain Somerhaugh declared that the British side was prepared to give a guarantee to ensure that any breach of the Danish prescriptive principle would be minimised. Accordingly one was prepared to let a Danish officer have a seat in the Court Martial, and one would if so wished, not execute the punishment, without the Danish authorities having had chance to consider the judgement. Group Captain Somerhaugh also referred to the fact that the war crimes of which Jepsen was accused were of such a nature that the limitations in the rules of extradition ought not to be enforced. The bringing to justice of war criminals should be put on the same footing as the fight against piracy, concerning which there was a recognized principle, that the punishment was an international matter. Assistant Secretary Schoen stated that the position, which so far had been assumed from the Danish side, depended on the resolution by the Ministry of Justice, before any departure from the agreement of fundamentals. Following discussion with Departmental Secretary Vedli in the Ministry of Justice the two English officers were referred to the officials in the Ministry to make their views known. The officers pointed out that the case was not urgent and they could wait one or two weeks for an answer from the Danes. The further discussions could be conducted with the local British military mission.

Gustav Jepsen was eventually convicted of war crimes. On 26 June 1947 he was hanged at Hameln prison along with a number of other Nazi war criminals executed that day. Walter's search for Jepsen in Denmark during 1946 was to have an unexpected twist. It was there in the spring of 1946 that he met his future wife, a Danish girl by the name of Annette Krarup. As a member of the ranking forces, Captain Walter Freud was invited to a reception aboard a British ship that was docked in the port of Copenhagen. Annette Krarup was also invited.

Annette Krarup was born on 25 March 1925 to Vibeke and Aage Krarup. She came from a non-Jewish family where on both sides there were prominent Danish judges and legal advisors. Vibeke, Annette's mother, was born Valentiner Branth in 1903, the daughter of a judge.[10] Annette's father Aage was born in Copenhagen in 1894, the son of Viggo and Hermandine Krarup. Viggo, Annette's paternal grandfather, was a highly respected High Court judge in Denmark, who died at the age of eighty-three in 1943. His wife Hermandine came from the Danish island of Bornholm in the Baltic Sea. Aage followed in his father's footsteps and studied law. Olaf Krarup, a family member who resides in Denmark, commented:

Once Aage had qualified he was considered a very bright legal adviser. After his exam he was employed in the government offices. The Labour party was for several years the leaders of the government and took on formulating the laws for the welfare state Denmark is known for. Aage did the job of formulating the bills, before they were passed by the parliament. It became a very time consuming job and Aage had many late evenings in his office.[11]

In 1935, Aage changed his profession to become the *stiftforvalter* (estate manager) of the estate of Vallø, a beautiful ochre-coloured Renaissance castle situated in south Zealand on the coast south of Copenhagen. The castle has a history going back five hundred years. During the 1580s it was the residence of Danish royalty. In 1737 Queen Sofia Magdalene, the wife of Christian VI, set up a trust with the estate as an insurance policy for aristocratic spinsters who could not afford an estate of their own. Fathers of Danish nobility would take out an insurance policy at birth for their daughters, then if they did not marry, they would be able to live at Vallø in retirement. In his new role as manager, Aage was engaged in the general running of the estate which included forestry and farming work as well as investing funds to make a profit for the foundation. With it came the official residence Skovhus, a detatched house with a large garden, situated in the forest. Aage worked as manager until his retirement in the 1970s.[12] Olaf Krarup recalls: 'They were all through the years very hospitable. Many of us nephews and nieces and our parents have stayed with them for long periods in both the summer and winter.'

Now in the rank of acting major, Walter began to correspond with his girlfriend. He headed his letters from 'Major A.W. Freud, War Crimes Investigation Unit, BAOR, Hamburg'.[13] He had returned to duties there, but was hopelessly missing Annette after their whirlwind romance. She was living at 24 Arnagh Falledoej in Copenhagen and working in the Foreign Office there. At the end of May Walter was back in London on leave, making preparations for his demobilisation, although it was still some weeks off. He had asked to be transferred off war crimes investigations because the psychological and emotional pressure had become too much. It was towards the end of his investigations into the Neuengamme concentration camp that he discovered the appalling suffering inflicted by the Nazis on French Jewish boys. This was for him the last straw. The Nazis were experimenting by cutting off parts of the boys' bodies and freezing them. He could tolerate no more. He later recalled to his family that the other distressing part about the investigations concerned the *kapos*, those Jews who were put in charge of other Jews. He found that they were more brutal than the Nazis and this shocked him to the core. His family urged him to write about it but he never could. On 31 May, during his last leave in London before being demobilised, he wrote to Annette from his father's home at 1 Holly Terrace, Highgate. The letter gives an insight into life in London after the war:

> London is slowly returning to peace-time life. An amazing activity is exhibited everywhere, transport is very good, shops are full but the food is worse now than during the war. But perhaps I am spoilt from Denmark.[14]

Walter then returned to Germany to complete his final tasks with the War Crimes Investigation Unit. This included the interrogation of minor Nazi war criminal Leopold Falkensammer, a former commander of Altengamme camp. Amongst Walter's papers lent by the family, there is an eighty to ninety-page typed manuscript in English entitled *The British Officer Told Me to Write My Story*. It is a full account written by Leopold Falkensammer of the war crimes which occurred at Altengamme, a sub-camp of the Neuengamme concentration camp. In the account he confesses to committing some of the atrocities, including cooperating with horrific medical experiments on POWs there. In July 1946 while Falkensammer was in custody in Fuhlesbuettel Prison, Hamburg, Walter persuaded him to write an account of everything he could remember. It begins:

> The British Officer has given me plenty of paper and a few pencils. He even told the guard to sharpen my pencils as I am not allowed a knife. Pencil sharpeners are not available here. It is winter now and my little cell is cold. I wish I knew how my wife was. The poor girl, she hasn't had much fun; but it was all her own fault, we could have been so very happy. The British Officer said that if I wrote a truthful account of my life I would be allowed to receive letters from my wife. I have no illusions about my eventual fate, so I shall write what I conceive to be the whole truth.[15]

Leopold Falkensammer was found guilty of war crimes against humanity and sentenced to death. He was executed by hanging at the prison in September 1946.

During July 1946, Walter suffered a car accident whilst on military duty in Germany. His father Martin wrote to his estranged wife Esti (Walter's mother) in America on 11 August with news that their son had had a serious accident. He wrote:

> The accident happened on 24th July; he overturned with his car when driving in Germany; he was on his own. The War Office sent me a telegram which really sounded as if there was very little hope left. But a few days later friends phoned from Germany and gave more reassuring news. On the 1.8 [1st August] Walter's Commanding Officer, a Colonel, phoned me and found me by coincidence at home. He had visited Walter on the same day and found him already in full recovery; the intention at this time had been to move him by plane to an English hospital but it seems now that he is recovering so quickly that they leave him where he is.

A travel permit has survived amongst Walter Freud's papers at the Imperial War Museum authorising him and Frank Kelley (a former SOE colleague) to travel to Czechoslovakia some time between 24–28 July 1946. It is not clear whether it was this journey that Walter was making when the accident happened. Another military entry permit also survives dated 14 July 1946 authorising Walter and Frank Kelley to attend the trials of leading war criminals at Nuremburg for two days from 14 July.

In September 1946 Walter was demobilised in the full rank of major as Major A. W. Freud and returned to England. In January 1947 he became engaged to his Danish girlfriend Annette Krarup and on 23 January his father wrote with his congratulations:

> Well, my congratulations und mein 'Segen'. Annette is an extremely nice girl and I think she is very fond of you and I hope you will treat her always very decently. It is early for a Freud to settle down at twenty-five, but your life was already so full of excitement that you may be mentally prepared for the restfulness of married life.

On 20 August 1947 Walter and Annette married in Denmark in the small church in Vallø. In years to come, it emerged that the Krarup family had played an extraordinary part in both the rescue of Danish Jews in 1943 and the Danish resistance during the Second World War. Both activities were highly risky and if caught by the Nazis they, like some other Danish resistance fighters, would have been sent to a concentration camp. Walter spoke about it in a video-interview recorded by the Jewish Museum, London:

> My wife was from an upper class Danish background. She was brought up in a
> big castle south of Copenhagen, and her father helped to evacuate the Danish
> Jews when they were threatened with deportation. He hid them in his castle.
> It was on the shores of the Baltic so when they had a group together [of Jews],
> they were rowed over to Sweden. Most of the Danish Jews survived the war
> in this way. I met her in Copenhagen. I was sent to Copenhagen. We wanted
> to extradite a Dane, who was instrumental in one of those death marches. At
> the end of the war he disappeared to Denmark, and we were very anxious to
> extradite him to Germany. So I went to Denmark.[16]

Nazi forces had invaded Denmark on 9 April 1940 and were met with little resistance. The Danish government yielded to the military might of Germany, although initially the country was permitted to self-govern under the ever-watchful eye of the occupying forces. British Prime Minister Winston Churchill referred to Denmark as 'Hitler's pet canary'. The country eventually could do nothing but sing to the tune of increasing Nazi demands. In 1941 the Danish resistance movement was formed after Germany interned members of the Danish Communist Party. Events took a turn for the worst for Danes in 1943. German demands had intensified to such an extent that the Danish government risked its own credibility and relationship with its people. Finally on 29 August 1943, Germany took control of the government and rounded up resistance members, transporting them to concentration camps. Olaf Krarup wrote of that period:

> The period of the war was of course special for all the Danes. The Germans
> occupied our country and Norway to 'protect' us from the British and
> Americans. They wanted to control the entrance to the Baltic Sea, but they

also wanted to make use of the well functioning Danish agriculture and industry. Therefore the Germans did not want to treat us ruthlessly and until August 1943 the Danish country kept its Navy, Army and Police. But we Danes did not like the Germans and all they did in Europe and their treatment of the Jews. The resistance movement had grown slowly and on the 31 August in 1943 navy officers decided to destroy the Danish warships, so they were sunk several places in Denmark. The Danish army and police were interned and the police was sent to German concentration camps.

That same year, 1943, the Danish resistance movement began to acquire explosives from England. By the end of 1944, the movement had carried out 1,500 acts of sabotage on railways and 2,800 on German-linked industry and shipping. Two years earlier in February 1942, the first two British SOE agents had been parachuted into Denmark. Only one survived, the other died when his parachute failed to open. According to Krarup oral family tradition, the men landed in or near the estate of Vallø.[17] Whilst family members do not know the names of the agents, they were thought to be British SOE agents Carl Johan Bruhn, a young doctor trained in England, and Mogens Hammer. Only Mogens Hammer survived. The men were found by the gamekeeper on the Vallø estate who reported immediately to Aage Krarup. Aage undertook to hide the surviving SOE man and buried his comrade; Aage was also part of the Danish resistance movement. This is known for sure because after the war he was a member of the Danish Home Guard and only members of the resistance during the war had the honour of being in the Home Guard at that time.[18] But this was not the full extent of Aage's wartime activities. Just before 1–2 October 1943, word circulated that the Germans were about to round up the country's Jews for deportation. There were some 7,000 Jews in Denmark, most of them living in Copenhagen. Due to the co-ordinated efforts of local Danes and the resistance movement, all but approximately 500 Danish Jews were able to be smuggled out of the country on fishing vessels to the safety of neutral Sweden. In October 1943, around 150 Jews were taken out of the country near the Gjorslev estate in Bogestrommen, just fifteen kilometres from Vallø. Prior to leaving they needed to be dispersed and hidden in the area. Some of those Jews were known to have been sheltered for a short time by

Aage Krarup in the ice house in woods on the Vallø estate. Olaf Krarup said of Aage's work during the war:

> Most Danes sympathised with the resistance movement and helped by hiding away 'the actives', who made life difficult for the German soldiers in Denmark. Being in the farming area and with forests around it was natural for Vibeke and Aage to take part in hiding the resistance people and help the Jews to get out of the country.

Maybe there was more to it than that for Aage Krarup. He had a choice – to be involved or not to be involved. He could have chosen a different path as a bystander; he risked his own life and that of his family through his involvement with hiding Danish Jews and the resistance movement. There is no record amongst family papers of his philosophy or his reasons for putting himself in that position. But for the moral standing and courage of people like Aage, the names of Danish Jews would have been added to the six million who perished in the Holocaust. At the time of writing this book, Aage Krarup has not been recorded as one of the Righteous Gentiles at Yad Vashem, Israel's Holocaust memorial museum.

Walter Freud was not the only one of Sigmund Freud's grandsons to have served in the British Forces during the Second World War. Ernst Freud's three sons Stephan, Lucian and Clement all served, albeit the artist Lucian Freud for only nine months in the Merchant Navy in 1941. They had come to Britain from Berlin in 1933; their parents initially renting rooms in Clarges Street in London's fashionable Mayfair. All three boys were educated at Dartington Hall near Totnes in Devon. Stephan, the eldest (born in Berlin in July 1921) continued his education at St Paul's in London; his brother Lucian (born in Berlin in December 1922) at Bryanston School in Dorset; and the youngest brother Clement (born in Berlin in April 1924) at the Hall, Hampstead in London. Since the family received British nationality before the outbreak of war, the three sons were not interned in the summer of 1940 like their uncle Martin Freud and cousin Walter Freud. After his schooling, Stephan Freud spent a year at Trinity College, Cambridge. Whilst there, he received his call-up papers and joined the Rifle Brigade. He was then posted to OCTU at Wrotham Heath in Kent and commissioned as a second lieutenant; afterwards he was sent to Catterick in Yorkshire, the largest artillery depot. In 1944 he was posted to Italy with a self-propelled field regiment with the Royal Artillery and at the end of the war, he was posted to the German Personnel Research Bureau, running examinations for important German civilians to ascertain whether they were suitable to work in a newly democratic state of Germany. Stephan was demobilised as a captain in 1946 and in civilian life took up publishing for eight years.

Clement Freud, the youngest of Ernst Freud's sons, received his call-up papers in 1942 at the age of eighteen and was sent for army training at Maryhill Barracks, Glasgow. Basic training consisted of route-marching, fixing and removing bayonets, as well as assembling a .303 rifle. In his autobiography *Freud Ego*, Clement narrates a humorous story regarding his surname. During a roll-call in training camp the sergeant called out 'Frood':

> I came to attention, said: 'Present, sergeant', and was on my way to the store building when I heard him shout 'Jung', looked around and saw that the man with whom I had travelled, had a coffee and shared a bacon butty was marching towards me. My tiredness disappeared and I said to him: 'This is the most extraordinary coincidence. You may have heard the man call me Frood; actually my name is Freud, and for a Freud and a Jung to be brought into such close contact is astonishing, don't you think?' He said: 'I don't know what you're on about. My name is Young.'[19]

Clement was eventually posted to the Royal Ulster Rifles. He spent five years in the army, holding ranks from rifleman to acting major. He did not experience front line fighting with the Royal Ulster Rifles and he himself commented: 'During my war I did not as far I can remember kill anyone, but was drunk a lot.'[20] At the end of the war, Clement was assigned to a number of different duties in the British occupation zone in Germany; it was a colourful time. For a while he was stationed in Bad Oeynhausen in charge of an employment exchange which used German POWs to serve in the British officers' mess. He was then briefly attached to Field Marshal Montgomery's staff as 'a sort of catering adviser. My job was to ensure that Montgomery was never given anything messed about or "frenchified" to eat; he was especially suspicious of salad dressing.'[21] In the winter of 1945 the entire sergeants' mess in Bielefeld contracted a sexually-transmitted disease from the same barmaid. For a period, Clement found himself VD officer. He recalled that he was:

> instructed how to give penicillin injections, slap the man on the bum, stick in the needle where you slapped and he is slightly anaethetised, pump in the penicillin and give the puncture point a wipe with cotton wool dipped in Dettol. I received one complaint during my short tenure of office. A soldier came to me confidentially to complain that he had gonorrhea and for his daily visits to the hospital had to share transportation with men who had syphilis. I called him a snob and told him to sod off.

The main part of Clement Freud's work was locating minor war criminals whose names appeared on a list issued by the International Military Tribunal in Nuremburg. This work included interrogation of suspects, some interpretation work, and collecting witnesses and escorting them to the trials. In October 1947 Clement was demobilised in the rank of lieutenant and returned to England. In post-war civilian life he became a journalist, television personality, broadcaster and Liberal MP.

By the end of the war, three of Sigmund Freud's grandsons had played their part by serving in various units of the British forces. After May 1945 each had been posted to the British occupation zone in Germany where they used their knowledge of German for war crimes investigations and interpretative work. Upon their demobilisation, they returned to England to rebuild their lives. Walter Freud, ever the deep thinker, reflected on the war and Hitler's defeat:

> The last war was such a close-fought battle that if the German Jews had been allowed to fight for Germany then she would certainly have won the war. Indeed, without the unnecessary, irrational and coarse anti-semitism the whole political climate against Germany in the West would have been more favourable and Germany's rightful claims might have had a more sympathetic hearing. But for the stupid and arrogant persecution of an imaginary and defenceless enemy, Hitler threw away the certainty of winning his war and realising his political dreams. The world can consider itself extremely lucky that he was mad enough to make enemies where there were none, and thus lose everything.[22]

Post-War Civilian Life

In September 1946 Walter Freud returned to England and was demobilised in the rank of major. That same month he resumed his studies at
Loughborough College, changing courses from aeronautical engineering
to chemical engineering. He faced adjustment to civilian life, having had
his formal education dislocated first by Hitler and second by internment
and five years in the British forces. In January 1947, whilst still at college, his naturalisation papers came through and he was formally granted
British citizenship.[1] In July that year he received a letter from the Ministry
of Pensions and National Insurance granting him a disablement pension
for the effects of a fractured skull which left him with bilateral deafness.
He was to receive £81 per annum in addition to his Army pension for the
period 24 December 1946 until 23 March 1948.[2] In the summer of 1949
he graduated from Loughborough. His father Martin sent a telegram to
him there: 'Congratulations today cheque two and half guineas on way.'[3]
His first job was with British Oxygen Company (BOC). He moved
with his wife of eighteen months to Hounslow, Middlesex. Before the
war, BOC imported oxygen machinery from Linde in Germany. The
company had a Jewish employee who had been at risk under the Nazis
in the early 1930s and had left Germany to emigrate to England where
he joined BOC. He had all the technical knowledge needed to extract
oxygen from the air. He started the air separation process in England,
and with his expertise BOC was able to devise its own oxygen plants

based on Shuften's original design. Walter and Annette purchased their first house at 4 Redfern Avenue in Hounslow. They had bought that particular one because it was the only one advertised as having central heating. Annette, having come over from Denmark, was used to properly insulated houses. The property in Redfern Avenue turned out to have only a couple of radiators, not proper central heating at all. In June 1950 their first child David was born in Hounslow.

The following year, in November 1951, Walter left BOC for better remuneration. He took up employment as a research engineer with British Nylon Spinners in the Welsh town of Pontypool. Nylon was catching on after the war, being used for stockings and carpets. His wife and son of sixteen months remained in Hounslow for a short time while he looked for suitable accommodation. On his first day at work he wrote to Annette: 'The only unpleasant thing about the factory, as far as I have been able to find out, is the strong acrid smell of "Dowtherm" from the heating units.'[4] Eventually they purchased Nidra House in Nevill Street, Abergavenny, a huge property which now houses the *Abergavenny Chronicle*. Two daughters were born in Abergavenny cottage hospital; the first, Ida, in July 1952 and the second, Caroline, in March 1955. While they were growing up, Annette remained at home. Later she became an educational welfare officer for a short time. She was always one to keep busy, and as Caroline remembers: 'She was such a warm, open and very socially orientated lady. She had a natural empathy for people. She was talented and artistic, taking up painting and sculpturing in her spare time. Later she completed a City and Guilds course in gardening.'

Walter stayed with British Nylon Spinners for seven years until the end of 1957 when he was head-hunted by British Hydro-Carbons in a joint venture between distillers and BP Chemicals. Walter was asked to do nylons and moved his family back to the London area. He and Annette bought Sandal Cottage, Kingswood Way, South Croydon. Between being with British Nylon Spinners and British Hydro-Carbons, a gap of about three months, the company decided not to go ahead with nylon. Walter therefore found himself employed by British Hydro-Carbons to do a job that never really occurred; he became a general chemical engineer across the spectrum. The company allocated him his own working room, but he was never part of any serious business hierarchy there. He was always valued for his intellect and skills in sorting out major projects. Living in

Sandal Cottage was in complete contrast to the two previous homes; the house in Hounslow had been terribly cold, the house in Abergavenny wet and damp such that the wallpaper on the walls of the thirty-metre-long corridors always peeled off. Walter was determined to make amends and install a central heating system in Sandal Cottage. This he did with the help of daughter Caroline who was six at the time. She recollects:

> He designed the whole heating system and put it in himself with some help from me. I was the only one who could fit under the floorboards, so it was my job to crawl under the floors and solder the pipes with a blow torch. I got quite proficient at this job.

Another project at Sandal Cottage was to install a swimming pool in the back garden with the help of Erik Valentiner-Branth, Annette's cousin, who was working in London at the time. He came down at weekends and helped Walter to dig out the pool. David Freud remembers:

> After weeks of digging, Dad and Erik had made little impact in the ground. There was a tiny hole, so builders were called in to help. The first thing the builder did was to fill in the hole and dig a new one. Dad laid the bricks and concrete for the pool, again with some help. He then made a filter for the pool which consisted of a dustbin full of coke, suspended in a tree above the pool with a hose pipe going around filtering the water. He got annoyed one day when he discovered there were squirrels nested in it. The squirrels weren't too impressed by his attempts to evict them. Squirrels weren't his only brush with nature during his projects. He was an enthusiastic bee-keeper. The honey was poor, partly because of the location of the bees in the garden. He never bothered to wear protection, saying to us children: 'They are my friends'. One day, I remember, he came running up the garden at full speed and jumped into the swimming pool because the bees had swarmed and were attacking him. After that he stopped being a bee-keeper.

Walter's three children have vivid memories of their summer holidays which were spent with the Krarup grandparents on the Vallø estate in Denmark. Expeditions and preparations for holidays had become something of a Freud family tradition which went right back to their grandfather Martin's memories of such times with his father, Sigmund.

The holidays in Vallø were usually for three weeks at a time. David recalls: 'It was a huge social whirl with all the extended family there. Aunts, uncles and cousins filled the house every day.' During these holidays their father used a cine camera to stage mini productions with the family as the cast. He produced one called *Football Pools* in which many Danish relatives were roped in. On another occasion one of David's parties saw the filming of the *Iliad* at Sandal Cottage. Troy was created out of paper and painted a garish red while the Trojan horse was designed out of a wheelbarrow. David's school friends came in costumes and mock battles were enacted. Walter devoted much time to his family as a high priority and enjoyed creating things for the children. Not that they always had chance to play with his latest project; David recalls: 'In about 1958–9 he built an incredibly complex model railway, but I never got to play with it. All the fun for him was in the challenge of the construction. He remained fascinated by railways, especially railway timetables.'

Something needs to be said about the life of Walter's father Martin after the Second World War. He was still working for the National Dock Labour Corporation (NDLC) until at least 1948. His qualifications as a lawyer were not recognised by the British authorities, something which many professional refugees also experienced. He considered himself too old to undergo further legal training again and eventually left the NDLC to open a tobacconist shop near the British Museum. One day while he was working in the shop, his estranged wife Esti stood unexpectedly in the doorway. He had no warning that she was over from America. Having not seen Martin since their separation in 1938, she stared at him and walked out without saying a word.[5] Letters from solicitors now in Walter Freud's archive at the Imperial War Museum indicate that Martin and Esti had sought legal advice about matrimonial matters, although they never actually divorced. Martin's main residence continued to be at 1 Holly Terrace in Highgate where he lived with his lady-friend Margaret.[6] David Freud explains:

> Margaret came down from Scotland to work in London and had nowhere to live so grandfather [Martin] had her to stay at 1 Holly Terrace. They became partners and she stayed with him for the rest of his life, eventually changing her name by deed-poll to Margaret Freud. In the 1950s they moved to Hove.

Martin never really settled after the death of his father. He would always be living in his father's shadow. He had been so dependent on him for acknowledgement and positive praise throughout childhood and into adulthood that carving out a confident independent identity was never going to be easy. When Sigmund died, Martin never really found himself. He took care of his father's literary estate and dealt with publishers of his father's works.[7] He also took it upon himself to be a kind of guardian of his father's image. This was demonstrated when he once objected to a TV production about his father called *The Wound Within* about which he wrote to *The Daily Mail*:

> Both of my parents were civilised adults who did not give vent to emotional outbursts. In the telefilm they quarrelled, shouted at each other and gave evidence of other instances of irritability, quite contrary to what happened in reality. My parents never behaved in such fashion. Children know such things! In the film, the young Freud rushes about in a state of uncontrolled excitation, throwing books about, hitting tables with his fist, leaping up and down stairs to emphasize a point, is insulting to senior colleagues and all together appeared to be an irritable, most undignified little chap. His wife is portrayed as a nagger who attempts to influence him when he has decided to sacrifice the easy career of a fashionable young doctor in the imperial residence to take the hard path of the rebel breaking medical tradition and facing ridicule and social boycott. I must insist this is utter nonsense! My dear mother would never have done such a thing! It is true that in the mornings mother would order my father's breakfast, order his clothing, lay out his shirt, trousers and socks. But she would never attempt to lay out his professional life. Whether this television production was successful as an explanation of psychoanalysis to the public, I do not know. However, in its attempt to portray the personalities of the two leading characters, Dr Sigmund Freud and his young wife, it has failed miserably.[8]

Martin wrote a number of short stories which were mostly unpublished.[9] A novel entitled *Any Suvivors?* set during the Second World War was also never published. But as has been mentioned in earlier chapters, two of his published books were his autobiography *Glory Reflected* and a novel, *Parole d'Honneur*, based on his experiences in the Austrian artillery in the First World War. Martin Freud died in Hove on 25 April 1967. After the funeral his ashes were placed at Golders Green Crematorium with those of the rest of the Freud family.

Less than three months after the death of his father, Walter Freud was honoured as a Fellow of the Chemical Society.[10] That autumn he launched one of his latest creative projects: a new brand of perfume which he named after his wife. It was registered on 27 September 1967 and called Annette Freud Perfume & Cosmetics.[11] His youngest daughter Caroline recalls:

> Through his working life, he tried to get businesses going to get out of the job he was in. At one time he created a perfume company. It had four basic fragrances which were mixed together in various potencies to a special scent. My job was to go into the hut at the bottom of the garden and screw all the lids on the bottles. The equipment consisted of a large bottle with alcohol in it, four little bottles with basic fragrances for mixing, an empty big bottle to put the mixture in, and a dropper and funnel. We had about 10 prototypes. Although it was not a success, it was taken up by Selfridges. We produced a total of around 2,000 bottles during the lifetime of the project. My mother had the task of marketing it.

In 1972 Walter and Annette moved to Stonehamme, an eighteenth-century coach house with two back-to-back cottages in Woodhurst Lane, Hurst Green, Oxted. Walter retired from BP Chemicals in 1976. He took up consultancy work for a time, some of it in India to look into possibilities of opening a new factory there. Life in retirement was never dull; there was always some project underway. Walter had all kinds of visionary schemes, like trying to invent photosynthesis to get energy and create starch to feed the starving millions in the world. Just before he died he was working on a fuel cell. Ida said: 'He lived to create something. He did all DIY jobs, from central heating systems to electrics.'

Walter remained utterly fascinated by the Second World War, accumulating a specialist library on wartime history, military biographies and diaries. On his death over 700 books on this alone were given to Essex University. Two main themes preoccupied his writing time in the latter years of his life: *Moses and Monotheism*, and the Second World War. He wrote an eighty-page manuscript for a book entitled *Paradoxes of the Second World War* which was never published. In it he posed a number of questions, one of which was: 'Why did the Germans, a cultivated and civilised people, vote for a gang of street-fighting bullies, who promised them ethnic cleansing and a war in the East?' In chapter 2 of his manuscript, he sets out his assessment of why the Nazi Party came to power in Germany in 1933. He lays the blame at the feet of the Weimar Republic for failing the people economically, rather than widespread support for Hitler's anti-Semitism:

> The reason was not so much Hitler's promises and demands, but the utter failure of the previous Weimar governments to improve Germany's lot, either at home or abroad. Instead the German economy had gone from bad to worse … In foreign relations too the Weimar governments had been impotent. They could not ease the huge burden of taxation imposed after World War I by the Allies at Versailles in order to pay for war reparations.[12]

Walter went on to argue:

> Many Germans who were attracted by Hitler's economic promises were repulsed by his anti-semitism. However there is a proverb in German *so rasch schiessen die Preussen nicht*, meaning the same as 'the soup is not eaten as hot as it is cooked'. In other words, it was expected that his anti-semitism would be much scaled down if and when he came to power. These people remember the Viennese mayor Karl Lueger who came to power on an anti-semitic ticket, but once there, forgot all about it and had no qualms in employing Jews when it suited him. The assumption by those dismayed by Hitler's Jew-baiting was that he would follow in Lueger's footsteps. This stifled their conscience.

Another temptation not to take Hitler's anti-Semitism too seriously was caused by a book published in 1923 called *Die Stadt ohne Juden* (The City without Jews). The author pictured the expulsion of the Jews from Vienna: 'Once they had gone, the Viennese found that they could not manage without them and pleaded with them to return. In a similar manner, many adherents of Hitler who were unhappy with his anti-Semitism thought that German Jews were much too important for Germany to be excluded.'[13]

In *Paradoxes of the Second World War*, Walter went on to show how, once in power, Hitler had no intention of governing democratically. Walter was not the only one of his SOE colleagues to continue to be fascinated by the events of the Second World War. Over a fifty-year period he kept in touch with his close friend from SOE training days, Eric Sanders. Eric reflected to Walter on the impact of Hitler on his own life in a letter written in 2000:

> Strange as it may seem, my personal life was actually improved by Hitler. It made me emigrate to England where I immediately felt good. My job on the farm milking the cows was an excellent experience as was the Pioneer Corps. There I had the environment of mostly well-educated men and there I started studying for matriculation which I passed literally days before being transferred to SOE. The period in the Pioneer Corps also led me to decide on teaching as a career. I found SOE exhilarating especially the parachuting. My year in Vienna with the British Occupation Forces was wonderful. I got a taste for the good life there.[14]

In 2007 Eric Sanders' autobiography was published in German, entitled *Emigration ins Leben: Wien-London und nicht mehr retour*. Other SOE colleagues from that group of ex-Austrians also wrote their memoirs: Fred Warner wrote *Personal Account of SOE Period*, a copy of which has been deposited in the archives at the Imperial War Museum; and Stephen Dale wrote *Spanglet or By Any Other Name*, privately published in 1993.

The second topic which Walter wrestled with, and wrote about, was the patriarch Moses who had led his ancestors out of Egypt thousands of years earlier. Walter studied in detail his grandfather's final work *Moses and Monotheism* and sought to fill the gaps in his theory. He wrote two treatments of the theme: one was a manuscript for a book called *Why We Created the Lord* and the second, a script for a play entitled *By the Waters of the Nile*. His basic hypothesis was to give reasons why the fourteenth-century BC pharaoh Akhenaten, together with Moses, replaced the longstanding polytheistic religion in Egypt with monotheism. He concluded that the economic upheavals in Egypt were the direct cause of this radical change, arguing:

> A new capital, Amarna, had to be built in the middle of Egypt to avoid the country splitting up again into two kingdoms. The only resources, particularly labour, available for such a large project belonged to the priests and they were reluctant to part with them. In order to overcome the priests' hostility, pharaoh Akhenaten abolished all gods but one; his sole God Aten, and made their priests redundant. Their property was confiscated and in this way the neces-

sary wherewithal for building the new capital was assured. The book makes comparisons with similar but more modern actions, such as those committed by Henry VIII who dissolved England's rich monasteries. The second subject which was explored centred on the reason why Moses, who according to Sigmund Freud was a high-born Egyptian, should be persuaded to become the leader of a group of slaves.[15]

The book concludes that Moses, an ardent monotheist, lost every-thing in the counter-reformation of the polytheistic priests, when his god Aten was toppled. His only chance of re-establishing himself to his former eminence was to re-initiate this God who became the Jewish Adonai. He secured their loyalty by introducing a seven-day week, a major advance to those used to working a ten-day week in Egypt at that time. In the concluding paragraph to the book, Walter could not resist making comparisons with his own Austria:

> It might be interesting to speculate what would have happened if the Hebrews had not adopted Adonai as their God, but had reverted to polytheism, together with the rest of Egypt. In that case Jewish identity would have disappeared. They would have become Egyptians, a desire they had expressed earlier by adopting the Egyptian custom of circumcision and other habits. I would like to compare this frustrated effort of assimilation with a more recent example of the same kind. Many Austrian Jews under Emperor Franz-Joseph desired to become 'real' Austrians. They furthered this aim by giving their children very Germanic names like Siegismund, Leopold and Ida, and avoided to have their sons circumcised. Both host countries, Egypt and Austria, were unim-pressed by such efforts of integration.[16]

The psychological trauma that affected the majority of refugees from Nazi oppression continued to be part of Walter's consciousness. He was especially sensitive to his German accent which he never really shed, in spite of taking numerous elocution lessons at various points in his life. He adopted England and felt terribly grateful to Britain for saving him from certain death. Only once did he ever go back to Vienna. The occa-sion was 1994; his son David had returned from a business trip to Austria and was just a stone's throw from Zeltweg, the airport which his father had captured in the war. He recalls:

I mentioned to Edmund Auli, the CEO of Austrian Industries that my father took Zeltweg aerodrome in the war. He didn't believe it initially. Then a couple of weeks later he came to me and said: 'I have looked up the files. Your father did indeed take the airfield. Bring me the Captain.'

I replied 'He won't come. He has never been back to Vienna.'

Auli replied: 'Bring me the Captain because we want to do a ceremony for the 60th anniversary of the end of the war.'

I said: 'He doesn't like to come back to Austria because he was rejected.'

His final words were: 'Well you bring me the Captain.'

When I returned to England, I told my father. He agreed to take part in the liberation ceremony. And so one day in May 1994 my father and mother flew to Vienna airport where they received VIP status. Two black Mercedes came up from Zeltweg to collect them. That evening there were big speeches and ceremony. The next morning there was a fly past in his honour. They stayed for a few days in Vienna with Edmund Auli. He took a walk down memory lane and visited his home and sites of his childhood for the first and only time since his expulsion in 1938. The ceremony at Zeltweg turned out to be a very important moment for him because it was the first time he was ever officially recognised for that achievement, albeit recognition by the other side! The British had never acknowledged what he had done at Zeltweg.

In 1997, Walter and Annette Freud celebrated their golden wedding anniversary with family and friends. Their fifty-year partnership had sustained a passionate and loving relationship which withstood many pressures. Three years later on 21 February 2000 Annette died at the age of seventy-four. Her funeral took place at the Surrey and Sussex Crematorium in Crawley. In recognition of her roots, a wreath of roses in the shape of the Danish flag was placed by the family on the coffin. Afterwards her ashes were taken to the Freud family resting place in Golders Green Crematorium.

Walter himself was already ill when his wife died. That same year he had a massive pleural effusion that was potentially fatal. Doctors drained the effusion and he was fit and well for another three and a half years. Then he developed secondary swellings and was in severe pain for six months. Walter died at home surrounded by family on 8 February 2004 at the age of eighty-two of mesothelioma (a form of asbestosis). His funeral at the Surrey and Sussex Crematorium in Crawley was a simple affair with a non-religious ceremony. The family also placed a wreath of flowers in the shape

of the Danish flag on his coffin to symbolise his connections and adoption
by the Danish side of the family. In a last poignant gesture of his Austrian
roots the ceremony ended with Johann Strauss's *The Blue Danube Waltz*.
His ashes were placed in the Ernst George Columbarium at Golders Green
Crematorium, London, with his wife Annette and other members of the
family, including his grandfather Sigmund Freud, grandmother Martha
and father Martin Freud. Walter's last will and testament encapsulated the
two most important characteristics for him, borne out from his experience
as a refugee. The first is the importance of the family, the second is the
deep suspicion of lawyers and anyone in authority. The latter comes from
his experience as a young man living under the Nazis. In clause 4 of his
will he stipulated that the bequest of £1,000 to each of his grandchildren
should 'be used for enjoyment, not saving,' and that they should be 'strongly
encouraged to make their permanent domicile in Great Britain. The roots
in this country which their forefathers have established with some difficulties should not be pulled up frivolously.' In clause 5 he expressed his desire
that the whole family should 'have an annual re-union at Easter-time. It will
be the duty of my oldest son and child David to hold the family together
through thick and thin. Alone one is nothing, as a family unit survival is
simplified.' In clause 13 came reference to Walter's suspicion of authority. It
read: 'Due to bad experience, I am urging my Executors to deal with this
will without the assistance of professional solicitors, except for purely technical questions.' Although Walter died a British citizen, having lived over
sixty years in Britain, he still felt an outsider. Being uprooted from Vienna
deeply affected his identity and feeling of acceptance. He once said:

> In a way, it's not what you feel – that doesn't count. It's what others think. And
> their first impression wouldn't be 'Oh, another Britisher'. One is an outsider and
> one has to stay an outsider until one dies. But it doesn't worry me too much.

Walter Freud is survived by his son David, Chief Executive Officer of
The Portland Trust; daughter Ida, a psychotherapist; daughter Caroline, a
family therapist and parenting facilitator; and nine grandchildren.

Seventy years after the flight of the Freuds from Vienna, their legacy
lives on. In 2005, the first university bearing Sigmund Freud's name and
dedicated to the study of psychoanalysis opened in Vienna.[17] The Nazis
may have burned his books, but ironically Sigmund Freud's gift to the

world in his theories of psychoanalysis are witness to the survival of such ground-breaking work in spite of attempts to eradicate it. Freud has now been seen rightly as a genius. Can Sigmund Freud be compared to the patriarch Moses? Moses – the figure that profoundly frustrated him for the latter years of his life? It is fair to say that Sigmund Freud has impacted on the secular world in a way that Moses did for the religious life of the Israelites and their descendants for thousands of years. His name has been assured an eternal remembrance. His grandson, the artist Lucian Freud, has also become a famous household name, maybe even a legend in his own right and the exceptional charismatic creativity of the Freud genes lives on in other descendants. Other branches of the family have made their own unique contribution to the world of finance, the arts, medicine, literature and economics. Through the pages of *Freuds' War*, a snap-shot of an extraordinary epoch in history has been viewed through the lens of one specific family, a family who survived two world wars. But that survival was not assured once Hitler annexed Austria in March 1938. Seventy years later, stories are emerging that demonstrate just how much danger Sigmund Freud was under at the time. David Freud recently met another David Freud whose grandfather experienced brutality at the hands of the Nazis just after the Anschluss:

'The "other" David Freud had a grandfather living in Vienna at the time of the Anschluss. He was also called Professor Freud. He went downstairs one day to help with a disturbance caused by some Nazis harassing the Jews immediately after the Anschluss. He thought of himself as high status and had fought in the First World War. The Nazis asked him who he was and he said "Professor Freud". They obviously thought he was Sigmund Freud and roughed him up severely. He managed to drag himself off upstairs but was badly hurt. It just shows the very real risk Sigmund was under, despite his status.'

What Sigmund Freud and his descendants have given, and continue to give, the world has been made possible by the sacrifice of others. Walter Freud's eldest daughter, Ida, poignantly concludes:

Our bloodline survives because of the courage of people like Princess Marie Bonaparte and Ernest Jones.

The Freud Family Legacy, by David Freud

'Your great grandfather was Sigmund Freud,' my father told me. 'Never forget it.'

It is one of my earliest memories, when I was three or four years old. And it was a message that I, and my sisters Ida and Caroline, were to hear often as we grew up, alongside details of the main psychoanalytic theories and our family history.

It was a testament to the magnetic personality and fame of Sigmund that his impact was still so powerful in the mind of my father in the mid-1950s, when he had been dead for fifteen years and more. That impact was stronger still for our grandfather, Martin, who had always remained strongly dependent on his father while he was alive and who never seemed to find his feet in his newly adopted country. As a result of this indoctrination, Sigmund's family legacy holds sway, even after three generations. His great grandchildren have a sense of identity grounded on their origins rather than on their position in a corporate hierarchy or social network. No doubt it was that sense of personal identity and the need to live up to such a high achiever that drove our father to attempt the seemingly suicidal capture of Zeltweg aerodrome single-handed.

Ironically, the fierce individualism and search for achievement evident among Sigmund's descendants in the UK has militated against close family links. The death of the patriarch in 1939 seemed to take the centre out of the family. His youngest child, Anna, who inherited his London house in Maresfield Gardens near Swiss Cottage, proved much more interested in pursuing her work in child psychoanalysis than spending time with family. Even though she died when I was in my early thirties I can remember only one serious conversation with her about my own plans and career. For a time Sigmund's youngest son, Ernst, filled the void. With his wife Lucy, whom we called Tante Lux, he hosted regular get-togethers of the extended family at his house in St John's Wood through the 1960s. They created a warm and inclusive atmosphere, whose wellspring was the devotion between Tante Lux and Ernst, obvious even to us children. That devotion was to have an unhappy outcome. When Ernst died in 1970 Tante Lux became virtually catatonic with grief and remained so till she died. Her depression is poignantly caught in a series of portraits by her son, the painter Lucian.

Neither Martin, nor our father, were in much of a position to take on the role, even though they represented the senior branch of the family. Martin had seen his own household break up and never communicated with his wife Esti after the war, even though they remained formally married. More disconcertingly he showed precious little interest in his daughter, Sophie, who stayed in the US with her mother. With his Austrian legal training redundant in the UK, he ran a tobacconist's shop in Holborn till he retired to Hove. As a child I remember him visiting us in Wales and being deeply impressed by his deep duelling scars. 'We used to rub salt in and open the wounds up to make them bigger,' he told me when I excitedly cross-examined him. But his life-long indifference to danger caught up with him when he had a motorbike accident in the 1950s. The impact to his head seemed to have the effect of accelerating senile dementia and our regular visits to Hove before his death in 1967 constituted a repetitive exercise in reminding him who we were.

Our father was little better placed. The difficulties of his upbringing – between two unhappy, warring parents – left him unsure of his place in the world. Rejection by one country (Austria) and the reluctant reception by another (which ordered his arrest as an enemy alien and despatched him to Australia) compounded a sense of insecurity that was probably greater than that of most refugees. Alongside the astonishing bravery, independence and determination, he could be obstinate and was deeply sensitive to imagined slights. It meant that he would find himself involved in intense rows with those who should have been close to him, not least with his mother and sister, as well as other members of his extended family. He was extremely lucky to have found a complementary partner in our mother, Annette, who inherited an outgoing relaxed approach and sophisticated social skills from her Danish upbringing. It allowed him to turn inward to the warmth of his own family and friends. He was also able to become part of a wider Danish family, which adopted him unreservedly.

He became devoted to his nine grandchildren and took great pride in them. Interestingly, however, he did not lecture them on the importance of the Freud name and their family legacy. Perhaps, after more than half a century, he had come to believe that they would be better off not carrying such a burden.

Notes

Chapter 1: The Early Years

1. *Glory Reflected*, p. 101.
2. *Ibid*, p. 11.
3. *Ibid*, p.11
4. *Ibid*, p.11
5. *Ibid*, p. 28.
6. *Ibid*, p. 30.
7. *Ibid*, p. 109.
8. *Ibid*, p. 110.
9. *Ibid*, pp 63–64.
10. *Ibid*, p. 63.
11. *Ibid*, p. 38.
12. *Ibid*, pp 32–33.
13. *An Austrian Grandfather*, chapter 10, p. 9.
14. *Ibid*, chapter 10, p. 3.
15. *Glory Reflected*, p. 31.
16. *Ibid*, p. 32.
17. *Ibid*, p. 40.
18. *Ibid*, p. 42.
19. *Ibid*, p. 51.
20. *Ibid*, p. 52.
21. *Ibid*, pp 57–58.
22. Quoted in *Glory Reflected*, p. 63.
23. *Glory Reflected*, p. 64.
24. Jones, vol. 2, p. 434.
25. *Glory Reflected*, p. 102.

26. *Ibid*, p. 169.
27. *Ibid*, pp 171–172.
28. *Ibid*, p. 156.
29. *Ibid*, p. 171.
30. *Ibid*, pp 175–177.
31. *Ibid*, p. 176.
32. *Ibid*, p. 176.
33. *Ibid*, p. 158.
34. *Ibid*, p. 158.
35. *Ibid*, p. 164.
36. *Ibid*, p. 165.
37. *Ibid*, pp 165–166.
38. Original letter in The Freud Museum.
39. *Glory Reflected*, pp 156–157.
40. *Ibid*, p. 168.

Chapter 2: The First World War

1. Quoted in Ernest Jones, vol. II, p. 192.
2. Jones, vol. 2, pp 229–230.
3. Walter Freud, *An Austrian Grandfather*, chapter 11, p. 3.
4. Jones, vol. 2, p. 203.
5. Sigmund Freud to Martin Freud, 26 August 1914.
6. These annotated notes are amongst the Freud family papers lent by Caroline Penney.
7. *Glory Reflected*, p. 180.
8. *Ibid*, p. 181.
9. Confirmed by letters held at the Freud Museum, London.
10. Walter Freud, *My Austrian Grandfather*, unpublished memoirs.
11. *Glory Reflected*, p. 89.
12. *Ibid*, pp 181–183.
13. *Ibid*, p. 154.
14. *Ibid*, p. 183.
15. *Ibid*, pp 184–185.
16. Sigmund Freud to Eitingon, 9 May 1915. See Jones, vol. II, p. 202.
17. Sigmund Freud to Sándor Ferenczi, 15 November 1915. Quoted in Jones, vol. 2, p. 203.
18. *My Austrian Grandfather*, p. XI/4.
19. *Living in the Shadow of the Freud Family*, p. 42.
20. Esti Drucker to Martin Freud, 6 February 1918.
21. *Parole d'Honneur*, pp 83–84.
22. *Ibid*, pp 91–92. Sachertorte refers to the rich iced chocolate cake for which the Hotel Sacher in Vienna is world famous.

23. *Ibid*, pp 95–96.
24. *Ibid*, pp 97–98.
25. *Living in the Shadow of the Freud Family*, p. 47.
26. *Ibid*, p. 46.
27. *Ibid*, p. 46.
28. *Ibid*, pp 47 and 49.
29. *Ibid*, pp 123–124.
30. *Ibid*, p. 144.
31. *Ibid*, p. 143
32. *Ibid*, p. 133.
33. *Glory Reflected*, p. 187.
34. Martin Freud to Sigmund Freud, 11 October 1918.
35. Martin Freud to Sigmund Freud, 25 October 1918.
36. *Parole d'Honneur*, p. 157.
37. *Ibid,* p. 160.
38. *Ibid*, p. 159.
39. Sigmund Freud to Alexander Freud, 18 November 1918, *An Austrian Grandfather*, chapter 11, p. 5.
40. Sigmund Freud to Ernest Jones, 15 January 1919. Quoted in Jones, vol. 2, p. 231.
41. *Parole d'Honneur*, p. 206.
42. *Living in the Shadow of the Freud Family*, p. 57.
43. Sigmund Freud to Ferenczi, 24 January 1919.
44. *Glory Reflected*, p. 188.
45. *An Austrian Grandfather*, chapter 11, p. 6.

Chapter 3: The Inter-War Years

1. *Glory Reflected*, p. 192.
2. *An Austrian Grandfather*, chapter 6, p. 7.
3. *Ibid*, chapter 6, pp 9–10.
4. *Ibid*, chapter 6, pp 4–5.
5. *Ibid*, chapter 6, p. 6.
6. *Before the Anticlimax*, pp 43–44.
7. *An Austrian Grandfather*, chapter 15, pp 4–5.
8. *Ibid*, chapter 9, pp 2–3.
9. *Ibid*, chapter 15, p. 5.
10. Quoted in *Living in the Shadow of the Freud Family*, p. 91. Sophie Freud comments on her mother's boyfriend on pp 91 and 95.
11. *An Austrian Grandfather*, chapter 6, p. 6.
12. *Ibid*, chapter 9, p. 1.
13. *Glory Reflected*, p. 202.
14. *Ibid*, p. 200.

15. Marie Bonaparte's introduction to *Glory Reflected*, p. 6.
16. *An Austrian Grandfather*, chapter 11, pp 6–7.
17. Sigmund Freud to Jeanne Lampl de Groot, 1 February 1933.
18. Sigmund Freud to Jeanne Lampl de Groot, 9 March 1933.
19. *An Austrian Grandfather*, chapter 12, p. 4.
20. Sigmund Freud to Eitingon, 3 April 1933.
21. Quoted in Michael Molnar (ed.), *The Diary of Sigmund Freud*, p. 143.
22. Their sons Stephan, Clement and Lucian were at Darlington Hall, near Totnes in Devon.
23. He became Chancellor of Austria on 20 May 1932.
24. Sigmund Freud to Arnold Zweig, 30 September 1934.
25. Sigmund Freud to Ernest Jones, 15 October 1933.
26. *Glory Reflected*, p. 196.
27. Sigmund Freud to Smith Ely Jelliffe, 2 August 1934.
28. Sigmund Freud to the Royal Society of Medicine, 25 May 1935.
29. Sigmund Freud to Marie Bonaparte, 26 March 1936.
30. Printed in *The Times,* 5 May 1936, the day before Freud's birthday.
31. Sigmund Freud to Ernst Freud, 6 June 1934.
32. Marie Bonaparte to Sigmund Freud, 6 September 1937.
33. *An Austrian Grandfather*, chapter 15, p. 6.
34. From a lecture given to the Jewish Museum, London by Walter Freud on 9 July 2002, p. 10.

Chapter 4: Finis Austriae

1. *Last Waltz in Vienna*, p. 167. On 12 February 1938, Churchill made a significant speech about the Austrian situation in the House of Commons in London.
2. Anna Freud to Ernest Jones, 20 February 1938.
3. *The Times*, 12 March 1938, p. 12.
4. Quoted from correspondence with the author.
5. *Glory Reflected*, p. 205.
6. *Ibid*, p. 206.
7. *Ibid*, p. 206.
8. Quoted in Jones, vol. III, p. 236. Sigmund Freud was alluding to 70 AD when Roman Emperor Titus destroyed the Temple in Jerusalem and expelled Jews from the city after the First Jewish Revolt against the Romans in Judea.
9. *Glory Reflected*, p. 206.
10. Extract from an unpublished lecture given by Martin Freud in America, amongst papers lent by Caroline Penney.
11. *Glory Reflected*, p. 211.
12. *Ibid*, p. 211.

13. Quoted in Michael Molnar (ed.), *The Diary of Sigmund Freud*, p. 229.
14. *Glory Reflected*, p. 208.
15. Jones, vol. 3, p. 233.
16. *Ibid*, p. 233.
17. *Glory Reflected*, p. 209.
18. *Ibid*, p. 210.
19. Reported in *The Times* the following day, 16 March 1938.
20. Jones, vol. 3, p. 235.
21. Michael Molnar (ed.), *The Diary of Sigmund Freud*, p. 232.
22. Princess Marie Bonaparte in the Introduction to *Glory Reflected*, p. 7.
23. *Diary of Sigmund Freud*, p. 232.
24. Jones, vol. 3, p. 239.
25. *Glory Reflected*, p. 212.
26. Extract from an unpublished lecture given by Martin Freud in America, amongst papers lent by Caroline Penney.
27. Ernest Jones to Sigmund Freud, 28 April 1938.
28. *Diary of Sigmund Freud*, p. 234.
29. Jones, vol. 3, p. 240.
30. *Ibid*, p. 214.
31. *Ibid*, p. 237.
32. *Ibid*, p. 214.
33. *The Diary of Sigmund Freud*, p. 232.
34. *Glory Reflected*, pp 215–216.
35. *Ibid*, p. 233.
36. *An Austrian Grandfather*, chapter 16, pp 8–9.
37. *Ibid*, chapter 16, p. 3.
38. *Ibid*, chapter 13, p. 1.
39. Quoted by Martin Freud in *Glory Reflected*, p. 218.
40. Actually reported in *The Times* the following day, 6 June 1938.
41. Sigmund Freud to Eitingon, 6 [7] June 1938. See *Diary of Sigmund Freud*, p. 239.
42. Two letters from Barclays Bank to Martin Freud amongst the Freud family papers.
43. *An Austrian Grandfather*, chapter 16, pp 8–9.
44. Sigmund Freud to Marie Bonaparte, 8 June 1938.
45. Quoted in *An Austrian Grandfather*, chapter 12, p. 4.
46. *An Austrian Grandfather*, chapter 12, p. 4.
47. Sigmund Freud to Lampl de Groot, 13 June 1938. Quoted in *Diary of Sigmund Freud*, p. 239.
48. *Before the Anticlimax*, p. 44.
49. Their story is told in detail by Sophie Freud in *Living in the Shadow of the Freud Family*.
50. *An Austrian Grandfather*, chapter 16, pp 8–9.
51. Sigmund Freud to Eitingon, 3 November 1938.
52. *The Night Hitler Lost His War*, an unpublished paper by Walter Freud.

53. Sigmund Freud to Marie Bonaparte, 12 November 1938.
54. Max Eitingon to Sigmund Freud, 12 December 1938. Quoted in *Diary of Sigmund Freud*, p. 251.
55. *An Austrian Grandfather*, chapter 16, p. 10.
56. *The Times*, 17 March 1939.
57. Reported in *The Times*, 17 March 1939, p. 9.
58. *The Observer*, 1 October 1939.
59. *An Austrian Grandfather*, chapter 16, p. 11.
60. *Ibid*, chapter 1, p. 3.
61. Quoted by Walter Freud in *An Austrian Grandfather*, chapter 13, p. 3.
62. *Daily Herald*, 25 September 1939.
63. *Glory Reflected*, p. 218.
64. Jones, vol. 3, pp 263–264.
65. *The Listener*, 5 October 1939.
66. *The Palestine Post*, 26 September 1939.
67. *British Medical Journal*, 30 September 1939.
68. *News Chronicle*, 25 September 1939.
69. *The Lancet*, 20 September 1939, p. 765.
70. *The Times*, 25 September 1939, p. 10.
71. *News Chronicle*, 25 September 1939.
72. *An Austrian Grandfather*, chapter 16, p. 9.

Chapter 5: His Majesty's Loyal Enemy Aliens

1. Amongst Walter Freud's papers at the Imperial War Museum.
2. Anna Freud to Leonard Woolf, 21 August 1940.
3. Martin Freud, *The Alien*, an unpublished short story lent by Caroline Penney.
4. *Ibid*.
5. Walter Freud to Martin Freud, 29 June 1940.
6. After the war the *Dunera* became a floating educational ship; it was sold in 1967 to a Spanish concern in Bilbao and scrapped.
7. Report by Walter Freud written in Hay, Australia, March 1941. Copy in the Imperial War Museum.
8. *Ibid*.
9. *Before the Anticlimax*, p. 18.
10. *Ibid*, p. 18.
11. Amongst unpublished papers of Martin Freud, lent by Caroline Penney.
12. Amongst papers lent by Caroline Penney.
13. *Glory Reflected*, p. 204.
14. Letter amongst Walter Freud's papers, The Imperial War Museum.
15. Letter dated 7 June 1941, Walter Freud's papers, The Imperial War Museum.

16. Martin Freud to Princess Marie Bonaparte, 23 March 1942.
17. Martin Freud to Walter Freud, 3 October 1941.
18. See *North Devon Journal*, 27 November 1941, p. 3.
19. *Before the Anticlimax*, pp 20–21.
20. *Ibid*, pp 25–26.
21. Letter from Martin Freud to Walter, 7 May 1942.
22. Martin Freud, *Strawberries*, an unpublished short story.
23. Garry Rogers, *Interesting Times*, pp 124–125.
24. Ref: E. Coll. Grave 16b–16r.
25. Correspondence with the author in May 2008.
26. PRO, ref: HS 9/544/3.
27. *Before the Anticlimax*, p. 26.

Chapter 6: Special Operations Executive

1. Correspondence between Eric Sanders and the author during 2007 and 2008.
2. Martin Freud to Walter Freud, in Freud's papers, The Imperial War Museum.
3. Written by CSM Webb on 18 February 1943.
4. Copy in his file, PRO HS 9/544/3.
5. *Before the Anticlimax*, p. 30.
6. Stephen Dale, *Spanglet or By Any Other Name*, p. 80.
7. *Before the Anticlimax*, p. 33.
8. *The Failure of a Mission*, an unpublished paper written by Walter Freud. Lent by Ida Fairbairn.
9. *Before the Anticlimax*, p. 30.
10. *Spanglet or By Any Other Name*, p. 81.
11. Martin Freud to Walter Freud, 13 August 1943.
12. *Before the Anticlimax*, pp 34–35.
13. Correspondence with the author.
14. Postcard from Martin Freud to Walter, 13 April 1944.
15. Martin Freud to Walter, 23 April 1944.
16. *Before the Anticlimax*, p. 32.
17. Correspondence with the author.
18. *Before the Anticlimax*, pp 35–36.
19. Form AP/6 in Walter's personal file at PRO, HS 9/544/3.
20. *Before the Anticlimax*, pp 35–36.
21. As confirmed in his secret personal war file, PRO, HS 9/544/3.
22. *Before the Anticlimax*, p. 37.
23. Martin Freud to Walter, 7 October 1944.

Chapter 7: Behind Enemy Lines

1. *Before the Anticlimax*, pp 36–37.
2. Unpublished memoirs, *Before the Anticlimax: With Special Operation Executive in Austria*, p. 32.
3. *Before the Anticlimax*, pp 34–35.
4. The information here on Charles Kaiser and Harry Williams has been supplied by Dr Elisabeth Lebensaft and Christoph Mentschl from the Austrian Academy of Sciences in Vienna.
5. *Before the Anticlimax*, p. 43.
6. *Ibid*, pp 46–47.
7. Freud, *op. cit.*, p. 52ff.
8. Original message in PRO, ref: HS 9/544/3.
9. *Before the Anticlimax*, pp 60–61.
10. The notification, written in German, survives in Walter Freud's SOE personal file.
11. Amongst letters and papers lent by Caroline Penney.
12. Discussions with the author, May 2008.

Chapter 8: War Crimes Investigation Unit

1. He died on 16 January 1950.
2. *The Arms of Krupp*, p. 657.
3. Video interview with Walter Freud by Bea Lewkowicz, The Jewish Museum, London.
4. *An Austrian Grandfather*, chapter 1.
5. PRO, ref: WO235/83.
6. *An Austrian Grandfather*, chapter 1, pp 4–5.
7. From vol. VIII of International Military Tribunal of the Major War Criminals I–XLII, Trial of Nuremburg.
8. *An Austrian Grandfather*, chapter 12, p. 8.
9. I am grateful to Ulla Harvey for translating this document from Danish into English.
10. She died in Denmark in 1968.
11. Correspondence between the author and Olaf Krarup during 2008.
12. Aage died in Copenhagen in 1981.
13. Private love letters exist in the Freud family archive.
14. Walter Freud to Annette Krarup, 31 May 1946.
15. *The British Officer Told Me to Write My Story*, p. 1.
16. Video interview with Bea Lewkowicz.
17. Information provided by Olaf Krarup and Eric Valentiner-Branth.
18. Information provided by Eric Valentiner-Branth.

19. *Freud Ego*, p. 52.
20. *Ibid*, p. 55.
21. *Ibid*, p. 62.
22. *An Austrian Grandfather*, chapter 12, p. 8.

Chapter 9: Post-War Civilian Life

1. His oath of allegiance is dated 29 January 1947, amongst papers lent by David Freud.
2. Letter dated 12 July 1947.
3. The date on the telegram is not legible.
4. Walter Freud to Annette Freud, 1 November 1947.
5. Information given by David Freud.
6. Her surname cannot be remembered by the second generation members of the family. They all remember her as Margaret Freud, having changed her name by deed-poll.
7. Numerous business letters exist in the Freud Museum, London and amongst papers held by the Freud family.
8. Letter from Martin Freud to *The Daily Mail*, 21 September 1958. Amongst Freud family papers lent by Caroline Penney.
9. There were a few exceptions, but generally Martin was unable to place his stories for publication.
10. Letter to Walter Freud from The Chemical Society, dated 6 July 1967. Papers lent by David Freud.
11. Registration document amongst papers lent by David Freud.
12. *Paradoxes of the Second World War*, pp 6–7.
13. *Ibid*, pp 7–8.
14. Eric Sanders to Walter Freud, 3 October 2000. Original letter in A.W. Freud papers at the Imperial War Museum.
15. Introduction to *Why We Created the Lord*.
16. *Why We Created the Lord*, p. 82.
17. See also an article in *International Herald Tribune*, 5 June 2008.

Selected Bibliography

Archives

Miscellaneous documents, papers and letters of Anton Walter Freud at the
Imperial War Museum, London, ref: 05/78/1
Unpublished letters from Martin Freud to Sigmund Freud 1914–1919, the
Freud Museum, London
Secret Service file for Walter Freud, Public Record Office, ref: HS 9/544/3
Selection of unpublished short stories by Martin Freud, in the possession of
Caroline Penney
Miscellaneous papers lent by Caroline Penney and Ida Fairbairn
Lecture entitled 'Freud and his Family at Home in Vienna' given by Anton
Walter Freud to the Jewish Museum, London on 9 July 2002, copy lent
by Caroline Penney
Bea Lewkowicz, Video Interview with Anton Freud, The Jewish Museum,
London

Books and Memoirs

Bailey, Roderick, *Forgotten Voices of the Secret War: An Inside History of Special
Operations during the Second World War*, Ebury Press, 2008
Bentwich, Norman, *I Understand the Risks: The Story of the Refugees from
Nazi Oppression who Fought in the British Forces in the World War*, Victor
Gollancz, 1950

Berghahn, Marion, *Continental Britons: German-Jewish Refugees from Nazi Germany*, Berg Publishers, 1988

Brook-Shepherd, Gordon, *The Austrians: A Thousand-Year Odyssey*, Harper Collins, 1996

Clare, George, *Last Waltz in Vienna: The Destruction of a Family 1842–1942*, Pan Books, 1990 edition

Cresswell, Yvonne, *Living With the Wire: Civilian Internment in the Isle of Man during the two World Wars*, Manx National Heritage, 1994

Dale, Stephen, *Spanglet or By Any Other Name*, privately published memoirs, 1993

Frankl, Viktor, *Man's Search for Meaning*, Rider, 2004 edition

Freud, Anton Walter, *Before the Anticlimax: with Special Operations Executive in Austria*, unpublished memoirs, copies in The Freud Museum and The Imperial War Museum

Freud, Anton Walter, *An Austrian Grandfather*, unpublished manuscript dated May 1988, lent by Ida Fairbairn

Freud, Clement, *Freud Ego*, BBC, 2001

Freud, David, *Freud in the City*, Bene Factum Publishing, 2006

Freud, Esti, *Vignettes of My Life*, lent by David Freud

Freud, Martin, *Glory Reflected. Sigmund Freud – Man and Father*, Angus & Robertson, 1957

Freud, Martin, *Parole d'Honneur*, Victor Gollancz, 1939

Freud, Sophie, *Living in the Shadow of the Freud Family*, Praeger, 2007

Fry, Helen, *The King's Most Loyal Enemy Aliens: Germans who Fought for Britain during the Second World War*, Sutton, 2007

Fry, Helen, *Jews in North Devon during the Second World War*, Halsgrove, 2005

Gillman, Peter and Gillman, Leni, *Collar the Lot: How Britain Interned and Expelled its Wartime Refugees*, Quartet Books, 1980

Glendinning, Victoria, *Leonard Woolf*, Simon & Schuster, 2007

Grenville, Anthony, *Continental Britons: Jewish Refugees from Nazi Europe*, The Jewish Museum, London, 2002

Johnson, Marilyn, 'Freud – a courageous gentleman', in *Alumni Magazine*, University of Loughborough, July 2004, pp 5–6

Jones, Ernest, *Sigmund Freud: Life & Work, Vol. 1: The Young Freud 1856–1900*, The Hogarth Press, 1953

Jones, Ernest, *Sigmund Freud: Life & Work, Vol. 2: Years of Maturity 1901–1919*, The Hogarth Press, 1955

Jones, Ernest, *Sigmund Freud: Life & Work, Vol. 3: The Last Phase 1919–1939*, The Hogarth Press, 1957

Kemp, Anthony, *The Secret Hunters*, Michael O'Mara Books, 1986

Lafitte, F., *The Internment of Aliens*, Harmondsworth, 1940

Manchester, William, *The Arms of Krupp: The Rise & Fall of the Industrial Dynasty that armed Germany at War*, Michael Joseph, 1969

Molnar, Michael, *The Diary of Sigmund Freud 1929–1939: A Record of the Final Decade*, Scribner, 1992

Pearl, Cyril, *The Dunera Scandal,* Angus & Robertson, 1983
Sanders, Eric, *Emigration ins Leben: Wien-London und nicht mehr retour*, Czernin, Wien, 2007
Snowman, Daniel, *The Hitler Emigrés*, Pimlico, 2003
Stent, Ronald, *A Bespattered Page? The Internment of 'His Majesty's most Loyal Enemy Aliens'*, Andre Deutsch, 1980
Warner, Fred, *Personal Account of SOE Period*, unpublished memoirs, copy in The Imperial War Museum and courtesy of Eric Sanders
Weyr, Thomas, *The Setting of the Pearl: Vienna under Hitler*, OUP, 2005

Unpublished Writings of Martin Freud

Any Survivors? Manuscript of a novel, 357 pages

Short stories

The Alien, a short story, based on experiences of internment
Cinderella Psycho-analysed, copy in The Freud Museum, based on an incident in the Pioneer Corps
Strawberries, based on an incident in Highgate in 1942
The Thousandth Week
With Whom We Live
Foreign Nurse
The Grey Lady
The Blind Cyclist

Unpublished Writings of Walter Freud

Paradoxes of the Second World War, 80 pages
Why We Created the Lord, 82 pages, September 1998
The Origin of Monotheism, a short paper
The Failure of a Mission, 4 pages about Walter's SOE comrades Peter Priestley and Stephen Dale
The Night Hitler Lost his War, 4 pages about Kristallnacht

Index